ELEMENTS OF ACCOUNTING

Philip Cahill

Department of Accounting and Management Science
University of Portsmouth

THE McGRAW-HILL COMPANIES

London · New York · St Louis · San Francisco · Auckland · Bogotá · Caracas
Lisbon · Madrid · Mexico · Milan · Montreal · New Delhi · Panama · Paris
San Juan · São Paulo · Singapore · Sydney · Tokyo · Toronto

Published by

McGraw-Hill Publishing Company

Shoppenhangers Road, Maidenhead, Berkshire, SL6 2QL, England
Telephone 01628 502500
Facsimile 01628 770224

The LOC data for this book has been applied for and may be obtained from the Library of Congress, Washington, D.C.

A catalogue record for this book is available from the British Library.

Further information on this and other McGraw-Hill titles is to be found at
http://www.mcgraw-hill.co.uk

McGraw-Hill

A Division of The McGraw-Hill Companies

Typeset by Mackreth Media Services, Hemel Hempstead

Printed and bound in Great Britain by the University Press, Cambridge
Printed on permanent paper in compliance with ISO Standard 9706

ELEMENTS OF ACCOUNTING

CONTENTS

PREFACE   vii

1. WHY STUDY ACCOUNTING ?
    Key concepts in accounting. Approaches to learning. Key points   1

2. ELEMENTS OF AN ACCOUNTING SYSTEM
    Learning objectives—Case 1: a market trader—Case 2: a trading company—
    Elements of an accounting system—The effect of computerisation—Control
    features—Key points   5

3. DOUBLE ENTRY ACCOUNTING 1
    Learning objectives—A brief history of double entry—Dual nature of
    transactions—Debit entries—Credit entries—Key points—Questions   12

4. DOUBLE ENTRY ACCOUNTING 2
    Learning objectives—More complex double entry—Credit transactions—
    Sales and purchase returns—Posting summaries—The accounting system
    and double entry—The trial balance—Key points—Questions   26

5. BASIC ACCOUNTING STATEMENTS
    Learning objectives—The Profit & Loss Account—The Balance Sheet—Key
    points—Questions   42

6. THE ACCOUNTS PRODUCTION PROCESS
    Learning objectives—An overview—Accounting for period end adjustments—
    Comprehensive example—Key points—Questions   58

7. MORE COMPLEX ACCOUNTING STATEMENTS
    Learning objectives—Partnership accounts—Company accounts—The
    appropriation of profit—Share capital and reserves—Debentures—Format of
    company accounts—Comprehensive example—Key points   73

8. PUBLISHED COMPANY ACCOUNTS
    Learning objectives—The annual report—Who reads annual reports ?—
    Narrative reports—Numerical reports—Key points—Questions   93

9. CASH FLOW STATEMENTS
    Learning objectives—Why produce cash flow statements?—Format of the
    cash flow statement—Notes to the cash flow statement—Key points—
    Questions   102

10. INTERPRETING FINANCIAL STATEMENTS
    Learning objectives—Who interprets accounts ?—Reporting the results of
    analysis—Techniques of interpretation—Key points—Questions   129

11. THE MANAGEMENT ACCOUNTING PERSPECTIVE
Learning objectives—Financial and management accounting tasks—Cost
control—Forecasting—Key points   157

12. THE CLASSIFICATION OF COST
Learning objectives—Cost classification—The problem of overheads—
Overhead absorption rates—Comprehensive example—Key points—Questions 163

13. TECHNIQUES FOR SHORT TERM DECISIONS
Learning objectives—Short term decisions—Terminology—The use of variable
costing for decision making—Limitations of variable costing techniques—Key
points—Questions   181

14. PLANNING AND CONTROL 1: BUDGETING
Learning objectives—The budget preparation process—Comprehensive
example—Zero based budgeting—Budgetary control—Key points—Questions   203

15. PLANNING AND CONTROL 2: STANDARD COSTING
Learning objectives—Variance analysis—Operating statements—Investigation
of variances—Interpreting variances—Key points—Questions   222

16. CAPITAL INVESTMENT APPRAISAL
Learning objectives—Capital expenditure decisions—Techniques—Choice of
method—Key points—Questions   240

    APPENDIX 1   Answers to end of chapter questions   259

    APPENDIX 2   Discount tables   364

    APPENDIX 3   Glossary of accounting terms   365

    INDEX   373

PREFACE

This book sets out to explain accounting processes and techniques to the non-specialist reader. This is a difficult task in that a balance must be struck between exposition and conciseness.

The text covers the traditional topic areas of introductory financial accounting and management accounting. Some readers may question the inclusion of double-entry accounting in a text aimed at non-accounting students. In fact, this book supports both the aficionados of double-entry and those who find 'T' accounts an anathema . Most of the financial accounting material is presented in a way that does not assume a detailed knowledge of double-entry accounting. The chapter on cash flow statements shows workings in two formats; tabulation and 'T' accounts.

The management accounting section of the book explains the essential differences between financial accounting and management accounting. In addition to coverage of the basic topic areas appropriate to first year undergraduate study, there are chapters on standard costing and capital investment appraisal. These are designed to cover the needs of diploma, post-experience and MBA courses.

Finally, in accordance with Oscar Wilde's notion that the one thing worse than being talked about is not being talked about, comments and suggestions from readers are encouraged.

Philip Cahill
University of Portsmouth

DATE CONVENTION

Accounting texts traditionally represent years in general terms only. Thus, an accounting period ending on 31 December 19X8 is represented instead of a year ended 31 December 1998. As this book is being published near to the turn of the century, it has been decided to adopt a date convention based upon the years in the 21st century. Accordingly, accounting periods in this book will be identified as relating to 20X1, 20X2, and so on.

WHY STUDY ACCOUNTING?

This is a book about ideas. Specifically, it is a book about the elements of structuring, representing, and reporting the financial aspects of commercial activity. Ideas in accounting are manifested in accounting statements. These are numerical tabulations which purport to tell a story about the past, the present, or the future. Numbers have the appearance of mathematical certainty and, indeed, students new to accounting often confuse the subject with mathematics. This author suggests that accounting is not a mathematical discipline because it is too imprecise in its measurements and inconsistent in its use of terminology.

A key element in accounting is profit. This may be expressed by some accountants as a formula:

$$Revenues - Expenses = Profit$$

A mathematician would argue that this is too imprecise. There is no indication of the time period during which revenues are earned or expenses incurred. In addition, there may be situations where expenses exceed revenues so that the formula should read:

$$Revenues - Expenses = Loss$$

There is no indication of which portion of business activity is being measured. Is it the whole of a business or a section of a business which is being measured? There is no indication of the monetary units being employed in the measurement of profit or loss. There is no indication whether these currency units represent historical values, inflation-adjusted values or estimates of future revenues and expenses. A further defect of the above formulae is that the owner of the profits or losses is not identified.

Other key elements in accounting are assets and liabilities. A favourite expression in accounting texts is the so-called accounting equation:

$$Assets = Liabilities$$

Assets represent things owned by a business while liabilities represent things owed by a business to third parties. Assets may therefore comprise: buildings, computers, vehicles,

1

inventories, bank balances or investments. Liabilities, on the other hand, may include such items as: loans, overdrafts, bills due to suppliers of goods or services, and a special class of liability known as capital. This is a representation of the owner's interest in the business.

Quasi-mathematical formulae, of the kind indicated above, can represent a convenient shorthand for the expression of some of the key ideas in accounting, but accounting is not mathematical and we must start to explore some of the ideas contained in the expressions:

$$\text{Revenues} - \text{Expenses} = \text{Profit (or loss)}$$

and

$$\text{Assets} = \text{Liabilities}$$

Fundamental to accounting is the notion that monetary values can be used to describe the operation of a business. An electrical retailer may sell computers, televisions, and radios, and may purchase buildings, vehicles, office equipment, and the services of staff. The measurement of these different items of revenue and expenditure may be conveniently expressed in monetary terms.

Another idea implicit in the above discussion is the conception that there should be a separation between the financial affairs of a business and the financial affairs of the owners of a business. A visit to the cinema by the owner of a shoe shop should not result in the cost of the ticket being included in the calculation of business profits. Thus, a business is considered by an accountant to be a separate entity from its owner or owners.

Accounting is a framework for the measurement of business activity. It employs money as a common unit of measurement and it separates the affairs of the business from the purely private affairs of business owners. An important element in this framework is the notion of the accounting period. This is a defined period of time over which accounting measurements may be made. Most businesses present their results in respect of an accounting year. This period need not coincide with the calendar year. A business may chose any period of twelve months as its accounting year. The choice may be made because, for example, the business commenced trading on a particular date. Thus, a business which commences trading on 1 April 20X1 may produce its first annual accounts for the year ended 31 March 20X2, and subsequent accounts to 31 March in the following years. The choice of accounting year may be made for administrative convenience or because the owners feel that the selection of a particular period most accurately reflects the annual operating cycle of the business. Whatever period of account is chosen, it must be consistently applied. A business may not prepare accounts to 31 March in one year and then to 31 December in a subsequent year, although this general rule may be modified in exceptional circumstances where, for example, an interest in a business changes hands.

We now need to consider the types of measurement that accounting techniques can facilitate. In general terms, the range of accounting measurements may be indicated as follows:

1. A measurement of the whole business profit or loss over a full accounting year.
2. The valuation of assets and liabilities at the start and end of the accounting period.
3. A measurement of business profit or loss over part of the accounting year. This may be weekly, monthly, quarterly or six-monthly.
4. A measurement of the costs and/or revenues of some part of the business. This may include departmental results or results by product line or service.
5. Some combination of (2)–(4) above.

6. A measurement of current costs and revenues for a specified portion of the business. This may include detailed calculations of the unit costs of materials, sub-assemblies or labour hours.
7. A measurement of expected future costs and revenues.

In the first part of the book, we will consider accounting measurements of the kind indicated in (1) and (2) above. This is a branch of accounting known as financial accounting. It is concerned with writing up a record of the activities of the business for the accounting period. It is a historical record which has some similarities to a ship's log. It records where the business has travelled in its economic environment. This record must be created after the end of the accounting period. Thus, financial accounting statements in respect of the year ended 31 March 20X2 can only be completed after that date.

The other accounting measurements associated with (3)–(7) above are largely the province of what is known as management accounting. This type of accounting seeks to provide information to assist in the management and control of the business. Thus, if financial accounting is the ship's log, management accounting represents its navigational charts.

1.1 BUT WHY STUDY ACCOUNTING?

We have seen that accounting is not the mere application of arithmetic. It has a set of rules and procedures different to other disciplines. It is not possible to delegate accounting tasks to computer software any more than it is possible to delegate the writing of text to word-processing software.

Accounting rules and procedures must be studied, and a tried and tested way that lecturers use to explain accounting is the illustrative method. A topic area is described in outline and then an example is used to illustrate the detail. In the subject area covered by this book, much of the illustrative examples are numerical. This deters some students who may try to adopt the approach of seeking an understanding by reading through the illustrative examples. Unfortunately, this is not the most effective learning strategy to adopt. The situation is somewhat similar to learning how to play a computer game. The user manual for the game will describe the basic rules, how to fly your aircraft, how to steer, accelerate, and brake your racing car, or how to navigate your spacecraft. However, it is only when the game is loaded into the computer that players will really learn how to play. In accounting, students need to get inside the numbers by working through examples. A learning strategy for readers to adopt would be to pause at each numerical example and to work through the numbers using a calculator. The book also contains a large number of chapter end questions and fully worked answers are given in Appendix 1. These questions represent a vital part of the learning process in this subject and a suggested method of working through them is as follows:

1. Attempt to answer enough questions to consolidate your understanding of the topic area, taking one question at a time.
2. For each question you should review the suggested answer, noting areas that need further work. At this stage you should try to understand how the answer was arrived at by re-reading the question and, if necessary, the relevant chapter.
3. Put aside the answer and attempt the question again.
4. If problem areas remain, repeat (1)–(3).

KEY POINTS

1. Accounting has a set of rules which are unlike those of any other discipline.
2. Profit is a key concept. Accounting profit, or loss, may be calculated as revenues — expenses.
3. Assets are items owned by a business.
4. Liabilities are items owed by a business to third parties.
5. Accounting measures business activity in monetary terms.
6. The business is treated as a separate entity from its owners.
7. An accounting period is a period of time defined for the purpose of accounting measurement. It need not coincide with the calendar year.
8. Financial accounting may be likened to the preparation of a ship's log.
9. Management accounting may be likened to the preparation of the navigational charts of a ship.

ELEMENTS OF AN ACCOUNTING SYSTEM

LEARNING OBJECTIVES

After reading this chapter you should:

- Understand that accounting activity is based upon a financial information system that is closely linked to organizational structure.
- Understand some of the environmental factors that shape the design of accounting systems.
- Understand the major types of transaction dealt with by an accounting system.
- Have an overview of the main elements of an accounting system.

In this chapter we will consider two very simple organizations and look at how their accounting systems are constituted.

Case 1: Harry Main

Harry Main sells fruit and vegetables from a market stall. The market takes place every Thursday, Friday, and Saturday in Brunswick Street in the city of Calchester. This is a small coastal city (population 200,000), surrounded mainly by farmland and light industry. Harry pays a licence fee and rent to the local authority. He operates his business from a stall on plot 17 of the market and tows his barrow to the site on market days using a 15-year-old Ford van.

The Brunswick Street market is situated very close to a large fruit and vegetable wholesaler, Davis & Pope Ltd. Harry is able to buy much of his merchandise from the wholesaler, but he also buys direct from some of the local farmers. At certain times of the year, their prices undercut the wholesaler by a large enough margin to allow Harry to benefit from direct purchase, even though he incurs extra costs in collecting and storing the farmers' produce.

Harry employs his son, William, on Saturdays and during the school holidays, and he also employs Vera, his sister, on a casual basis to help out at busy times of the year and when William is not available.

5

Harry does have a bank account for the business (he pays the wholesaler by cheque), but he likes to trade in cash. This, to Harry, means banknotes. Customers pay him in cash and he pays the running costs of his business in cash. Harry is extremely reluctant to accept cheques from customers and sometimes adjusts his prices to reflect what he calls the 'administrative inconvenience' of processing cheques.

ACTIVITY

You may wish to pause here and consider the following questions before proceeding with the chapter:
1. What sort of accounting system do you think would be appropriate to Harry's needs?
2. Why do you think Harry is reluctant to accept cheques?
3. Is there any difference in the meaning of the word 'cash' in the following phrases:
   (a) cash and cheques
   (b) cash and credit.

2.1 WHAT IS THE PURPOSE OF AN ACCOUNTING SYSTEM?

This important question must be answered before we can examine the accounting system of any organization. We could consider the answer to this question from a number of perspectives. We could, for example, consider the question from the point of view of: a philosopher; an organizational theorist; an engineer; or an accountant. We would get very different answers, but each could be a valid answer to the question. A good way to solve this problem is to consider what sort of answer Harry would regard as valid.

We might, therefore, say to Harry that the purpose of an accounting system is to:

- Record accounting transactions.
- Keep track of the assets and liabilities of the business.
- Ensure the business debts are paid when due.
- Ensure money owing to the business is paid when due.
- Allow profit statements and other accounting reports to be prepared.

Harry's accounting system

The business is so small that Harry can keep most of the information about it in his head. He remembers how much he has paid for his vehicle and his other assets. He knows all his suppliers and many of his customers by sight. He remembers how much he has agreed to pay his employees and when they should be paid. He can tell by looking at his stall when he needs to order more stock. He does, however, need to write a few things down. He needs to record his income and expenditure, and he needs to file his invoices and bank statements.

He also needs to decide on his accounting period. This, in Harry's case, will be a period of 12 months which need not coincide with the calendar year. Harry actually started trading on 1 July 20X1 and so he has decided to make up his accounts to 30 June every year.

The part of the accounting system not existing in Harry's head could comprise of a cash book and a file for his invoices, bank statements, and other business documents for the accounting period.

2.2 THE CASH BOOK

Accounting terminology differentiates between cash (payment now) and credit (payment in the future) rather than the form of payment. An accountant may think of cash as representing cheques and bank notes.

Harry does not own a computer. His cash book is a physical book of about A4 size. The left-hand pages of his book are used to record receipts and the right hand-pages are used to record payments.

This may be represented as follows:

Harry Main: cash book

Left-hand page	*Right-hand page*
Cash received from customers	Cash paid to suppliers, employees, and for business expenses

Payments and receipts are normally listed in date order. Cash payments and receipts include those payments with cheques and with bank notes.

Case 2: Stocker & Shaw Ltd.

James Stocker and Terry Shaw are the shareholders and directors of a small engineering company. The company employs 50 people and is based in purpose-built premises at Manville (population 8,000) which is about 10 miles from Calchester.

Stocker & Shaw Ltd. produce storage cabinets, trolleys, and storage boxes. These are used on passenger aircraft for the service of food, drinks and duty-free goods. During the last 20 years, the company has built up a reputation as a high-quality supplier in this niche market. The reason why the company has been so successful is partly due to its size. It is small enough to service its market efficiently. Product demand from the airlines has two components. There is a fairly steady demand for the replacement of cabinets, trolleys, and boxes which wear out in use, but there are periods of high demand when the airlines replace or upgrade their aircraft. Stocker & Shaw Ltd. can react very quickly to sudden increases in demand. It can incorporate design changes into its products at very short notice and at various stages in the production process. All the company's products are fabricated at the Manville site (from stainless steel, tubular steel, and plastic) using computer-controlled machine tools. These are then delivered to customers utilizing the company's small fleet of delivery vehicles. The company is fortunate in being located only 80 miles from two major international airports.

James Stocker tends to stay at the Manville site and divides his time between the factory floor and the office in roughly equal proportion. Terry Shaw spends most of his time travelling to meet customers. His job is to negotiate technical details with the airlines and to act as a troubleshooter for the company. The accounting system of this company has to be able to deal with a number of information-processing tasks. The most important of these tasks are shown in Table 2.1.

Table 2.1   Information processing tasks in an accounting system

Task	Transaction type	Accounting system elements
250 invoices are received every month: the company has 500 suppliers, and invoices must be paid within two months	Credit purchases	Invoice listings Supplier account details Cash payment records
35 sales invoices are sent out each month: The company has 100 customers and requires payment within one month	Credit sales	Invoice listings Customer account detail Cash receipt records
Payment of weekly wages and monthly salaries to 50 employees, and payment of tax and social security deductions to government	Payroll	Personnel records Tax and social security details
Control of assets: this includes the vehicle fleet, plant and equipment, office equipment, and freehold premises	Fixed asset accounting	Asset listing
Control of raw materials, and stocks of partly finished and finished goods	Inventory (stock) accounting	Inventory listing
Calculation of profit, and evaluation of assets and liabilities	Financial reporting	Transaction summary

An accounting system capable of dealing with the above tasks might be represented as shown in Figure 2.1.

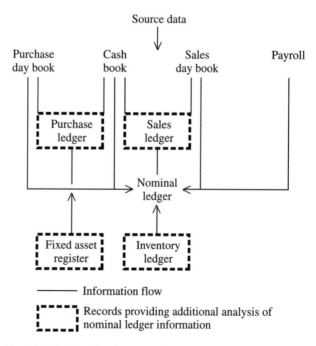

Figure 2.1   Stocker & Shaw Ltd. Outline of main accounting system elements

Notes

1. For the sake of clarity, some minor records such as returns day books and petty cash have been omitted, as have details of document files.
2. Source data include: cheques, bank notes, monetary transfers, invoices, and credit notes. This is the point at which transactions enter the accounting system.
3. Day books are used to list invoices for subsequent summary and analysis.
4. Cash book. This contains details of cash receipts and payments. Cash in the Stocker & Shaw system will, in the main, be represented by transactions passing through the business bank account. Very few transactions will employ bank notes.
5. Payroll comprises a number of records, and is used to determine net wage and salary payments, and amounts due to the government for payroll taxes and social security.
6. Purchase/sales ledgers. These contain lists of supplier and customer accounts, and are used to compare invoices with cash settlement on an individual supplier or customer basis.
7. The fixed asset register is a listing of the major assets owned by the company.
8. Inventory ledger. This is a listing of the components of inventory such as stocks of raw materials, and stocks of partly finished and finished goods. These stocks change continually during the accounting period.
9. Nominal ledger. This summarizes all the other elements of the accounting system, and is used as the basis for the preparation of profit statements and balance sheets.

2.3 COMPUTERIZATION OF ACCOUNTING SYSTEMS

We have not been told whether the Stocker & Shaw Ltd. accounting system is a manual or a computerized system. However, this should not alter the fundamental elements of the accounting system. A paper-based and a computer-based system have, essentially, the same tasks to complete.

In practice, an accounting system could exist in manual form or on computer, or be a hybrid of manual and computerized elements. Many smaller businesses use a payroll package, for example, in tandem with manual system elements.

2.4 CONTROL FEATURES OF ACCOUNTING SYSTEMS

You will recall that Harry Main had the perfect accounting control system. He could see all aspects of his business and he personally controlled most of the accounting transactions. In Stocker & Shaw Ltd., this close attention to detail is not possible due to the volume of transactions.

A key element in the control of accounting transactions is that there should be segregation of duties so that employees act as a cross-check on each other. The person ordering goods should not be the person writing out the cheques and signing them. A useful control technique is to compare information from different parts of the accounting system. Thus, payroll amounts can be compared with cash book payments, and cash book amounts can be compared with bank statements.

Other controls may relate to the movement of goods in and out of the business. Purchase invoices should be authorized for payment after examination of documentary, or other, evidence of the satisfactory receipt of goods. The dispatch of goods to customers should only be permitted if the credit rating of the customer is satisfactory.

In addition to the control techniques of comparison and the examination of evidence, another useful technique is physical security procedures. This may mean having secure fences, doors, windows, and locks, but it can also mean periodic counting of inventory or the indelible marking of company assets.

Some of the control features of the Stocker & Shaw Ltd. system are shown in Table 2.2.

Table 2.2   Stocker & Shaw Ltd. accounting controls

Transaction type	Control features
Credit purchases	Evidence of receipt of goods of acceptable quality. Authorization of payment.
Credit sales	Evidence of acceptable credit rating of customers. Authorization of refunds or special prices. Evidence of payment for goods.
Payroll	Evidence of rates of pay and employee status. Authorization of overtime and changes in rates of pay. Comparison between payroll and cash book.
Fixed assets	Physical security. Indelible marking. Periodic checks.
Inventory	Physical security. Periodic count and comparison with inventory ledger.
Reporting	Comparison with expectations and previous period results.

It should be stressed here that these are not all the possible controls which could be employed by Stocker & Shaw Ltd. The above chart merely serves to indicate the variety of control features in the Stocker & Shaw system.

2.5   CONCLUSION

The business environment is a major determinant of the design of accounting systems. These systems are deeply embedded in the structure of organizations. They adapt, change, and grow organically over time in response to environmental stimuli. This includes legal, regulatory, technological, and social change. Systems are also modified by the working practices and prejudices of a succession of employees.

Therefore, in many businesses, the detail of accounting systems is not formally recorded. Auditors will record an outline of an accounting system and its control features, but much of the detail of a system exists as a collection of records, and the explicit and tacit working practices of employees.

An accounting system can be seen, therefore, as the basis for the measurement of business activity in numerical form.

KEY POINTS

1. The purpose of an accounting system is to:
   - Record accounting transactions.
   - Keep track of business assets and liabilities.
   - Ensure business debts are paid when due.
   - Ensure customers settle their accounts when due.
   - Form the basis of financial reporting.

2. Control features of an accounting system include the following:

- Segregation of duties.
- Comparison of different parts of the system.
- Examination of evidence for transactions.
- Authorization of transactions.
- Physical security procedures.

3. The business environment is a major determinant of accounting system design.

THREE

DOUBLE-ENTRY ACCOUNTING 1

LEARNING OBJECTIVES

After reading this chapter you should:

- Understand the importance of double-entry in accounting.
- Understand the meaning of the terms debit and credit.
- Understand how transactions are recorded using double entry.

The double-entry system of recording accounting transactions has a long and distinguished history in the Western accounting world. It is thought that forms of double-entry accounting had been in use for about 200 years when in 1494 a text on mathematics was published in Venice. The *Summa de Arithmetica, Geometria, Proportioni et Proportionalitia* by Luca Pacioli contained a section called 'De Computis et Scrituris' which represented the first printed explanation of double-entry bookkeeping.

The essence of the system is for a list of assets and liabilities to be made, and the preparation and maintenance of three account books. The first of these books, the memorandum, was designed as a comprehensive book of prime entry to record the full details of transactions as they take place. One of the problems encountered by 15th century Venetian bookkeepers was the variation of monetary units used. A common currency did not exist and each city often had its own mint. The memorandum helped to deal with this problem by containing a full narrative of transactions, thus allowing entries to be made in different currency units.

The second of the Venetian account books, the Journal, was designed to summarize the entries in the memorandum, and to render the transactions into a common currency unit. The third book, the ledger, was described by Pacioli in a way that would be familiar to many modern accountants. He stated that for every entry that was made in the journal two must be made in the ledger. This double-entry system is quite simple in concept. Every transaction that a business makes, for example paying rent or selling goods, must be written down twice. A transaction is written once as a debit entry and once as a credit entry. This provides an important cross-check on accounting transactions, and also provides a framework which can be used to describe and explain such transactions.

We will now consider the meaning of the terms debit and credit before we examine how double-entry accounting is used today.

3.1 DEBIT AND CREDIT

One problem with these terms is that they are used incorrectly in everyday language. In fact, debit means to receive or value received and credit means to give or value given. Misunderstanding of the meaning of these terms arises because most private individuals receive accounting statements which have been prepared by a variety of commercial enterprises. One of the most common forms of accounting statement is the bank statement. This is a copy of a record from the bank's accounting system. The bank will therefore record debit and credit transactions from its perspective, and not from the perspective of the individual customer.

Example

Janice has a bank account with Bartons Bank. They send her a statement at the end of every month. This is a copy of information contained in their accounting system. The statement contains the following information:

Bartons Bank Plc
Bank statement
September 20X1

Debit entries	*Credit entries*
Money paid back to Janice:	Money paid in by Janice:
Cheques and other monetary	Salary and other income.
transfers initiated by her.	

As far as the bank is concerned, they are required to give value to Janice. They must give her money back to her, and this is recorded as a credit entry in their books. This requirement to give value to Janice is reduced when there are cheques or other transfers out of the account. This is a receipt of value by the bank and is recorded as a debit entry in their books.

If Janice wanted to keep her own records in respect of this account, she would produce a statement which shows the transactions from her point of view:

Janice: Statement of account with Bartons Bank Plc

Debit entries	*Credit entries*
Money received by Janice:	Money paid by Janice:
Salary and other income.	Cheques and other monetary
	transfers.

When Janice receives value, it is a debit entry in her books. When she gives value, it is a credit entry in her books.

The above statement is in respect of a bank account. If Janice was running a business, she would keep a bank account in her nominal ledger. In fact, Janice would keep a number of ledger accounts in her nominal ledger if she was running a business.

3.2 LEDGER ACCOUNTS

A ledger account is used to record each part of the double-entry for each transaction in an accounting system. Ledger accounts can be represented as follows:

Name of account

Debit side   *Credit side*

This form of representation is known as a 'T' account. This is the way that ledger accounts are represented in most accounting textbooks. Debit entries are entered on the left-hand side of these accounts, and credit entries are entered on the right-hand side of 'T' accounts.

Ledger accounts are used to record double-entry transactions. Therefore, accounting transactions need to be assigned to particular ledger accounts. The total number and type of ledger account will depend partly on the nature of the business and partly on the amount of information required by the owner or manager of the business. Thus, a small business will have a small number of ledger accounts, sufficient only to deal with the major categories of transactions and, for example, a single ledger account may be sufficient to record motor expenses. A larger business may require detailed information about such expenses. It may, therefore, use a ledger account to record the running costs of individual vehicles. Thus, details of motor expenses for this business may be recorded in several ledger accounts.

There are, however, a number of ledger accounts which are common to most business entities. These are:

Sales account
Used to record sales made by the business.

Purchases account
Used to record the purchase of goods for resale.

Overhead expense accounts
Individual accounts are used to record each category of overhead expense such as: insurance, rent, salaries, and motor expenses.

Fixed asset accounts
Individual accounts are used to record each class of fixed asset, such as: vehicles, computers, and machinery.

Current asset accounts
Individual accounts are used to record each class of current asset such as: stock, debtors, bank, and cash.

Current liability accounts
Used to record each class of current liability such as: creditors, and bank overdrafts.

Capital account
This records the owner's interest in the business. In essence, it shows how much the business owes to its owner or owners. This type of account can vary widely in its description, depending upon the legal nature of the owner(s)' interest in the business.

Drawings account
In non-incorporated businesses (i.e. businesses which are not set up as companies), money which is paid to the owners is described as drawings. This represents money which is returned to owners, normally as a payment in advance in respect of profit. In practice, the owner of a business would not wait until the end of the accounting year, when profit is calculated, before drawing money for living expenses.

3.3 DOUBLE-ENTRY ACCOUNTING

The kind of double-entry accounting which is presented in this book is a simplification of the complexity of real-world accounting. Even quite small businesses have a large volume of transactions which have to be processed during an accounting period. In addition, real-world accounting transactions have to be checked, summarized and analysed before double-entry processing can begin. We will, therefore, concentrate on double-entry accounting in the nominal ledger and reduce the number of transactions to a minimum.

The nominal ledger contains a number of accounts which represent the history of defined categories of revenue, expenditure, assets, and liabilities. Each transaction will affect two accounts. A revenue transaction will require an entry in a revenue account and an entry in an asset account. Thus, a sales transaction of £500 will require an entry in the sales account and an entry in the bank account. Value has been received in the bank account, this will be the debit entry. Value has been given by the business in the form of a sale, there will be a credit entry in the sales account. A purchase transaction of £250 will require an entry in the purchases account and an entry in the bank account. In this case, value has been received in the purchases account in the form of goods. There will be a debit entry in the purchases account of £250. Value has been given in the form of a payment out of the bank account. There will be a credit entry in the bank account. These ideas may be made clearer with an example of the processing of some simple double-entry transactions.

Example

Let us assume that Janice has decided to open up a new business. In order to keep things simple, we will look at her transactions for the first ten days of trading only.

We can start by listing out her transactions:

Day 1   Janice pays £10,000 into the business bank account.
Day 2   She buys a second-hand car for £4,000. This vehicle will be used in the business.
Day 3   She buys goods for £2,000.
Day 4   She pays rent of £500.
Day 5   She pays the telephone installation bill of £350.
Day 6   She sells goods for £3,500 and receives a cheque from the customer.
Day 7   She pays wages of £200 to her assistant.
Day 8   She pays £600 for insurance.
Day 9   She pays £750 for advertising.
Day 10   She pays herself £500.

There are now two stages which we can work through in order to deal with these transactions.

Stage 1:
Which two accounts are affected by each transaction?

Stage 2:
For each transaction, which account will have a debit entry and which account will have a credit entry?
    You may wish to attempt to answer these questions yourself before reviewing the suggested answer.

Stage 1
The following accounts are affected:

Day 1   Bank account and capital account.
Day 2   Motor vehicle account and bank account.
Day 3   Purchases account and bank account.
Day 4   Rent account and bank account.
Day 5   Telephone account and bank account.
Day 6   Bank account and sales account.
Day 7   Wages account and bank account.
Day 8   Insurance account and bank account.
Day 9   Advertising account and bank account.
Day 10 Drawings account and bank account.

Stage 2
The debit and credit entries are as follows:

Day	Debit	Credit
1	bank	capital
2	motor vehicle	bank
3	purchases	bank
4	rent	bank

5	telephone	bank
6	bank	sales
7	wages	bank
8	insurance	bank
9	advertising	bank
10	drawings	bank

The 'T' accounts for these transactions would be as follows:

Bank account

Debit side					*Credit side*	
		£				£
Day 1	Capital	10,000	Day 2	Vehicle		4,000
Day 6	Sales	3,500	Day 3	Purchases		2,000
			Day 4	Rent		500
			Day 5	Telephone		350
			Day 7	Wages		200
			Day 8	Insurance		600
			Day 9	Advertising		750
			Day 10	Drawings		500

Capital account

		£			£
			Day 1	Bank	10,000

Motor vehicle

		£		£
Day 2	Bank	4,000		

Purchases

		£		£
Day 3	Bank	2,000		

Rent

		£		£
Day 4	Bank	500		

Telephone

		£		£
Day 5	Bank	350		

Sales

	£			£
		Day 6	Bank	3,500

Wages

		£		£
Day 7	Bank	200		

Insurance

		£		£
Day 8	Bank	600		

Advertising

		£			£
Day 9	Bank	750			

Drawings

		£			£
Day 10	Bank	500			

Notice that in each of the ledger accounts, transactions are identified with the name of the account containing the corresponding entry. This facilitates the checking of entries when processing errors have been made.

We can now describe some general rules for debit and credit entries.

Debit entries

- Increase an asset account.
  The value in the bank and motor vehicle accounts have been increased by debit entries.
- Increase an expense account.
  Purchases, rent, telephone, wages, insurance, and advertising have all been increased by debit entries.
- Increase the drawings account.

Credit entries

- Increase a revenue account.
  The sales account has been increased by a credit entry.
- Increase the capital account.
- Decrease an asset account.

We will return to these general rules at the end of the next chapter. At this stage, you should consider the notion that some accounts tend to have debit balances because they represent assets of the business and expenses incurred by the business, and other accounts tend to have credit balances because they represent liabilities of the business and revenues.

The double-entry system can seem incomprehensible to the layman. One of the reasons for this is that accounting is the kind of subject that is best learned by practice, by working through examples. This chapter is designed to provide a general introduction to the basic ideas in double-entry accounting. The most important part of the learning process is in working through the chapter end questions.

KEY POINTS

1. In double-entry accounting, each transaction is written down twice: once as a credit and once as a debit.
2. The terms debit and credit tend to be used incorrectly by the layman. This is because private individuals receive copies of the accounting records of organizations. These organizations present accounting information from their perspective.
3. Nominal ledger accounts are used to record the history of the different categories of revenue and expenditure which are appropriate in describing the financial affairs of the business.
4. A debit entry indicates that value is received in an account.
5. A credit entry indicates that value is given by an account.
6. An understanding of double-entry accounting is greatly assisted by the working through of examples.

QUESTIONS

3.1 Chantall Shoes manufactures high-quality fashion shoes for women. In a typical week, the following types of transaction are processed by the accounts department:

(a) Purchase of raw materials
(b) Payment of wages
(c) Income from sale of shoes
(d) Purchase of stationery
(e) Payment of advertising costs

Which accounts in the nominal ledger should be debited and which accounts should be credited in respect of each of the above transactions? Assume that all the above transactions are reflected in the business bank account.

3.2 Franco has just started a restaurant 'La Bella Napoli'. He asks your advice about entering transactions in his nominal ledger using the double-entry system. What advice would you give him in respect of the following transactions?

(a) Cash paid into the business by Franco
(b) Purchase of eggs, flour, fish, and meat
(c) Cash received from customers
(d) Cash withdrawn by Franco for his personal living expenses
(e) Purchase of a pizza oven

3.3 Julia started trading as a music teacher in January 20X0. State which account should be debited and which account should be credited in respect of the following transactions:

(a) Fees from pupils
(b) Rent
(c) Electricity
(d) Gas
(e) Purchase of sheet music
(f) Purchase of grand piano

3.4 Tarquin runs the Eagleburger Hotel. Using the pro-forma below, write up his business bank account in the nominal ledger for February 20X1.

The source data are:

		Payments	Receipts
20X1 February			
1.	Accommodation		850
2.	Wine	200	
3.	Foodstuffs	300	
4.	Wages	1,500	
5.	Wedding reception		2,500
6.	Advertising	500	

Eagleburger Hotel nominal ledger (extract)

Bank account

Debit		Credit
	£	£

3.5 Using the information in question 3.4, complete the double-entry postings to the Eagleburger Hotel nominal ledger.

3.6 Skin Deep is a hair and beauty salon in the West End of London. The property insurance premium of £10,000 is paid by cheque on 31 May 20X1. Show the double-entry for this transaction in the nominal ledger of Skin Deep.

3.7 Akiro runs a sports shop specializing in the sale of martial arts equipment. In August 20X3, he pays the following bills by cheque:

(a) Burglar alarm repair £570
(b) Telephone bill £450
(c) Advertising £120

Show the double-entry for these transactions in Akiro's nominal ledger.

3.8 Tirana Travel is a business specializing in selling package holidays to Albania. Silvana, the bookkeeper, has written up the nominal ledger for March 20X8, but she is not sure whether her entries are correct. She summarizes the transactions on a piece of paper and sends it to you. Can you indicate to her if any of her double-entry transactions have been incorrectly entered and write out the correct entries.

Bank

		£				£
(1)	Sales	13,000	(4)	Sales		5,000
(2)	Rent	1,000	(5)	Advertising		350

Sales

		£			£
(4)	Bank	5,000	(1)	Bank	13,000

Electricity

		£			£
			(3)	Bank	700

Rent

		£		£
(2)	Bank	1,000		

Advertising

		£			£
(5)	Bank	350	(3)	Electricity	700

(*n*) = transaction number

3.9 James Clay is the general manager of a sports centre. Correct the following entries in his nominal ledger.

Bank account

		£			£
20X3			20X3		
December			December		
1	Subscriptions received	1,500	10	Purchase of equipment	4,500
2	Grant from Athletics Council	8,000	12	Purchase of bar Supplies	1,700
3	Wages paid	2,500	15	Bar sales	3,850
4	Subscriptions refunded	120			

3.10 It is May 1496 at the University of Milan. Luca Pacioli is visited by his friend Leonardo da Vinci. Leonardo has come to show Pacioli preliminary sketches for some illustrations he is contributing to Pacioli's book, *De Divina Proportione*. Naturally, the great men fall into a long discussion about the nature of artistic representation and accounting. A (rough) translation of part of their discussion is as follows:

Leonardo: What do you know about drawings?
Pacioli: I will answer your question with a number of statements. Some of these statements I regard as false and some I regard as correct. My statements are:

One   Drawings are not artistic representations
Two   Drawings represent a payment on account of profit to the owner of a business
Three   Drawings are wages paid to the owner of a business
Four   Drawings should be debited to the drawings account
Five   Drawings can represent cash taken out of the business by the owner and also goods taken out of the business for the owner's personal use.

Which statements do you think Pacioli regards as correct and which do you think he regards as false?

3.11 You are a contestant in a television game show based upon accounting theory. At the end of the final round, you have exactly the same number of points as your opponent. You must face a sudden-death play off by making the responses 'true' or 'false' to the following statements about nominal ledger entries.

(a) For every debit entry there must be a corresponding credit entry.
(b) Expenses such as rent are always represented by debit entries in the bank account.
(c) Electricity payments are always represented by debit entries in the electricity account.
(d) Sales are always represented by credit entries in the sales account.
(e) Purchases for resale must be credited to the purchases account.

3.12 Dragonquest is a producer of computer games. On 30 October 20X5, £8,700 must be paid for packaging costs; £25,000 for software; £97,500 for salaries; £10,000 for rent, and £3,700 for electricity. At the close of business on 29 October 20X5, the balance on the business bank account was £37,500 debit.

   You are required to show the nominal ledger accounts for the above transactions and to calculate the closing balance on the bank account at the end of October 20X5.

3.13 Goldenear is a business set up to manage the production of the film 'Webmaster' a spy thriller staring the Irish–American superstar Piers Mahon. It is 30 June 20X9 and the following payments must be made:

		£
(a)	Aviation fuel	72,000
(b)	Film	110,000
(c)	Equipment repairs	12,500
(d)	Stuntmen fees	65,000
(e)	Location catering	95,000
(f)	Aircraft hire	200,000
(g)	Vehicle leasing	30,000
(h)	Legal fees	57,000
(i)	Scriptwriters' fees	1,250

Show the nominal ledger entries for the above transactions.

3.14 Simon Davis began trading on 2 January 20X1. The transactions for the first week of trading were as follows:

20X1
January
2   Payment by Simon of £1,000 into the business bank account.
     Withdrawal of £40 for petty cash.
3   £371 paid to Thompson & Co. for goods supplied.
4   Cheques received from A. Davis £10 and M. Jones £345.
5   £30 paid for postage stamps.
6   £80 paid for stationery.
7   D. Thomas paid the business £8.
8   £112 paid for goods supplied.

Assume that all payments, apart from the payment for postage stamps, have been made by cheque from the business bank account. Assume all receipts are for sales.

Required

1. Which accounts are to be debited and which accounts are to be credited in each of the above transactions?
2. Write out the 'T' accounts for each of the above transactions.

3.15 You have been approached by John who is thinking of starting a business as a mobile motor mechanic. He has read a little bit about the double-entry system, but he is confused about the meaning of the terms debit and credit, which he says do not make sense to him. He shows you his bank statement which clearly indicates to him that money received into the account is a credit entry. According to John's reading of double-entry texts, money received by him should be a debit entry.
   Write a letter to John explaining your understanding of the terms debit and credit, and why he might have been confused by the bank statement.
NB Explain to John using words, not numbers or diagrams.

3.16 Ivan is a systems analyst who specializes in accounting systems. He does not like double-entry accounting and says that the system was designed centuries ago as a method of exercising control over monetary transactions, and that in the computer era the double-entry system is obsolete.

Why do you think the use of the double-entry system has persisted, despite the widespread use of computers in accounting? Write down your reply to Ivan in the form of notes.

FOUR

DOUBLE-ENTRY ACCOUNTING 2

LEARNING OBJECTIVES

After reading this chapter you should:

- Understand the double-entry procedures required to deal with credit transactions.
- Be able to process transactions and balance off accounts.
- Be able to construct a trial balance.
- Understand the importance of the trial balance.

4.1 MORE COMPLEX DOUBLE-ENTRY

Up to now, we have been processing double-entry transactions which have passed through a bank account or a cash account. These are described as cash transactions in accounting terminology. Remember that accountants differentiate between cash (settlement now) and credit (settlement in the future) rather than the form of monetary transfer.

Credit transactions require a more complex set of entries than cash transactions because settlement of invoices is not immediate. Invoices are paid after a time interval. In addition, defective goods may be returned to suppliers or returned by customers. We will first look at situations where there are no returned goods. A good starting point is to consider in more detail the nature of credit transactions.

4.2 CREDIT TRANSACTIONS

Goods may be purchased on credit or sold on credit.

Example

Navistar makes navigation equipment for yachts and pleasure cruisers. It purchases components from a range of suppliers. It sells its products to dealers and yacht chandlers in the UK, Continental Europe, Scandinavia, and the Far East.

In reality, it is quite a simple business. Components and sub-assemblies are purchased from suppliers, and Navistar assembles these into finished products.

The main items purchased by the business are:

Product	Supplier	Credit terms
Components	Axis Ltd.	30 days
Sub-assemblies	Brownscombe & Co.	60 days
Packing materials	Challis Plc	90 days

The main items sold are:

Product	Supplier	Credit terms
Navistar 2000	IMG Dealers Ltd.	30 days
Satnav 500	Seacorp.	30 days

The suppliers (Axis Ltd., Brownscombe & Co., and Challis Plc) are known as creditors in accounting jargon. They are owed money by Navistar Ltd. The customers (IMG Dealers Ltd., and Seacorp) are called debtors in accounting terms, they owe money to Navistar Ltd.

Double-entry for credit transactions

We now need to look at how Navistar records its credit transactions using double-entry, but first we need to make a simplifying assumption. In practice, a firm such as Navistar would have a large number of creditors and debtors. It would therefore need to keep individual accounts for each creditor in the purchase ledger, and individual accounts for each debtor in the sales ledger. We will assume that Navistar has only three suppliers and two customers. This means that it can dispense with the need to keep a purchase ledger and a sales ledger, and therefore can record its credit transactions in the nominal ledger only. We will make the additional assumption that Navistar uses one nominal ledger account for its creditors and one account for its debtors.

Credit transactions for purchases

In August 20X5, Navistar had the following transactions:

August 1	Cheque paid for goods £250.
August 3	Goods purchased on credit from Axis Ltd. £750.
August 31	Cheque paid to Axis Ltd.

The double-entry for the transaction on August 1 is quite simple. There is a debit entry in the purchases account and a credit entry in the bank account.

Purchases			
	£		£
Aug 1 Bank	250		

	Bank		
	£		£
	Aug 1	Purchases	250

The credit transaction on August 3 is more complex. The payment for the goods does not occur until August 31. There is a debit to the purchases account of £750 on August 3, but no credit entry in the bank account. Instead, there is a credit entry in the creditors account, indicating that money is owed to Axis Ltd. When the money is paid on August 31, there is a credit to the bank account and a debit to the creditors account, which indicates that money due to Axis Ltd. has now been paid. The double-entry accounts to reflect this are as follows:

		Purchases		
		£		£
Aug 1	Bank	250		
Aug 3	Creditors	750		

		Creditors		
		£		£
			Aug 3 Purchases	750
Aug 31	Bank	750		

		Bank		
		£		£
			Aug 1 Purchases	250
			Aug 31 Creditors	750

The creditors account has been used to record the timing difference between the obligation to pay for the goods and payment for the goods. A similar idea is used for dealing with credit sales. In this case, the debtors account is used to record the difference in time between the issue of a sales invoice and payment for the goods by the customer.

Credit transactions for sales

In September 20X5, Navistar had the following transactions:

September	1	Cash sales	£1,500.
September	4	Credit sale to Seacorp	£3,750.
September	30	Seacorp pays Navistar	£3,750.

The double-entry transactions are:

Bank

		£			£
Sept 1	Sales	1,500			
Sept 30	Debtors	3,750			

Sales

		£			£
			Sept 1	Bank	1,500
			Sept 4	Debtors	3,750

Debtors

		£			£
Sept 4	Sales	3,750	Sept 30	Bank	3,750

Sales and purchase returns

In the above cases, the transactions were completed when payment was made for the goods. In practice, problems often arise which result in the return of goods by customers or the return of goods to suppliers. Unfortunately, this complicates the recording of credit transactions using double-entry.

Sales returns

You will recall that Navistar's debtors account for September 20X5 looked like this:

Debtors

		£			£
Sept 4	Sales	3,750	Sept 30	Bank	3,750

We will now assume that on September 30 20X5 there was a problem and Seacorp did not pay Navistar £3,750. In fact, goods to the value of £750 were returned by Seacorp. The nominal ledger would now contain the following entries:

Debtors

		£			£
Sept 4	Sales	3,750	Sept 30	Bank	3,000
			Sept 30	Sales returns	750

Sales returns

		£		£
Sept 30	Sales	750		

A new account has been opened to record the return of goods by customers. The sales returns account could be described as a 'negative' sales account. We could have debited the returned goods to the sales account, but the use of the sales returns account allows the situation to be highlighted for control purposes. It should be clear that the return of goods is a situation which should require the attention of business owners and managers. If returned goods are debited to the sales account there is a danger that problems in this area might be overlooked with adverse long-term consequences for the business. In the above example, the revised bank account has not been shown.

Purchase returns

In this case, the treatment of goods returned to suppliers is to open a purchase returns account which is credited with returned goods and there is a debit entry in the creditors account. Purchase returns is therefore a 'negative' purchases account.

Comprehensive example

In October 20X5 Navistar has the following transactions:

October	1	Credit purchases £1,250.
October	2	Credit sales £5,000.
October	3	Goods returned to supplier £600.
October	4	Goods returned by customer £1,750.
October	31	The debtor pays the amount due and Navistar pays its creditor the amount due.

Purchases

		£			£
Oct 1	Creditors	1,250			

Creditors

		£			£
Oct 3	Purchase returns	600	Oct 1	Purchases	1,250
Oct 31	Bank	650			

Sales

		£			£
			Oct 2	Debtors	5,000

Debtors

		£			£
Oct 2	Sales	5,000	Oct 4	Sales returns	1,750
			Oct 31	Bank	3,250

Purchase returns

		£			£
			Oct 3	Creditors	600

Sales returns

		£			£
Oct 4	Debtors	1,750			

	Bank				
		£			£
Oct 31	Debtors	3,250	Oct 31	Creditors	650

Summary

The double-entry for credit transactions is as follows:

	Debit	*Credit*
Credit purchases		
On receipt of goods	Purchases	Creditors
On payment for goods	Creditors	Bank
Credit sales		
On despatch of goods	Debtors	Sales
On receipt of payment	Bank	Debtors
Purchase returns	Creditors	Purchase returns
Sales returns	Sales returns	Debtors

4.3 BALANCING OFF LEDGER ACCOUNTS

At the end of an accounting period, the accounts in the nominal ledger must be balanced off. In other words, we must find out how much has been expended and received in respect of all the defined categories of revenue and expenditure that are represented by the nominal ledger accounts. We must look at each ledger account and calculate the balance on that account. This serves both to check the accuracy of the double-entry postings and forms a basis for the preparation of the financial statements.

We will now look at two methods of balancing off ledger accounts. The first is the formal accounting method and the second is a short cut method, the Hicks Method, which some students prefer to the more traditional method.

The formal accounting method of calculating ledger account balances

Accountants have developed methods of recording and processing transactions which have been proved by centuries of use. An example of this is the formal method of determining the balances in ledger accounts which is described below. We will use as an example the bank account of Navistar for November 20X5. At the end of the month, the account contains the following transactions:

	Bank				
		£			£
Nov 1	Balance brought down	2,600	Nov 3	Purchases	1,800
Nov 15	Sales	3,000	Nov 14	Rent	1,000
Nov 30	Debtors	5,500	Nov 30	Creditors	3,200

Step 1

The first stage in the balancing procedure is to calculate sub-totals on each side of the account. You will also notice that the Navistar bank account for November contains an item described as balance brought down. This is the balance on the account at the end of October which has been brought down as the opening balance for November.

	Bank				
		£			£
Nov 1	Balance brought down	2,600	Nov 3	Purchases	1,800
Nov 15	Sales	3,000	Nov 14	Rent	1,000
Nov 30	Debtors	5,500	Nov 30	Creditors	3,200
		11,100			6,000

Step 2

The largest of the two sub-totals is written at the bottom of the account as a grand total.

	Bank				
		£			£
Nov 1	Balance brought down	2,600	Nov 3	Purchases	1,800
Nov 15	Sales	3,000	Nov 14	Rent	1,000
Nov 30	Debtors	5,500	Nov 30	Creditors	3,200
		11,100			6,000
		11,100			11,100

Step 3
The account is made to balance by the insertion of a balancing figure. This is the difference between the sub-total and the grand total. In this case, there is no difference on the debit side of the account so the balancing figure is entered on the credit side of the account. This balancing figure is described as the balance carried down. It is the balance on the account at the end of the period.

Bank

		£			£
Nov 1	Balance brought down	2,600	Nov 3	Purchases	1,800
Nov 15	Sales	3,000	Nov 14	Rent	1,000
Nov 30	Debtors	5,500	Nov 30	Creditors	3,200
		11,100			6,000
			Nov 30	Balance carried down	5,100
		11,100			11,100

Step 4
The balance carried down is now taken out of the account and placed on the opposite side. It becomes the balance brought down at the start of the next period.

Bank

		£			£
Nov 1	Balance brought down	2,600	Nov 3	Purchases	1,800
Nov 15	Sales	3,000	Nov 14	Rent	1,000
Nov 30	Debtors	5,500	Nov 30	Creditors	3,200
		11,100			6,000
			Nov 30	Balance carried down	5,100 --┐
		11,100			11,100
	Balance brought down	5,100 --┘			

In this case, the balancing figure had to be inserted on the credit side of the account. It could have been inserted on the debit side if the sub-totals were different. It is clear that there is a debit balance on this account as more has been received in the period than paid out. The balance brought down is the balance on the account at the end of the current accounting period, and also the balance on the account at the start of the next accounting period.

A further point to mention at this stage in relation to balancing ledger accounts is that, in practice, accountants do not show sub-totals in their ledger accounts and as students become more adept at balancing accounts they are often encouraged to omit these sub-totals from their 'T' accounts. The balancing procedures shown above and below are designed to provide a systematic way of calculating the balance on a ledger account and determining if the balance is a debit or a credit balance. If there is only one entry in an account, the balance has, in effect, been calculated and it is clear whether or not it is a debit or a credit balance. In such cases, there is no need to employ a balancing procedure.

The Hicks method

An alternative to the formal accounting method of calculating ledger account balances is the Hicks method. Step 1 of this method is similar to the accounting method in that sub-totals are calculated for each side of the ledger account. Step 2 is to take the smallest of the two sub-totals over to the other side of the account and to calculate a balance. Thus, the balance on the account can be calculated very quickly and it is immediately clear if the balance is a debit or a credit balance.

		£			£
Nov 1	Balance brought down	2,600	Nov 3	Purchases	1,800
Nov 15	Sales	3,000	Nov 14	Rent	1,000
Nov 30	Debtors	5,500	Nov 30	Creditors	3,200
		11,100			6,000
		6,000			
		5,100			

Bank

In the above example, the smallest sub-total is on the credit side. Thus, £6,000 is taken over to the debit side and deducted from the larger sub-total. The resulting figure is clearly a debit balance and can be calculated very quickly. The disadvantage of this method is that it is possible to omit opening balances in subsequent accounting periods.

The trial balance

A major purpose of accounting is to produce financial statements. A key element in the process of preparing accounting statements is the trial balance. This is a list of the balances extracted from nominal ledger accounts at the end of the accounting period. The trial balance is used to check the accuracy of double-entry postings in the nominal ledger. If the double-entry transactions have been correctly processed, and if the account balances have been correctly extracted from the ledger accounts, then the trial balance should balance. That is to say that the total of the debit balances should equal the total of the credit balances. It is possible, however, for a trial balance to balance and for errors to have occurred in the processing of transactions. Debit and credit entries could have been posted the wrong way round, errors could arithmetically compensate each other, or transactions could be omitted in their entirety. We will return to this problem later, but for the moment we will consider a simple example which should serve to consolidate the work we have covered in this chapter.

Example

Visconti has the following transactions for March 20X3:

March 1	Started business with £25,000. This was paid into the business bank account.
March 2	Purchased goods on credit for £17,000.
March 10	Purchased a motor vehicle for £10,500. Payment for the vehicle was by cheque.
March 18	Paid rent by cheque £3,750.
March 28	Paid salaries by cheque £5,250.
March 31	Sold goods on credit £32,000.

The double-entry for these transactions is as follows:

Bank

		£			£
March 1	Capital	25,000	March 10	Motor vehicle	10,500
			March 18	Rent	3,750
			March 28	Salaries	5,250
			March 31	Balance carried down	5,500
		25,000			25,000
Balance brought down		5,500			

Capital

		£			£
			March 1	Bank	25,000

Purchases

		£		£
March 2	Creditors	17,000		

Creditors

	£				£
			March 2	Purchases	17,000

Motor vehicle

	£			£
March 10 Bank	10,500			

Rent

	£			£
March 18 Bank	3,750			

Salaries

	£			£
March 28 Bank	5,250			

Sales

	£				£
			March 31	Debtors	32,000

Debtors

	£			£
March 31 Sales	32,000			

As all the transactions have been entered for March 20X3, we can now extract the balances on the accounts and produce a trial balance. Notice that we have only used the formal balancing procedure in respect of the bank account. All the other accounts have single entries, therefore it would be pointless to go through the balancing procedure. We know the amount of the balances on these accounts, and we know if the balances are on the debit or the credit side.

Visconti: Trial balance as at 31 March 20X3

	Debit £	Credit £
Bank	5,500	
Capital		25,000
Purchases	17,000	
Creditors		17,000
Motor vehicle	10,500	
Rent	3,750	
Salaries	5,250	
Sales		32,000
Debtors	32,000	
	74,000	74,000

The total of the debit balances equals the total of the credit balances. We are now ready to commence the preparation of financial statements. In fact, the real importance of the trial balance for students is that it forms the basis of financial accounts, and many assessment and examination questions are presented in the form of a trial balance. The purpose, therefore, of learning double-entry can be seen as a method of obtaining an understanding of the trial balance.

KEY POINTS

1. The term credit transactions describes a situation where there is a timing difference between the obligation to pay or receive payment and the actual payment or receipt.
2. In the case of credit purchases, a creditors account is used to account for the timing difference.
3. In the case of credit sales, a debtors account is used to account for the timing difference.
4. Goods may be returned to suppliers or returned by customers.
5. A purchases returns account is used to deal with returns to suppliers.
6. A sales returns account is used to deal with returns by customers.
7. Review the methods of balancing ledger accounts.
8. A trial balance is a list of balances on the nominal ledger accounts at the end of the accounting period.
9. A trial balance is the starting point for the production of financial accounting statements.

QUESTIONS

4.1 Michelle Lee trades as a stationery supplier. Show the 'T' account entries for the following transactions:

20X3
June   1   Started business with £1,500 paid into the
                 business bank account.
         3   Cheque paid for goods £ 255.
         7   Goods purchased on credit £348.
         10   Cheque from customer £126.
         14   Goods returned to supplier £84.
         18   Bought goods on credit £294.
         21   Goods returned to supplier £57.
         24   Goods sold on credit £165.
         25   Creditor paid £88.
         30   Debtor paid £55.

4.2 Pandro Goodlad sells garden furniture. Write up the following transactions in his nominal ledger:

20X5
July   1   Business started with £5,000 capital.
         2   Goods purchased on credit £390.
         3   Second-hand delivery van purchased for
                 £2,500.
         5   Goods purchased by cheque £275.
         10   Sold goods on credit £490.
         12   Returned goods to supplier £90.
         19   Cash sales £140.
         22   Purchase of computer by cheque £750.
         24   Loan from Arthur Smith £500.
         29   £300 paid to creditor.

4.3 The bank account in Tara McCarthy's nominal ledger for July 20X3 is as follows:

Bank account

20X3			£	20X3			£
July	3	Sales	75	July	1	Balance brought down	1,500
	5	Debtors	125				
	6	Loan	1,000		4	Purchases	248
	7	Sales	50		7	Creditors	710
	9	Sales	65		23	Creditors	489
	15	Debtors	1,175		31	Creditors	527
	22	Sales	205				
	25	Debtors	310				

Calculate the balance on this account as at 31 July 20X3. Is this balance a debit balance or a credit balance?

4.4 The creditors account in David Smith's nominal ledger for August 20X5 is as follows:

Creditors account

20X5			£	20X5			£
Aug 1	Purchase returns		100	Aug 5	Purchases		475
				17	Purchases		321
8	Purchase returns		15	23	Purchases		407
10	Bank		360	25	Purchases		835
31	Bank		321	25	Purchases		915
				27	Purchases		1,127

Calculate the balance on this account as at 31 August 20X5.

4.5 Pamela Tanzer runs Creative Canopies, a business which sells a range of decorative blinds, canopies, and awnings. Show the nominal ledger entries for the following transactions:

20X6
September   1   Started business with £50,000 paid into the business bank account.
                     2   Loan from Brian Hope £2,000.
                     3   Goods purchased on credit £22,200
                     4   Cash sales £1,000.
                     5   Credit sales £2,000.
                   11   Bought goods on credit £1,850.
                   12   Goods returned by customer £200.
                   14   Credit sales £2,550.
                   15   Goods returned to supplier £700.
                   17   Purchase of van on credit £13,000.
                   19   Purchased office furniture for cash £3,000.
                   20   Returned goods to supplier £550.
                   21   Goods purchased by cheque £1,100.
                   25   Payment to supplier £5,350.
                   26   Goods returned by customer £150.
                   27   Payment for van £13,000.

4.6 Using your answer to question 4.5 above extract a trial balance as at 30 September 20X6 from Pamela Tanzer's nominal ledger.

4.7 Write up the following transactions in David Jensen's nominal ledger for May 20X4 and extract a trial balance as at 31 May 20X4:

20X4

May	1	Started business with £20,000 capital.
	2	Credit purchases £11,500.
	5	Cash sales £1800.
	6	Return of goods to supplier £400.
	7	Credit purchases £1,900.
	10	Credit sales £3,900.
	12	Cash sales £2,100.
	21	Cash purchase of machinery £5,500.
	22	Credit sales £2,200.
	23	Goods returned by customer £1,400.
	28	Goods returned to supplier £300.
	29	Cheque payment to creditor £8,600.
	31	Purchase of computer on credit £2,700.

BASIC ACCOUNTING STATEMENTS

LEARNING OBJECTIVES

After reading this chapter you should:

- Understand the difference between capital and revenue transactions.
- Understand the elements of the calculation of profit.
- Understand the structure of basic financial statements.
- Be able to construct simple profit and loss accounts, and balance sheets.

5.1 ACCOUNTING FOR THE RESULTS OF BUSINESS ACTIVITY

It is normal for most businesses to prepare accounting statements. These statements may be prepared at intervals of six months, quarterly or monthly, but almost all businesses will use a twelve month accounting period as the main accounting period for which to prepare accounts. We will, therefore, concentrate on the preparation of accounts which disclose the results of business activity in respect of an accounting year.

5.2 THE CALCULATION OF PROFIT

The profit (or loss) made by a business during the accounting year is not the same as the difference between cash received and cash paid. In general terms, profit is the difference between revenues and expenditures, but we need to consider the meaning of these terms closely. An important concept in the calculation of profit is the distinction that is made between revenue and capital items. Revenue means income; let us now define it further as income from trading activities. Thus, a shoe shop will derive revenue income from selling shoes. The shoe shop may, at some stage, sell its business premises and purchase a new outlet in a different location. The sale of the business premises is clearly not income from trading activities. Accountants would call such income capital income. In a similar way, expenditures can be classified into those that are related to the day-to-day operation of the business and those that are not. Expenditures that are related to the generation of trading income are called revenue expenses, whereas expenditures which are related to the purchase of assets for long-term use in the business are known as capital expenditures.

We can, therefore, refine our definition of profit as the difference between revenue income and revenue expenditure.

Example

On 1 January 20X1, Henry Jackson commenced trading as an employment agency specializing in supplying systems analysts and programmers to the computer industry. He started the agency with a cash injection of £20,000 and during the year he has drawn out £15,000 for living expenses. He has prepared a profit statement for the year ended 31 December 20X1.

Henry Jackson: profit statement for the year ended 31 December 20X1

	£	£
Income: Cash received in year		300,000
Expenditure		
Cash paid in year:		
Wages	205,000	
Drawings	15,000	
Office expenses	45,000	
Cost of new motor vehicle	25,000	
		290,000
Profit for the year		10,000

Henry's profit statement is incorrect. His income figure includes the money he paid into the business bank account to start the agency. He has included personal drawings and capital expenditure on a motor vehicle in his calculation of profit. If we look at the other expenses, it should be clear that wages and office expenses are the day-to-day running expenses of the business, but the vehicle will still exist at 31 December 20X1. In fact, the vehicle is likely to be used in the business for a number of years. Thus, the 20X1 profit figure has been distorted by the inclusion of the cost of an asset which will be used in subsequent accounting periods.

Henry's profit statement is also incorrect for another reason. He has used cash receipts and cash payments for his income and expenditure figures. Henry has not calculated a profit figure, he has calculated a cash surplus. We need to arrive at a more accurate figure of profit than that provided by Henry.

The first thing we could do is to eliminate the initial cash injection, the drawings, and the expenditure in respect of the vehicle. In the next chapter, we will look at ways in which the use of assets can be reflected in the calculation of profit, but for the moment we will ignore this complication.

The next thing we could do is to consider whether or not there are any debtors or creditors which need to be taken into account at 31 December 20X1. That is to say, fees earned in the year, but which have not been received by 31 December 20X1 or expenditures incurred in the year which have not been paid by the year end date. We can represent the year end position as follows:

Debtors at 31 December 20X1
Fees receivable £35,000.
Creditors at 31 December 20X1
Wages £ nil
Office expenses £ 5,000

Accountants call the profit calculation statement the profit and loss account because it shows how the profit or loss for the accounting period has been calculated. Henry's profit and loss account for 20X1 is as follows:

Henry Jackson: profit and loss account for the year ended 31 December 20X1

	£	£
Income		
(300,000 − 20,000 + 35,000)		315,000
Expenditure		
Wages	205,000	
Office expenses		
(45,000 + 5,000)	50,000	
		255,000
Profit for the year		60,000

The adjustments we have made to Henry's calculation are:

(a) The exclusion of the capital injection, personal drawings and capital expenditure.
(b) The inclusion of income due but not yet received at the year end (debtors).
(c) The inclusion of expenditure payable but not yet paid at the year end (creditors).

5.3 THE BALANCE SHEET: A LIST OF ASSETS AND LIABILITIES

After profit has been calculated, it would be useful for Henry to have an idea of his assets and liabilities at the end of the accounting period. This presents an indication of the health of the business by showing what is owned by and owed by the enterprise.

Assets

These are items of value owned by the business. The information provided above indicates that Henry's business has the following assets:

	£	
Motor vehicle	25,000	
Debtors	35,000	
Bank balance	10,000	(the cash surplus from Henry's 'profit' calculation)

The vehicle is of a different character to the other assets. It will last for a number of accounting periods. It is, therefore, known as a fixed asset. The other assets will be used up in the day-to-day running of the business. In the subsequent accounting period, debtors will pay the amounts they owe to the business, and the cash balance will be increased and decreased by trading activity. These assets are known as current assets.

Liabilities

These are items owed by the business, At 31 December 20X1, the liabilities are as follows:

	£
Creditors	5,000
Capital account	65,000

The creditors are in respect of office expenses. They are short-term liabilities and are known as current liabilities. The capital account is the liability of the business to its owner. In this case, the balance on the account represents the initial amount paid in by Henry to start the business, his personal drawings, and the profit earned by the business during the year.

We are now in a position to prepare a balance sheet. You should notice that the balance sheet is presented in a vertical format like the profit and loss account. This vertical format is easy to read because the figures are presented in a logical sequence and are spread over two columns. If the figures had been presented in a single column they would be much harder to read. In addition, you should also note that in a 'T' account and on a trial balance the position of a number (on the left or on the right of an account or a balance listing) indicates whether the number is a debit or a credit. This is NOT the case with vertically presented financial statements. The use of columns is a matter of presentation only.

Henry Jackson: balance sheet as at 31 December 20X1

	£	£
Fixed assets		
Motor vehicle		25,000
Current assets		
Debtors	35,000	
Bank	10,000	
	45,000	
Less: current liabilities		
Creditors	5,000	
		40,000
		65,000
Capital account		
Capital introduced January 1 20X1		20,000
Add: Profit for the year		60,000
		80,000
Less: Drawings		15,000
		65,000

The balance sheet balances because it is based on the principles of double-entry accounting. In the above example, we did not look at the relationship between double-entry and the financial statements. We now need to look at a more detailed example which links the trial balance with the profit and loss account and the balance sheet.

Up to now, we have looked at the calculation of profit as a simple statement of income minus expenses. Accountants like to present their profit statements in slightly more formal terms in what is known as a profit and loss account.

5.4 THE PROFIT AND LOSS ACCOUNT

In strict accounting terminology, there can be two elements to a profit calculation. These are:

1. *A trading account*
   This is used for the calculation of gross profit. That is to say, sales minus the costs which vary with sales.
2. *The profit and loss account*
   This takes gross profit as its starting point. Overhead expenses are deducted from gross profit and net profit is calculated.

Thus, a business needs to prepare a trading and profit and loss account. In this book, we will use the term 'profit and loss account' to cover the calculation of gross profit and net profit, in order to keep things simple.

The format of a typical profit and loss account is as follows:

[Business name]
Profit and loss account for the year ended [accounting period]

	£	£
Sales		X
Less cost of sales:		
Opening stock	X	
Plus purchases	X	
	—	
	X	
Less closing stock	(X)	
	—	(X)
		—
Gross profit		X
Less overhead expenses:		
[Category of expense]	X	
[Category of expense]	X	
[Category of expense]	X	
[Category of expense]	X	
[Category of expense]	X	
[Category of expense]	X	
	—	(X)
		—
Net profit		X
		=

[ ] = detail to be inserted by accounts preparer
(X) = number deducted to arrive at total

Notice that we start with sales and deduct items from the sales figure in order to arrive at profit. Also, we use two columns because this makes the profit and loss account easier to read. If we put all the figures into one column, it would be quite hard to spot the most important figures—sales, gross profit and net profit.

Why calculate two types of profit?

Gross profit is the profit earned by the business from its trading activities before the overhead expenses (such as rent, power, wages and travelling expenses) are deducted. In the basic format shown above, a cost-of-sales figure is calculated. The cost-of-sales figure represents the costs that vary directly with sales. We will make the simplifying assumption that the costs that vary directly with sales are the costs of materials which have been purchased for resale. Thus, if a business sells 1,000 units of its product in an accounting period, this would be represented in the profit and loss account as follows:

Sales	(1,000 units at selling price)
Cost of sales	(1,000 units at cost)

You will notice, however, that the cost of sales figure must be calculated by adding together the opening stock of materials and purchases of materials during the accounting period. Opening stock represents the cost of materials purchased in previous accounting periods. Opening stock is last period's purchases which will (normally) be sold in the current accounting period.

Closing stock is deducted from the total of opening stock plus purchases. This represents materials purchased in the current (and previous) accounting period(s) which have not been sold at the balance sheet date.

Gross profit is a useful calculation. It allows readers of accounts to compare the trading activities of a business over time and to compare the results of different businesses. The tax authorities also take a keen interest in gross profit as it is well known that a business which is in a particular industry will tend to have a particular level of gross profit.

Net profit shows the effect on profitability of overhead expenses. A business owner wishing to increase his profits by reducing his costs is likely to consider how to reduce his overhead costs before attention is focused on other costs.

5.5 THE BALANCE SHEET

At the end of the accounting period a list of assets and liabilities is drawn up. The format of a simple balance sheet is shown below. We will modify this format slightly in subsequent chapters.

[Business name]
Balance sheet as at [last day of accounting period]

	£	£
Fixed assets		
[Category]		X
[Category]		X
		—
		X
Current assets		
Stock (Closing stock)	X	
Debtors	X	
Bank and cash	X	
	—	
	X	
	—	
Current liabilities		
Creditors	X	
Bank overdraft	X	
	—	
	(X)	
	—	
Net current assets		X
		—
Net assets		X
		=
Capital account		
Opening balance		X
Plus net profit (or minus Loss)		X
		—
		X
Less drawings		(X)
		—
		X
Long-term loans		
Bank loan		X
		—
		X
		=

Example

George Armitage manufactures a range of high-quality clothes for the young adult/youth market. He uses mainly denim and leather to produce the famous GA classics range of jeans, shirts, and jackets. The key to George's success as a clothing manufacturer is his innovative use of fabric and colour to create eye-catching designs, and his insistence upon using high-quality materials. George also insists upon exceptionally high production standards which he enforces with rigorous quality controls. His trial balance for the year ended 30 September 20X5 is as follows:

	£'000s Debit	£'000s Credit
Sales		975
Purchases	320	
Stock at 1 October 20X4	52	
Wages	175	
Rates and water	37	
Light and heat	22	
Repairs and renewals	15	
Insurance	12	
Freehold property at cost	150	
Professional fees	25	
Postage and stationery	7	
Advertising	40	
Telephone	34	
Motor vehicles at cost	60	
Machinery at cost	250	
Travelling expenses	18	
Drawings	65	
Capital account		378
Debtors	120	
Creditors		45
Bank overdraft		5
Cash	1	
	1,403	1,403

There was no stock at 30 September 20X5

With this information, we are now ready to prepare a profit and loss account, and balance sheet. It is best to break this exercise down into a number of simple steps. These are:

Step 1 Classify the trial balance items into those that belong to the profit and loss account, and those that belong to the balance sheet. Mark the face of the trial balance.

Step 2 Start with the profit and loss account. Calculate gross profit.

Step 3 Bring in the overhead expenses and calculate net profit.

Step 4 Move on to the balance sheet. Start with fixed assets. List the categories of fixed assets and make a sub-total.

Step 5 Move on to current assets and current liabilities. Make a sub-total of each and deduct total current liabilities from total current assets.

Step 6 Calculate net assets. This is normally done by adding the product of step (5) to the fixed assets sub-total. Where current liabilities exceed current assets, the product of step (5) is deducted from the fixed assets sub-total.

Step 7 Complete the other side of the balance sheet.

The accounts for George Armitage for 20X5 should look like this:

George Armitage
Profit and loss account for the year ended 30 September 20X5

		£'000s	£'000s
	Sales		975
Step			
	Less cost of sales:		
2	Stock at 1 October 20X4	52	
	Purchases	320	
		———	
		372	
	Less stock at		
	30 September 20X5	–	
		———	372
			———
	Gross profit		603
	Less overhead expenses		
Step	Wages	175	
	Rates and water	37	
3	Light and heat	22	
	Repairs and renewals	15	
	Insurance	12	
	Professional fees	25	
	Postage and stationery	7	
	Advertising	40	
	Telephone	34	
	Travelling expenses	18	
		———	385
			———
	Net profit		218
			═══

George Armitage
Balance sheet as at 30 September 20X5

		£'000s	£'000s
	Fixed assets		
Step	Freehold property		150
	Motor vehicles		60
4	Machinery		250
			——
			460
	Current assets		
Step	Stock at 30 Sept 20X5	——	
	Debtors	120	
5	Cash	1	
		——	
		121	
		——	
	Current liabilities		
	Creditors	45	
	Bank overdraft	5	
		——	
		50	
		——	
Step	Net current assets		71
6			——
	Net assets		531
			==
	Capital account		
Step	Opening balance		378
7	Plus profit		218
			——
			596
	Less drawings		65
			——
			531
			==

KEY POINTS

1. Profit is the difference between revenue income and revenue expenditure.
2. Assets are items of value owned by the business.
3. Liabilities are financial obligations of the business.
4. The capital account is the liability of the business to the owner.
5. The calculation of profit is presented in the profit and loss account.
6. Assets and liabilities are listed on the balance sheet.
7. Review the profit and loss account and balance sheet formats.

QUESTIONS

5.1 Distinguish between capital expenditure and revenue expenditure.

5.2 Hillary Hedgemead runs a small shop. At the end of her accounting period, 31 December 20X8, she has produced the following profit statement.

Hillary Hedgemead
Profit and loss account for the year ended 31 December 20X8

	£
Stock at 1 January 20X8	1,300
Purchases	8,000
Drawings	1,625
Motor vehicle at cost	1,500
Wages	4,375
Light and heat	550
Insurance	300
Advertising	1,000
Telephone	850
	19,500
Less sales	24,375
Profit for the year	4,875

There was no stock at 31 December 20X8. Hillary is not sure whether her profit statement is correct. She asks for your advice. You are required to:

1. Write a memo explaining to Hillary how an accountant would normally construct a profit statement.
2. Produce a corrected profit and loss account.

5.3 Cherie's trial balance for the year ended 31 October 20X5 is as follows:

Advertising	Professional fees
Bank overdraft	Postage and stationery
Capital account	Sales
Cash	Stock at 1 November 20X4
Creditors	Travelling expenses
Drawings	Wages
Debtors	
Freehold property	
Insurance	
Machinery	

You are required to classify these accounts into items which will appear in the profit and loss account, and items which will appear on the balance sheet (use the abbreviations P&L for profit and loss and BS for balance sheet).

5.4 Robert sends you an urgent fax from his yacht which is cruising around the Canary Islands. He asks two questions:

1. What is a balance sheet?
2. How should a balance sheet be set out?

Reply to Robert's questions.

5.5 Explain what is meant by the following terms:

1. Fixed assets
2. Current assets
3. Current liabilities
4. Capital account

5.6 The following trial balance has been extracted from Norma's accounting system in respect of the year ended 31 May 20X9:

	£	£
Sales		48,750
Stock at 1 June 20X8	2,600	
Purchases	16,000	
Overhead expenses	19,250	
Motor vehicles	20,000	
Office equipment	3,000	
Debtors	5,750	
Creditors		2,500
Bank	250	
Cash	50	
Capital account		18,900
Drawings	3,250	
	70,150	70,150

There was no stock at 31 May 20X9.

You are required to produce Norma's profit and loss account for the year ended 31 May 20X9 and a balance sheet at that date.

5.7 Using the following trial balance, prepare a profit and loss account and balance sheet for John.

John

Trial balance as at 30 June 20X4

	£	£
Capital account		42,875
Rent	15,000	
Motor vehicles	9,500	
Purchases	47,000	
Sales		72,000
Wages	19,250	
Stock at 1 July 20X3	3,250	
Debtors	6,000	
Bank	500	
Creditors		3,750
Drawings	18,125	
	118,625	118,625

There was no stock at 30 June 20X4.

5.8 Tony's trial balance for the year ended 31 August 20X8 is as follows:

	£	£
Sales		121,875
Purchases	40,000	
Stock at 1 September 20X7	6,500	
Wages	21,875	
Rates and water	4,625	
Light and heat	2,750	
Repairs and renewals	1,875	
Insurance	1,500	
Freehold property at cost	31,250	
Professional fees	3,125	
Postage and stationery	875	
Advertising	5,000	
Telephone	4,250	
Motor vehicles at cost	7,500	
Machinery at cost	18,750	
Travelling expenses	2,250	
Drawings	8,125	
Capital account		47,250
Debtors	15,000	
Creditors		5,625
Bank overdraft		625
Cash	125	
	175,375	175,375

There was no stock at 31 August 20X8.
  Prepare Tony's profit and loss account and balance sheet for 20X8.

5.9 1. Distinguish between drawings and wages.
  2. Prepare a set of accounts using the following trial balance:

Harold
Trial balance as at 31 December 20X7

	£	£
Advertising	1,150	
Bank	150	
Capital account		25,950
Cash	50	
Drawings	8,500	
Electricity	650	
Office equipment	5,000	
Machinery	10,000	
Purchases	10,700	
Sales		31,500
Stationery	450	
Creditors		2,600
Debtors	3,250	
Wages	19,350	
Stock at 1 January 20X7	800	
	60,050	60,050

There was no stock at 31 December 20X7.

5.10 Mary's trial balance in respect of her accounting period ended 31 July 20X5 is as follows:

	£'000s	£'000s
Stock at 1 August 20X4	1,184	
Purchases	5,937	
Sales		9,461
Wages and salaries	1,931	
Rent	152	
Insurance	39	
Motor expenses	332	
Office expenses	108	
Heat and light	83	
General expenses	514	
Freehold premises	2,500	
Motor vehicles	900	
Office equipment	175	
Debtors	1,948	
Creditors		865
Bank	241	
Drawings	600	
Capital		6,318
	16,644	16,644

Stock at 31 July 20X5 was £1,473,000

Prepare a profit and loss account for the year ended 31 July 20X5 and a balance sheet at that date.

THE ACCOUNTS PRODUCTION PROCESS

LEARNING OBJECTIVES

After reading this chapter you should:

- Understand the process of constructing a set of financial statements.
- Understand the relationship between the accounting system and the financial accounting statements.
- Understand the nature and purpose of period end adjustments.
- Reinforce your understanding of financial accounting statements.

6.1 THE ACCOUNTS PRODUCTION PROCESS

This chapter draws together some of the ideas presented in previous chapters. These ideas can be summarized as follows:

ACCOUNTING SOURCE DATA
are
processed
in
THE ACCOUNTING SYSTEM
a
TRIAL BALANCE
is produced
FINANCIAL STATEMENTS
are produced
from the trial balance

This chapter will introduce a further stage in the accounts production process: period end adjustments.

The process can now be represented as follows:

ACCOUNTING SOURCE DATA
THE ACCOUNTING SYSTEM
TRIAL BALANCE
PERIOD END ADJUSTMENTS
FINANCIAL STATEMENTS

PERIOD END ADJUSTMENTS

These adjustments are necessary because some of the information required for the preparation of accounts only becomes available after the end of the accounting period. In addition, certain judgements need to be made concerning the use of fixed assets, the status of debtors and the valuation of closing stock.

Period end adjustments may be classified as follows:

1. Depreciation—which seeks to measure the cost to the business of the wearing out or loss in value of fixed assets.
2. Accruals—which are additional items of expenditure relevant to the current accounting period, but which have been omitted from the trial balance.
3. Pre-payments—which are items of expenditure contained in the trial balance which belong to a subsequent accounting period.
4. Debtors adjustments—these take the form of accounting adjustments for non-paying customers (bad debts) and for potentially non-paying customers (doubtful debts).
5. Stock—materials unsold at the end of the accounting period must be valued and carried forward into the subsequent accounting period so that the cost of such materials can be matched with the relevant sale proceeds.

These adjustments will now be considered in more detail.

Depreciation

Chapter 5 introduced fixed assets. These assets, whether they are vehicles, computers or machinery, will wear out and lose value as they are used by the business.

Example

Benjamin is a freelance consultant. He has just purchased equipment costing £16,000 for use in his business. He estimates that this equipment will last for four years and have a residual or scrap value of £1,000. Charging the full cost of this asset against Benjamin's profit in the current accounting year would not make sense. The asset will be used in the generation of profits over four years. In order to match like with like, the cost of acquiring the equipment should be charged over its useful life in the business. The amount charged against profits to reflect the cost of using assets is known as deprecation. We need to consider how Benjamin could calculate the amount of depreciation to charge to profit over the next four years.

Straight line and reducing balance methods of depreciation

Benjamin could have chosen a number of methods in order to calculate his annual depreciation charge. In practice, the two main methods used by businesses are the straight line method and the reducing balance method.

The straight line method charges the profit and loss account with an equal amount of depreciation each year over the useful life of the asset. The annual depreciation charge may be calculated using the following formula:

Annual depreciation charge using the straight line method

$$\frac{\text{Cost} - \text{residual value}}{\text{Useful life}}$$

Benjamin's equipment has cost £16,000, it has a residual value of £1,000, and it will last for four years. The annual depreciation charge for each of the four years of ownership will be:

$$\frac{£16,000 - £1,000}{4} = £3,750 \text{ pa}$$

He could have chosen to use the reducing balance method which charges large amounts of depreciation in the early years of ownership of the asset and smaller amounts of depreciation in later years of ownership. The calculations for depreciating Benjamin's vehicle on a reducing balance basis are slightly more complex. The reducing balance method takes into account depreciation charged in previous accounting periods. Thus, in year one the depreciation charge is based on cost and in year two the charge is based on cost minus the year one depreciation charge. Any residual value is reflected in the rate of depreciation. This means that, strictly, the percentage rate of depreciation must be calculated which reduces the value of the asset to its residual value at the end of its useful life. This can be calculated using the following formula:

Annual depreciation rate using the reducing balance method

$$r = 1 - \sqrt[n]{s/c} \qquad \text{or one minus the } n\text{th} \\ \text{root of s over } c$$

where r = rate of depreciation
n = the useful life of the asset
s = the residual or scrap value of the asset
   (where there is no residual value $s = 1$)
c = the cost of the asset

The only difficulty with the formula is that it requires the calculation of the nth root. This is easy with a scientific calculator, however, where the useful life is two years (or a multiple thereof) the nth root can be found using the square root key. (If the key is pressed twice, the fourth root is found and so on.)

Annual depreciation charge using the reducing balance method
The above formula does not give the depreciation charge for the year, it merely gives the depreciation rate. The annual depreciation charge is:

Cost − depreciation charged in previous year(s) × depreciation rate.

The calculations for depreciating Benjamin's asset over four years are as follows:

(a) Calculation of depreciation rate

$$r = 1 - \sqrt[n]{s/c}$$

$$r = 1 - \sqrt[4]{1000/16,000}$$

$$r = 1 - \sqrt[4]{0.0625}$$

$$r = 1 - 0.5$$
$$r = 0.5 \text{ or } 50\%$$

(b) Depreciation charge

Year		£
0	Cost	16,000
1	charge = 16,000 × 50%	8,000
		8,000
2	charge = 8,000 × 50%	4,000
		4,000
3	charge = 4,000 × 50%	2,000
		2,000
4	charge = 2,000 × 50%	1,000
	residual value	1,000

The straight line method charges an equal amount of depreciation during each year of useful life. The reducing balance method charges a higher amount of depreciation in the early years of ownership of the asset.

Which method to use?
In practice, each asset (or class of asset) is considered and a method of depreciation is chosen which most accurately reflects the cost of using that particular asset during its useful life.

Assessment exercises will always make it clear which method of depreciation should be used and some will require students to use both methods in respect of different classes of asset.

Example
The following is an extract from the trial balance of Katherine for the year ended 31 December 20X1:

	£	£
Motor vehicles: cost	25,000	
Accumulated depreciation (at 1 January 20X1)		12,500
Plant and equipment: cost	10,000	
Accumulated depreciation (at 1 January 20X1)		4,000

Depreciation is to be provided on motor vehicles at 25% on cost, and on plant and equipment at 20%, using the reducing balance method.

The annual charge for depreciation may be calculated as follows:

Motor vehicles (straight line method): £25,000 × 25% = £6,250
Plant and equipment (reducing balance method):
  Cost   10,000
  Less depreciation previously charged   4,000
                                                       ─────
                                                       6,000 × 20% = £1,200
                                                       ─────
                                                                £7,450
                                                                ─────

Disposal of an asset

The sale of an asset by the business during an accounting period requires the accountant to calculate the profit or loss on disposal. This is done by comparing the sale proceeds of the asset with the net book value at the date of disposal. In assessment exercises, a simplifying assumption is often made that no depreciation is provided in the year of disposal.

Example

Miles sells a vehicle he has been using in his business for £7,000. The vehicle cost him £18,000 and the accumulated depreciation provided in respect of this vehicle is £13,500.

The result of this transaction is as follows:

	£
Cost of vehicle	18,000
Accumulated depreciation	13,500
	─────
Net book value	4,500
Sale proceeds	7,000
	─────
Profit on sale	2,500
	─────

The cost and accumulated depreciation in respect of this vehicle will be removed from Miles's balance sheet and the profit on sale will be shown in the profit and loss account.

Other period end adjustments

Depreciation requires a more detailed explanation than the other period end adjustments.

We will now, briefly, examine the other categories of adjustment before we consider a comprehensive example.

Accruals

The end of an accounting period of a particular business may not coincide with the billing frequency of other businesses. A 31 December year end may not, for example, coincide with the quarterly billing periods used by utility companies. A £300 electricity bill for the three months ended January 20X2 may be received (by a business having a 31 December 20X1 year end) in February 20X2. This bill must be subdivided so that the charge in respect of November and December 20X1 may be included in the 20X1 profit and loss account. This charge is known as an accrual. It appears in the profit and loss account as part of overhead expenses, and on the balance sheet as a current liability.

Pre-payments

A pre-payment is similar, in many respects to an accrual. However, in this case, an item of expenditure has been paid by the business which relates partly to the current accounting period and partly to a subsequent accounting period. A £1,200 annual insurance premium paid on 1 April 20X1 would, at 31 December 20X1, result in the profit and loss account containing an insurance charge in respect of the period January to March 20X2. This prepaid amount must be deducted from the profit and loss account charge and added to current assets in the balance sheet as a pre-payment.

Example

Pandro is producing the accounts for his business (a bar, restaurant, and gambling club) in respect of the year ended 31 December 20X1. During the year, he paid on 1 April an insurance premium of £1,200 for the period 1 April 20X1 to 31 March 20X2. In February 20X2, he receives his quarterly electricity bill of £300 in respect of the three months ended 31 January 20X2.

In order to calculate the correct amounts to show in his profit and loss account for the year ended 31 December 20X1, he must make the following adjustments:

1. He must calculate the accrued expense for electricity:
   £300 × 2/3 = £200   This is the charge for November and December 20X1.
2. He must calculate the pre-payment for insurance:
   £1,200 × 3/12 = £300   This represents insurance for the three months ended 31 March 20X2.

Debtors adjustments

Debtors owe money to the business. These debts may be bad or doubtful. A bad debt occurs when the customer will not pay, either because of a dispute or bankruptcy. A bad debt must be written off as an overhead expense in the profit and loss account.

A debt is doubtful when the owner of the business decides that the customer might not pay. In practice, businessmen know by experience that a certain percentage of debtors are likely not to pay their bills. Instead of trying to identify such debtors individually, a general provision for doubtful debts can be created. This provision is a credit balance and remains on the balance sheet as a deduction from the debtors figure in current assets. Any increases or decreases in this provision are charged or credited to the profit and loss account. Where a provision is created for the first time, it is effectively increased from zero to the full amount of the provision. Thus, in the year of its creation, the whole of the doubtful debts provision is charged to the profit and loss account. In subsequent years, only changes in the provision pass through the profit and loss account.

Stock

A manufacturing business will buy raw materials in order to produce goods for resale. At the end of the accounting year, some of these materials may not have been used. This stock of raw materials must be counted and valued. Once this is done, the value of these materials must be deducted from raw material purchases made in the year and included in the balance sheet under current assets. Raw materials are not the only form of stock. A business may also have stocks of partly finished goods (sometimes called work in progress) and stocks of finished goods. The accounting treatment of these stocks is similar to the treatment of raw material stocks.

Comprehensive example

The stages in the accounts production process may now be illustrated by means of the following example:

Dax
Trial balance as at 31 December 20X7

	£	£
	Debit	Credit
Bank	35,300	
Capital account		19,300
Drawings	16,000	
Insurance	1,800	
Long-term loan from bank		50,000
Loan interest	7,500	
Miscellaneous expenses	7,700	
Office equipment:		
Cost	40,000	
Accumulated depreciation		19,000
Provision for doubtful debts		2,000
Purchases	320,000	
Rates	10,000	
Sales		372,000
Stock (1 January 20X7)	36,000	
Trade creditors		105,000
Trade debtors	93,000	
	567,300	567,300

The following information is given as the basis for period end adjustments:

1. Stock at 31 December 20X7 is £68,000.
2. At 31 December 20X7, an accrual for rates of £2,000 was calculated and in addition it was discovered that insurance pre-paid amounted to £200.
3. Office equipment is depreciated at a rate of 25% per annum on a straight line basis.
4. Specific bad debts of £13,000 are to be written off.
5. The provision for doubtful debts is to be made equal to 10% of the outstanding trade debtors as at 31 December 20X7.

In order to produce financial statements for Dax, the accounting treatment of the period end adjustments must be established as follows:

1. *Stock*
   The closing stock at 31 December 20X7 is deducted from the total of opening stock and purchases in the profit and loss account. The closing stock figure is also included as a current asset in the balance sheet.
2. *Accruals and pre-payments*
   The rates accrual of £2,000 represents an additional amount due in respect of rates at the end of the accounting period. This amount is added to the trial balance figure of £10,000, giving a figure of £12,000 as the overhead charge in the profit and loss account. The accrual of £2,000 is then included in the balance sheet under current liabilities.

   The insurance pre-payment of £200 is deducted from the trial balance figure of £1,800 giving an overhead charge of £1,600 in the profit and loss account. The pre-payment of £200 will then appear under current assets in the balance sheet.
3. *Depreciation*
   The depreciation charge for the year is £40,000 $\times$ 25% = £10,000
   This is charged to the profit and loss account.

In order to show the correct figure of accumulated depreciation on the balance sheet, a further adjustment must be made as follows:

	£
Accumulated depreciation per trial balance	19,000
Depreciation for year	10,000
Accumulated depreciation at 31 December 20X7	29,000

4. *Specific bad debts*
   In this particular situation, the bad debts of £13,000 must be deducted from the debtors figure and shown in the profit and loss account as an overhead charge. In many trial balances presented to students, bad debts are shown on the trial balance as a debit entry and the figure of debtors given is after bad debts have been deducted. The adjustment for Dax is as follows:

	£
Debtors per trial balance	93,000
Bad debts charged to profit and loss account	13,000
Debtors at 31 December 20X7	80,000

5. Provision for doubtful debts

	£	
Provision required at 31 December 20X7	8,000	(80,000 × 10%)
Provision per trial balance	2,000	
Increase in provision	6,000	

The increase in provision of £6,000 will be charged to the profit and loss account, and the provision of £8,000 will appear on the balance sheet at 31 December 20X7
The financial statements can now be constructed.

Dax
Profit and loss account for the year ended 31 December 20X7

	£	£
Sales		372,000
Less cost of sales:		
Opening stock	36,000	
Plus purchases	320,000	
	356,000	
Less closing stock	68,000	
		288,000
Gross profit		84,000
Less overhead expenses:		
Depreciation	10,000	
Insurance (1,800 − 200)	1,600	
Loan interest	7,500	
Miscellaneous expenses	7,700	
Rates (10,000 + 2,000)	12,000	
Bad debt	13,000	
Increase in doubtful debt provision	6,000	
		57,800
Net profit for the year		26,200

Dax
Balance sheet as at 31 December 20X7

	£ Cost	£ Accumulated depreciation	£ Net book value
Fixed assets:			
Office equipment	40,000	29,000	11,000
Current assets:			
Stock		68,000	
Debtors	80,000		
Less provision	8,000		
		72,000	
Bank		35,300	
Pre-payments		200	
		175,500	
Less current liabilities:			
Creditors	105,000		
Accruals	2,000		
		107,000	
			68,500
Net assets			79,500
Capital account			
Balance at 1 January 20X7			19,300
Add profit for the year			26,200
			45,500
Less drawings			16,000
			29,500
Long-term-loan			50,000
			79,500

KEY POINTS

1. The stages in the accounts production process are as follows:

- Source data
- Processed in accounting system
- Trial balance extraction
- Period end adjustments
- Financial statements

2. Period end adjustments comprise:

- Depreciation
- Accruals
- Pre-payments
- Debtors adjustments
- Stock

3. Depreciation measures the wearing out or other loss of value of fixed assets.
4. Accruals are additional items of expenditure which belong to the current accounting period.
5. Pre-payments are items of expenditure which belong to the subsequent accounting period.
6. A bad debt is written off as an overhead expense.
7. Doubtful debts are debts which may not be paid. They are not specifically identified. Instead, a provision for doubtful debts is created. Increases or decreases to this provision are charged (in the case of increases) or credited (in the case of decreases) to the profit and loss account.
8. Closing stock at the end of the accounting period must be deducted from purchases and shown as a current asset on the balance sheet.

QUESTIONS

6.1 On 1 January 20X1, Andrew purchased a vehicle for use in his business. The vehicle cost him £24,000, and he estimates that it will have a useful life of 4 years and a residual value of £1,500.

Andrew is not sure whether to use the straight line method or the reducing balance method of depreciation.

Required
Calculate the depreciation charge for the accounting periods ending on 31 December 20X1, 20X2, 20X3, and 20X4 using both methods of depreciation (use a depreciation rate of 50% for the reducing balance method).

6.2 Edward is preparing his accounts for the year ended 30 September 20X8. The following is an extract from his trial balance:

Edward
Trial balance at 30 September 20X8 (extract)

	£	£
Plant and equipment		
Cost	200,000	
Accumulated depreciation		72,000
Motor vehicles		
Cost	75,000	
Accumulated depreciation		30,000

Depreciation is to be charged as follows:

1. Plant and equipment 20% on the reducing balance basis.
2. Motor vehicles 20% on cost.

Required
1. Calculate the amount of depreciation to be shown in Edward's profit and loss account for the year ended 30 September 20X8 in respect of each class of fixed asset.
2. Prepare the fixed assets section of Edward's balance sheet as at 30 September 20X8.

6.3 On 31 December 20X2, Charles sold an item of office equipment for £17,500. The equipment had cost £25,000 on 1 January 20X1. Charles uses the reducing balance basis to depreciate his office equipment. The item sold has been depreciated using an estimated useful life of four years and a residual value to £10,240.

Required
Calculate (1) the annual percentage rate of depreciation and (2) the profit or loss on sale in respect of the above asset.

6.4

Tomislav
Trial balance at 31 July 20X9 (extract)

	£
Light and heat	132,000
Insurance	200,000
Rates	80,000
Wages	334,000
Advertising	15,000
Telephone	125,000
Accruals at 31 July 20X9	
Light and heat	41,500
Rates	30,000
Pre-payments at 31 July 20X8	
Insurance	70,000
Advertising	1,000

Required
Using the above information, prepare extracts from Tomislav's profit and loss account and balance sheet for 20X9 to show how overhead expenses, accruals, and pre-payments should be disclosed in financial statements.

6.5 1. Explain the accounting treatment of:
(a) bad debts, and
(b) doubtful debts.
2. At 1 January 20X8, Elizabeth has a provision for doubtful debts of £8,000. At 31 December 20X8, her debtors are £100,000 and she requires a provision of 10% of outstanding debtors. Show how this provision is reflected in the 20X8 financial statements.
3. At 31 December 20X9, Elizabeth's debtors are £70,000. If she wishes to maintain a provision of 10% of outstanding debtors, show how this situation is reflected in the 20X9 financial statements.

6.6 Rupert's trial balance as at 31 December 20X2 is as follows:

	£	£
Bank	17,650	
Capital account		9,650
Drawings	8,000	
Insurance	900	
Long-term loan from bank		25,000
Loan interest	3,750	
Miscellaneous expenses	3,850	
Motor vehicles:		
Cost	20,000	
Accumulated depreciation		9,500
Provision for doubtful debts		1,000
Purchases	160,000	
Rates	5,000	
Sales		186,000
Stock at 1 January 20X2	18,000	
Creditors		52,500
Debtors	46,500	
	283,650	283,650

Additional information
1. Stock at 31 December 20X2 is £34,000.
2. At 31 December 20X2 insurance pre-paid amounted to £100, and rates accrued amounted to £1,000. There were no other accruals or pre-payments.
3. Motor vehicles are depreciated at a rate of 25% per annum on a straight line basis.
4. Bad debts of £6,500 are to be written off.
5. The provision for doubtful debts is to be made equal to 10% of the outstanding debtors at 31 December 20X2.

Required
Prepare Rupert's profit and loss account for the year ended 31 December 20X2, and a **balance sheet** at that date.

6.7 Anne's trial balance for the year ended 30 June 20X6 is as follows:

	£	£
Advertising	4,500	
Bank	600	
Capital		110,250
Drawings	15,000	
Electricity	4,800	
Furniture and fittings		
Cost	18,000	
Accumulated depreciation		2,700
Administration expenses	43,350	
Provision for doubtful debts		3,450
Purchases	975,000	
Rates	9,000	
Sales		1,234,200
Stock	76,500	
Telephone	1,950	
Creditors		19,500
Debtors	63,000	
Vehicles		
Cost	52,500	
Accumulated depreciation		10,500
Wages and salaries	116,400	
	1,380,600	1,380,600

Additional information
1. Stock at 30 June 20X6 was £75,000.
2. Depreciation is to be charged at a rate of 15% on furniture and fittings on a straight line basis.
3. Depreciation is to be charged at a rate of 20% on vehicles on a reducing balance basis.
4. At 30 June 20X6, accruals and pre-payments were as follows:

Accruals	Pre-payments
Electricity £450	Rates £1,500

5. The provision for doubtful debts is to be 10% of outstanding debtors as at 30 June 20X6.

Required
Prepare Anne's profit and loss account for the year ended 30 June 20X6, and a balance sheet at that date.

6.8 Margaret's trial balance as at 31 December 20X3 is as follows:

	£	£
Capital		189,500
Cash at bank	1,200	
Rent received		3,900
Land and buildings at cost	50,000	
Plant and equipment		
Cost	165,000	
Accumulated depreciation		90,000
Motor vehicles		
Cost	192,000	
Accumulated depreciation		48,000
Office expenses	147,000	
Purchases	249,000	
Sales		492,000
Stock	8,400	
Debtors	39,600	
Creditors		28,800
	852,200	852,200

Additional information
1. Depreciation:

Asset	Rate	Basis
Land and buildings	–	no depreciation provided
Plant and equipment	30%	Cost
Motor vehicles	25%	Reducing balance

2. Stock at 31 December 20X3 was £47,400
3. At 31 December 20X3, accrued expenses amounted to £3,600 and pre-payments amounted to £1,000.
4. Office expenses include Margaret's drawings of £27,000.

Required
Prepare Margaret's profit and loss account for the year ended 31 December 20X3, and a balance sheet at that date.

SEVEN

MORE COMPLEX ACCOUNTING STATEMENTS

LEARNING OBJECTIVES

After reading this chapter you should:

- Understand how accounting statements deal with multiple-owner business enterprises.
- Understand the special accounting requirements of companies.
- Be able to prepare a set of partnership accounts.
- Be able to prepare a set of company accounts.

7.1 MORE COMPLEX ACCOUNTING STATEMENTS

In earlier chapters we have looked at methods of describing the results of the simplest form of business entity: the sole trader. This chapter will consider more complex business entities which are owned by more than one individual. These are partnerships and companies. It is useful to consider the accounting requirements of these entities in the following terms:

Single-owner entities	Multiple-owner entities
Capital is provided by an individual and recorded in a capital account	Capital is provided by a number of individuals. These interests must be recorded separately
Profit belongs to an individual	Profit must be divided between the owners of the business
Owner has clear ownership of the business	A variety of classes of ownership is permitted

7.2 PARTNERSHIPS

Partnerships, as the name implies, are businesses which are owned by more than one individual. This may be because individuals can combine differing talents, e.g. technical skill and management skill, or resources, e.g. financial resources and product knowledge.

In the UK, the number of people who can form a partnership is 20, although this limit does not apply in the case of professional partnerships such as solicitors and accountants.

Accounting problems

Problem	Solution
Multiple contributions of capital	A capital account is opened for each provider of capital
Profits and losses must be divided between the partners	A profit and loss appropriation account is used to divide profits between the partners

We need to modify our conception of capital in partnership accounts. You will recall that in the case of sole traders the capital account contained three main elements:

Capital introduced   This includes the initial amount of capital used to start the business (cash or assets) and any other amount of additional capital introduced in subsequent years.

Profits/losses   At the end of each accounting period, the net profit or loss is credited (or debited) to the capital account.

Capital withdrawn (drawings)   At the end of each accounting period, drawings are debited to the capital account.

In partnership accounts, each partner's capital account contains only the first element of capital: capital introduced. Profits/losses and drawings are contained in a new account, the current account.

Example

Abelard and Eloise are in partnership as a language school. On 1 January 20X0 Abelard introduces cash of £2,000, and freehold premises with an agreed valuation of £120,000. Eloise contributes cash of £50,000. At the end of their first year of trading, profits are £40,000, and drawings are £20,000 Abelard and £10,000 Eloise. They have agreed to share profits equally. Write up the capital and current accounts of this partnership as at 31 December 20X0.

Solution

Abelard and Eloise
Capital and current accounts as at 31 December 20X0

Capital account—Abelard

31.12.X0			1.1.X0		
Balance c/d	122,000		Bank	2,000	
			Freehold property	120,000	
	122,000			122,000	
			Balance b/d	122,000	

Capital account—Eloise

			1.1.X0		
			Bank	50,000	

Current account—Abelard

31.12.X0			31.12.X0		
Drawings	20,000		P&L appropriation account	20,000	

Current account—Eloise

31.12.X0			31.12.X0		
Drawings	10,000		P&L appropriation account	20,000	
Balance c/d	10,000				
	20,000			20,000	
			Balance b/d	10,000	

Abelard and Eloise agreed to share profits equally. There are, however, a number of other ways they could have divided up the profits. Eloise could argue that as she spends a great deal of her time administering the business, setting the timetable, arranging the advertising, and hiring staff, she should be entitled to a fixed amount regardless of the actual amount of profit in the year. Thus, she insists on receiving a salary of £7500 as compensation for her administrative tasks.

Abelard, on the other hand, could point out that he has contributed more to the business in terms of capital, and this should be compensated for by allowing interest on capital at the rate of 10% of the balance on the capital account at the end of the accounting period. The partners agree to share any remaining profit on a 50:50 basis as before, although Eloise may insist on a higher profit share in the future as the business continues to prosper due to her marketing and administrative skills.

Thus, partnership profits may be divided into:

- Partnership salary to one or all the partners
- Interest on capital
- Share of balance of the profits

If these profit-sharing arrangements had been in force during the year to 31 December 20X0, the result would have been:

Abelard and Eloise
Profit and Loss Appropriation account
For the year ended 31 December 20X0

	£	£
Net profit for the year		40,000
Less: shares of profit		
(a) Partnership Salary		
Abelard	–	
Eloise	7,500	
	———	7,500
		———
		32,500
(b) Interest on capital		
Abelard £122,000 × 10%	12,200	
Eloise £ 50,000 × 10%	5,000	
	———	17,200
		———
		15,300
(c) Share of balance of profits		
Abelard 50%	7,650	
Eloise 50%	7,650	
	———	15,300
		———
		–
		———

The current accounts would have been:

Abelard and Eloise
Balance sheet (extract) as at 31 December 20X0

	£	£	£
Current accounts	Abelard	Eloise	Total
Opening balance	–	–	
Partnership Salary	–	7,500	
Interest on capital	12,200	5,000	
Balance of profits	7,650	7,650	
	19,850	20,150	
Less drawings	20,000	10,000	
Closing balance	(150)	10,150	10,000

Summary —partnership accounts

The basic format of sole trader accounts is modified to deal with profit shares and multiple ownership by the use of:

1. A profit and loss appropriation account to show how the net profit is divided between the partners.
2. A capital account for each partner which is used to show the (relatively) fixed portion of capital introduced to start and expand the business.
3. A current account for each partner which deals with profit shares and drawings.

7.3 COMPANY ACCOUNTS

The major vehicle for trading in most modern economies is the Limited Company. As a business entity, it has a number of important characteristics which differentiate it from partnerships and sole traders. These are:

(a) legal personality
(b) limited liability of members
(c) regulatory control

The accounting importance of these characteristics is as follows:

(a) *Legal Personality*—expansion of the business entity concept
A company is a legal person distinct from its members. It can sue in its own name. It can be sued. It can outlast the lifetime of its founding members. A major accounting consequence of legal personality is that companies, like other individuals, must pay tax on income and capital gains. In the UK, the scheme of company taxation is known as corporation tax.
Another consequence of legal personality is the fact that a company must be named in such a way that clearly indicates its legal status. In the UK, companies are designated 'Limited' for private limited companies and 'Public' for public limited

companies. The essential difference between a public and a private company is that the former is permitted to sell its shares to the public in order to finance its activities.

(b) *Limited liability of members*

The owners of companies are shareholders. Capital is divided into a number of shares of different classes. If a company gets into difficulties and is unable to pay its debts, it may be wound up or liquidated by legal process. In these circumstances, shareholders may lose only their share capital (the amount they invested in the company). Their personal assets will be unaffected. Thus, in companies the liability for business debts of shareholders is limited to the capital contributed by them. We will discuss share capital in more detail below.

(c) *Regulatory control*

The form and content of company accounts is regulated by statute. Companies must provide accounting statements to shareholders at least once a year. These accounting statements must contain a specified amount of information which must be audited. We will consider these points in more detail in the next chapter.

7.4 FEATURES OF COMPANY ACCOUNTS

Share capital

In partnerships and sole traders, capital is represented by capital and current accounts. In companies, the capital is known as 'share capital'. There are two main types of share capital: ordinary shares and preference shares.

Ordinary shares have many of the characteristics of the capital accounts of partnerships or sole traders. Ordinary shareholders are the main owners of a company. They have a right to receive all or part of profits in the form of dividends, although it is rare for a company to distribute all of its profits to the ordinary shareholders.

We saw, above, that multiple-owner entities permit a variety of classes of ownership. Preference shares are an example of this. Preference shares entitle the holders to a fixed percentage share of profits. If a company is experiencing difficult trading conditions, the preference shareholders will receive dividends, while the ordinary shareholders may not. If a company goes into liquidation and ceases trading, the preference shareholders will be repaid the nominal value of their shares before the ordinary shareholders.

In many company balance sheets, shares are described as 'Authorized' and 'issued'. Authorized shares represent the amount of share capital that a company is allowed, by its constitution, to issue. A company may not issue all of its authorized share capital. Issued share capital represents the amount of shares that are actually issued. It is possible, therefore, that there will be different amounts of authorized and issued share capital. In assessment exercises, the authorized share capital is given by way of note and the issued share capital is shown on the trial balance. In this case, both authorized and issued share capital should be shown on the face of the balance sheet. A disclosure format (X Ltd.) is shown below.

Dividends

Partners receive profit shares, but shareholders in companies receive dividends. These profit shares depend upon shareholdings. Thus, dividends may be calculated:

(a) as pence per share, e.g. 100,000 shares × 20p = £20,000
(b) as a stated amount, e.g. £15,000
(c) as a percentage, e.g. £100,000 of shares × 10% = £10,000

The expression of dividends as a percentage is normally related to preference dividend payments. Dividends may be paid during the year, in which case they will appear on the trial balance. Dividends may also be paid after the end of the accounting period when profit is determined. These proposed dividends are creditors in the accounts. They are disclosed in the profit and loss account, and under current liabilities on the balance sheet.

Share premium account

A feature of the UK regulatory environment is that company shares are issued at a nominal value. A nominal value is the named or decided value for a particular type of share. A company may decide, for example, to designate all its share capital as £1 ordinary shares. This decision is made when the company is formed. £1 is therefore the nominal value of the company's ordinary shares. When the company comes to sell its shares, it will seek to sell them at the highest price. If we assume that the company actually receives £1.50 for each of its shares, the amount received in excess of the nominal value (50p per share) is known as the share premium. It is a convention that this premium is credited to the share premium account. In this introductory text, we will not consider any of the detailed accounting and legal rules relating to the use of the share premium account. The account will appear as a credit balance on the trial balance and should be shown on the face of the balance sheet as indicated below in the examples X Ltd. and Ergonomics Ltd.

Reserves

Companies are unlike other forms of business unit in that they need not distribute all of their profits to the owners of the business. Companies disclose this undistributed profit as retained profit in the profit and loss account and as a reserve on the face of the balance sheet. Thus, in the examples below, we see an amount described as 'profit and loss account' on the face of the balance sheet. This represents cumulative retained profits. Another type of reserve is the share premium account. In fact, there are a number of other reserves which companies may create. However, as this is a rather complex area of accounting, we will not explore this topic further. We will therefore consider reserves as being limited to the profit and loss account and the share premium account.

Debentures

A debenture is a legal document used to secure a loan. Debentures can be considered as a form of long-term loan. The lender is given security for his loan by being allowed rights to assets of the business if the borrower defaults. Interest on debentures is a charge against profit, not an appropriation of profit. Debenture interest payments should not, therefore, be confused with dividend payments.

Taxation

Companies are legally constituted persons. They must, therefore, pay tax. The special scheme of income tax for companies is called 'corporation tax'. This tax charge is based on profit, but the rules for calculating taxable profits are different from the rules for calculating accounting profit. The corporation tax liability cannot be calculated until accounting profit is calculated. Therefore, the tax liability must be a creditor. In company accounts, there is an additional period end adjustment which is the estimation of the corporation tax liability. This is shown in the profit and loss account as the taxation charge, and in the balance sheet as a current liability.

Directors

Directors manage the day-to-day affairs of the business on behalf of the shareholders. Directors' salaries, remuneration, emoluments or fees are an overhead expense in the profit and loss account, and not an appropriation of profit.

Published company accounts

It is useful at this stage to distinguish two types of accounting statement for companies: 'published' company accounts and internal company accounts. In this chapter, we will concentrate on the simple form of internal company accounts which are a variation on the basic format of partnership and sole trader accounts we have considered in this chapter and in previous chapters. Published company accounts are more complex and will be considered in more detail in the next chapter.

7.5 FORMAT OF INTERNAL COMPANY ACCOUNTS

The basic format of a company profit and loss account is similar to sole trader and partnership profit and loss accounts until we get to net profit. At this point, the format is as follows:

X Ltd.
Profit and loss account (extract)
For the year ended 30 June 20X5

	£'000s
Net profit before tax	375
Less corporation tax	130
Net profit after tax	245
Less dividends	50
Retained profit for the year	195
Retained profit brought forward	600
Retained profit carried forward	795

X Ltd.
Balance sheet as at 30 June 20X5

	£'000s	£'000s
Fixed assets		1,335
Current assets	300	
Current liabilities		
Creditors	100	
Accruals	10	
Corporation tax	130	
Proposed dividends	50	
	290	
		10
Net assets		1,345

Share capital	Authorized share capital	Issued share capital
Ordinary shares of £1 each	500	300
Reserves		
Profit and loss Account		795
Share premium account		150
		1,245
Long-term loan		
Debentures		100
		1,345

NB: In the above example, numbers are shown for illustrative purposes only.

Comprehensive example

Ergonomics Ltd. sells office furniture. The following trial balance has been extracted as at 31 December 20X5.

	Debit £	Credit £
Bank	34,000	
100,000 ordinary shares of £1 each		100,000
80,000 8% preference shares of £1 each		80,000
Freehold property	350,000	
10% Debenture loan stock		40,000
Office expenses	17,500	
Wages and salaries	32,500	
Directors' remuneration	75,000	
Purchases	140,000	
Sales		420,000
Share premium account		50,000
Creditors		18,000
Debtors	70,000	
Motor vehicles at cost	35,000	
Accumulated depreciation		21,000
Plant and equipment at cost	85,000	
Accumulated depreciation		17,000
Profit and loss account at 31.12.X4		128,200
Preference dividend paid	3,200	
Stock as at 31.12.X4	25,000	
Debenture interest paid	2,000	
Ordinary dividend paid	5,000	
	874,200	874,200

Notes
1. The authorized share capital of the company is 125,000 £1 ordinary shares and 100,000 8% preference shares of £1 each.
2. The directors of the company have decided not to depreciate the freehold property.
3. The debenture stock is repayable on 31 December 20X9. The rate of interest payable is 10%.
4. Corporation tax for the year has been estimated at £50,000.
5. Depreciation is to be provided as follows:

Motor vehicles:	20% on cost
Plant and equipment:	10% on the reducing balance

6. The directors have decided to pay a final dividend of 25p per share.
7. Stock at 31 December 20X5 was £30,000

Required
A profit and loss account for the year ended 31 December 20X5 and a balance sheet at that date.

Suggested solution
Ergonomics Ltd.
Profit and loss account for the year ended 31 December 20X5

	Tutorial note	£	£
Sales			420,000
Less cost of sales:			
Opening stock		25,000	
Plus purchases		140,000	
		165,000	
Less closing stock		30,000	
			135,000
Gross profit			285,000
Less overhead expenses:			
Debenture interest	(a)	4,000	
Office expenses		17,500	
Wages and salaries		32,500	
Directors' remuneration	(b)	75,000	
Depreciation:			
Motor vehicles (20% x £35,000)		7,000	
Plant and equipment			
(10% x (85,000—17,000))		6,800	
			142,800
Net profit before tax			142,200
Taxation			50,000
Net profit after tax			92,200
Less dividends			
Ordinary dividends paid		5,000	
proposed	(c)	25,000	
Preference dividends paid		3,200	
proposed	(d)	3,200	
			36,400
Retained profit for the year			55,800
Retained profit brought forward	(e)		128,200
Retained profit carried forward			184,000

Ergonomics Ltd.
Balance sheet as at 31 December 20X5

	Tutorial note	£	£	£
Fixed assets		Cost	Accumulated depreciation	Net book value
Freehold property		350,000	–	350,000
Motor vehicles		35,000	28,000	7,000
Plant and equipment		85,000	23,800	61,200
		470,000	51,800	418,200
Current assets				
Stock			30,000	
Debtors			70,000	
Bank			34,000	
			134,000	
Current liabilities				
Creditors		18,000		
Corporation tax		50,000		
Debenture interest	(a)	2,000		
Proposed dividends:				
Ordinary	(c)	25,000		
Preference	(d)	3,200		
			98,200	
				35,800
Net assets				454,000
Share capital:			Authorized	Issued
Ordinary shares of £1			125,000	100,000
8% preference shares of £1			100,000	80,000
			225,000	180,000
Reserves				
Share premium account				50,000
Profit and loss account				184,000
Loans				
10% debenture stock (repayable 20X9)				40,000
				454,000

Tutorial notes
(a) Debenture interest
£40,000 of loan stock has been issued. At an interest rate of 10%, the total interest charge for the year must be £4,000. If the trial balance shows that only £2,000 has been paid, the balance due of £2,000 must be a creditor.
(b) Directors are employees of the company. Their remuneration is an overhead expense, not an appropriate of profit.
(c) Ordinary dividend
100,000 shares × 25p per share = £25,000. This has not been paid at 31 December 20X5. It must therefore be a creditor.
(d) Preference dividend
£80,000 of 8% preference shares have been issued. The total dividends which must be paid in the year are £80,000 × 8% = £6,400. Only £3,200 has been paid by 31 December 20X5, therefore, the remaining £3,200 is a creditor.

KEY POINTS

1. Partnerships and companies are multiple-owner entities.
   The interests of owners must be recorded and profit must be divided between owners.
2. In partnerships, the interest of owners is recorded in capital accounts and current accounts. In companies, these interests are recorded in the form of share capital.
3. The major trading unit in most modern economies is the limited company.
4. A company has a legal personality distinct from its members. Company owners have limited liability.
5. Review the features of company accounts.
6. Review the format of company accounts.

QUESTIONS

7.1 Jake and Nog are in partnership. They share profits in the ratio: Jake 60% and Nog 40%. The following trial balance was extracted as at 31 March 20X6:

	£	£
Office equipment at cost	6,500	
Motor vehicles at cost	9,200	
Provision for depreciation at 31 March 20X5		
Motor vehicles		3,680
Office equipment		1,950
Stock at 31 March 20X5	24,970	
Debtors and creditors	20,960	16,275
Cash at bank	755	
Sales		90,370
Purchases	71,630	
Salaries	8,417	
Office expenses	1,933	
Current accounts at 31 March 20X5		
Jake		1,379
Nog		1,211
Capital accounts		
Jake		27,000
Nog		12,000
Drawings		
Jake	5,500	
Nog	4,000	
	153,865	153,865

Required
Draw up a set of final accounts for the year ended 31 March 20X6 for the partnership. The following notes are applicable at 31 March 20X6:

1. Stock was £27,340 at 31 March 20X6.
2. There were office expenses of £110 owing.
3. Provide for depreciation as follows: motor vehicles 20% of cost; office equipment 10% of cost.
4. Charge interest on capital at 10% per annum.

7.6 The following trial balance has been extracted from the books of account of Ramsey Ltd. as at 31 December 20X2:

	£'000s	£'000s
Administrative expenses	11,850	
Bank overdraft		650
Authorized and issued share capital:		
Ordinary shares of £1 each		4,000
10% cumulative preference shares		
of £1 each		1,000
Debtors and creditors	17,450	11,000
Distribution costs	4,500	
Furniture and fittings		
Cost	500	
Accumulated depreciation 1.1.X2		200
Interim dividend paid		
(10p per ordinary share)	400	
Plant and machinery		
Cost	35,000	
Accumulated depreciation 1.1.X2		20,000
Preference dividend paid	50	
Profit and loss account		15,000
Purchases	40,000	
Sales		66,000
Share premium account		1,900
Stock at 1.1.20X2	10,000	
	119,750	119,750

Notes
1. Stock at 31 December 20X2 £12m.
2. Depreciation is to be charged as follows: furniture and fittings 10% on cost; Plant and machinery 50% on a reducing balance.
3. The Corporation tax liability is estimated to be £2.65m.
4. The Directors propose to pay a final ordinary dividend of 20p per ordinary share.

Required
Prepare the Company's profit and loss account for the year to 31 December 20X2 and a balance sheet at that date.

7.7 Madge Ltd.'s trial balance, for the year ended 30 June 20X3, is shown below:

	£'000s	£'000s
Administrative expenses	420	
Called up share capital		
(£1 ordinary shares)		1,440
Bank	80	
Distribution costs	1,160	
Dividends received		8
Freehold property:		
Cost	400	
Accumulated depreciation		32
Profit and loss account 1 July 20X2		320
Purchases	2,720	
Sales		4,960
Stock	520	
Creditors		240
Debtors	900	
Motor vehicles		
Cost	1,400	
Accumulated depreciation		600
	7,600	7,600

Notes
1. Stock at 30 June 20X3 £2.25m.
2. Depreciation: freehold property 4% on cost; motor vehicles 25% on the reducing balance.
3. At 30 June 20X3: £20,000 was owing for office salaries £10,000 was paid in advance for motor vehicle licences.
4. Corporation tax based on the profit for the year estimated to be £110,000.
5. The directors propose to pay an ordinary dividend of 10p per share.

Required
Prepare the profit and loss account and balance sheet at 30 June 20X3.

EIGHT

PUBLISHED COMPANY ACCOUNTS

LEARNING OBJECTIVES

After reading this chapter you should:

- Understand the difference between published and internal company financial statements.
- Obtain an overview of the main elements of an annual report.

Companies publish the results of their commercial activities in the form of an annual report. This chapter is designed to illustrate the contents of an annual report.

8.1 WHAT IS AN ANNUAL REPORT?

In Chapter 7, a distinction was made between the simple form of company accounts, which are used for internal purposes, and accounting information which is provided for use by parties external to the company. In 1975, the UK accounting profession produced a document entitled 'The Corporate Report' which described an annual report as a 'comprehensive package of information of all kinds which most completely describes an organization's economic activity'.

The phrase; 'package of information of all kinds', is a clear indication of a fundamental difference between published and internal accounting reports. Internal reports are often little more than a profit and loss account and a balance sheet. External reports, on the other hand, contain narratives and explanatory notes which provide a framework to assist readers in understanding the economic performance of companies.

8.2 WHO READS ANNUAL REPORTS?

Accountants describe the readers of annual reports as 'users'. The Corporate Report, despite its age, is an extremely useful document. In addition to providing an excellent

definition of an annual report, it identifies seven groups that use published financial information. These are:

1. The equity investor group. These are existing and potential shareholders, essentially the current and future owners of a company.
2. The loan creditor group. This includes providers of short, medium and long-term finance. Suppliers of goods and services are not included under this heading. Loan creditors are, mainly, banks and other financial institutions which lend money to companies.
3. The employee group. This includes former, current and future employees who may derive income and benefits from a company.
4. The analyst advisor group. This wide-ranging group contains highly trained experts who supply information to other groups. The group includes financial analysts, stockbrokers, journalists, credit rating agencies, and other suppliers of financial advisory services.
5. The business contact group. This includes; customers, suppliers, trade creditors, and competitors.
6. The government. The tax authorities, and local, regional, and central government are included in this group, together with those government agencies charged with the regulation of business activity.
7. The public. This includes consumers, pressure groups, political groups and other associations of individuals with an interest in published accounting information.

It is not proposed at this introductory level to consider in much detail the information requirements of accounting users groups. It should be clear, however, that each of the different user groups have different information needs and different levels of accounting knowledge. The annual report has to present a variety of information to an audience which has varying degrees of interest and education. It is inevitable, therefore, that published accounting information is something of a compromise between the needs of the various user groups.

EXAMPLE

Tellos Plc is an international manufacturing group. It is not a single company. In common with many large businesses it is a group of companies. In practice, many annual reports present what is known as group accounts.

The structure of the Tellos group is as follows:

Tellos Plc

Tellos Handling Ltd.	Tellos Automotive Ltd.	Tellos Hardware Ltd.	Tellos Engineering Ltd.

Tellos Plc is a holding company, it owns the share capital of the four subsidiary companies. The results of the five companies are consolidated into one annual report and for this reason the accounts of a group of companies are sometimes known as consolidated accounts.

We will examine some extracts from the annual report for the year ended 31 December 20X5. It is convenient to divide this information into two main types:

1. Narrative information.
2. Numerical information.

Tellos Plc: narrative information in the 20X5 annual report.

1. *The chief executive's statement.* This is a description of the activities of the business during 20X5 and of the future prospects for the group.
2. *The directors' report.* The content of the chief executive's statement is not regulated by law, and therefore, the directors' report is a UK legal requirement which is designed to provide information that might otherwise be omitted from the annual report.
3. *The audit report.* In most jurisdictions, there is a requirement that the results of companies are audited. Independent external auditors are required to give an opinion about the truth and fairness of published accounting information. This opinion must be included in annual reports.

Tellos Plc
Chief executive's report

Introduction
The group achieved further substantial progress during 20X5. We continue with the core strategy of the group which is the development of four strategic business areas each with a leading position in their main geographical markets.
An introductory section outlines the strategy of the group.
Results
Pre-tax profits were 29% higher at £67.6m (£52.3m in 20X4) while the turnover was broadly unchanged at £798.6m (£794.5m in 20X4). The board is recommending a final dividend of 2.6p per share payable on 31 March 20X6. This makes the total dividend for the year 4.6p per share, an increase of 24% over 20X4. Net assets at 31 December 20X5 were £229.3m (£202.1m in 20X4).
A brief summary of the results for the year is given together with comparative figures for the previous year. Note that turnover is another word for sales.
Business review
The main markets for group products in the UK remained buoyant throughout the period and three business divisions; Handling Machinery, Automotive and Hardware all performed strongly. The Handling Machinery Division increased profits by 21% due to a very strong order intake in the UK. Since the year end we have completed the acquisition of the Zoltan Corporation which not only extends the Handling Machinery Division's portfolio but brings with it market leadership in both its main product areas of lifting equipment and waste management handling.
The Automotive Division increased its profits by 91% largely due to organic growth following the major reorganization of 20X3. Our strategy of creating product-based centres of excellence supported by international purchasing has built a platform for continuous productivity improvement and earnings enhancement.

The Hardware Division's profit grew by 94% as a result of the consolidation of production facilities at our new Malaysian manufacturing site.

Our smallest operation the UK based Engineering Division experienced difficult market conditions and this, following the disposal of the loss making process control operations, has led to a disappointing performance. However, orders received in the last quarter of the year showed signs of improvement and this together with changes in its management structure should lead to an improvement in performance in 20X6.

A statement of how the business has performed during the year. Note that reasons are given for the changes in performance and that the bad news about the Engineering Division is given at the end of the business review.

Outlook

The strategy of the group is now increasingly focused on enhancing the value of our company through capital investment aimed at future productivity gains. The continuing acquisition and investment programme aims to augment existing operations with complimentary businesses which will satisfy the key objectives of:

- *broadening the group's geographical spread*
- *increasing market share*
- *strengthening its competitive position*
- *widening the customer base.*

The directors believe that Tellos Plc is well positioned due to its carefully implemented strategy and accordingly looks forward to the future with considerable confidence.

A concluding statement providing an optimistic assessment of future prospects.

Tellos Plc
Directors' report

An outline of the content of the directors' report for Tellos Plc is as follows:

Principal activities.

This section of the report requires companies to indicate the nature of the business they are involved in and any material changes in those activities during the year. In the case of Tellos Plc, the chief executive's report contains a comprehensive review of business activities and therefore this section of the directors' report is required merely to direct the reader to the appropriate parts of the chief executive's report.

Dividends.

Details of the amounts paid and payable in respect of dividends.

Share capital.

This section provides information in respect of changes in the authorized or issued share capital of Tellos Plc.

Fixed assets.

Details of major acquisitions and disposals of fixed assets during the accounting period.

Directors.

In this section of the report, the directors of Tellos Plc are identified by name. In addition, a listing of directors' ownership of shares, share options and loan capital of the company is given.

Employment policy.
This section contains a formal statement of the policy of the company in respect of the provision of information to employees, health and safety matters, and training and development matters. The policy of the company in respect of the employment of disabled persons is also stated in this section.

Donations.
Details of political and charitable donations in excess of £200.

Auditors.
A feature of the UK regulatory regime is that auditors must be formally re-appointed by shareholders at the annual general meeting of the company. It is a requirement that the directors' report should record the annual re-appointment of auditors.

Tellos Plc
Auditors' report
Report of the auditors to the members of Tellos Plc.

We have audited the financial statements on pages xx to zz which have been prepared on the basis of accounting policies set out on page yy.
An opening sentence identifies the financial statements which have been audited. The auditors report to the members of the company. These are the shareholders.

The page references refer to the numerical accounting reports and their supporting notes, but not the narrative statements in the annual report.

Respective responsibilities of directors and auditors.
The company's directors are responsible for the preparation of financial statements. It is our responsibility to form an independent opinion, based on our audit, on those statements and report our opinion to you.

This section of the report says that auditors are not responsible for preparing the annual accounts of the company, they are merely responsible for giving an opinion on those accounts.

Basis of opinion.
We conducted our audit in accordance with Auditing Standards issued by the Auditing Practices Board. An audit includes an examination, on a test basis, of evidence relevant to the amounts and disclosures in the financial statements. It also includes an assessment of the significant estimates and judgements made by the directors in the preparation of the financial statements, and of whether the accounting policies are appropriate to the company's circumstances, consistently applied and adequately disclosed.

We planned and performed our audit so as to obtain all the information and explanations which we considered necessary in order to provide us with sufficient evidence to give reasonable assurance that the financial statements are free from material misstatement, whether caused by fraud or other irregularity or error. In forming our opinion we also evaluated the overall adequacy of the presentation of information in the financial statements.
This section of the report attempts to explain the nature of an audit of financial statements.

An audit is an examination of evidence of the veracity of the accounting numbers in the annual report. In forming their opinion of these accounting numbers, the auditors also consider the accounting judgements made by the directors.

Opinion.
In our opinion the financial statements give a true and fair view of the state of affairs of the company and the group as at 31 December 20X5 and of the group's profit for the year then ended and have been properly prepared in accordance with the Companies Act 1985.

This is a formal statement of the auditors opinion. Tellos Plc has received what is known as an unqualified audit report from its auditors who state that the accounts give a true and fair view of the results of trading activity for 20X5.

Tellos Plc: Numerical information in the 20X5 annual report
The main numerical reports produced by Tellos Plc present the results of the five group companies in one set of consolidated or group accounts. It is not intended at this introductory level to spend much time dealing with the intricacies of group accounts. There are however some general points which can be made:

1. Group accounts are designed to present the results of the group from the point of view of the holding company.
2. In addition to the preparation of group accounts, each of the subsidiary companies is required to produce its own individual annual report.
3. The results of Tellos Plc as an individual company are presented within the group annual report.

The main financial statements in the group annual report are:

1. A consolidated profit and loss account which discloses the profit made by the group in 20X5.
2. A consolidated balance sheet which discloses the assets and liabilities of the group as at 31 December 20X5.
3. A balance sheet for Tellos Plc as an individual company.
4. A consolidated cash flow statement.

We will consider the first two of these statements only. Notice that the terminology employed in the following statements differs from that used in internal company accounts. In the profit and loss account; sales is described as turnover, and interest payments are shown separately from other overhead expenses which are described as net operating expenses. Operating profit is shown explicitly in the profit and loss account.

The main figures are shown on the face of the statements and this allows the reader to see the significant figures clearly. Fuller details of the amounts presented are shown in notes to the statements and note number references are given (the detailed notes are not shown). It is a convention in the UK and many other jurisdictions that the first note to the financial statements explains to the reader the main accounting policies used in the preparation of the accounts. Thus, the first note reference shown on the face of the profit and loss account is to note 2.

Tellos Plc
Consolidated profit and loss account
For the year ended 31 December 20X5

Notes		£'000s
2	Turnover	798,618
3	Cost of sales	(602,456)
	Gross profit	196,162
4	Net operating expenses	(130,378)
5	Operating profit	65,784
6	Net interest payable	(10,414)
	Profit before taxation	55,370
7	Taxation	(20,485)
	Profit for the financial year	34,885
8	Dividends	(21,387)
	Retained profit for the financial year	13,498

Tellos Plc
Consolidated balance sheet as at 31 December 20X5

Notes		£'000s	£,000s
	Fixed assets		
9	Intangible assets		1,697
10	Tangible assets		210,262
11	Investments		15,980
			227,939
	Current assets		
12	Stocks	140,181	
13	Debtors	197,541	
	Cash at bank and in hand	133,080	
		470,802	
	Creditors		
14	Amounts falling due within one year	(252,859)	
	Net current assets		217,943
	Total assets less current liabilities		445,882
	Creditors		
15	Amounts falling due after more than one year		(216,534)
	Net assets		229,348
	Capital and reserves		
16	Share capital		44,819
17	Share premium account		15,048
18	Profit and Loss account		169,481
			229,348

In the balance sheet, fixed assets have been divided into intangible assets and tangible assets. The two types of fixed assets may be distinguished as follows:

1. *Intangible assets.* These are assets that have no physical substance, and include such things as development costs, patents and trademarks.
2. *Tangible assets.* These are assets such as buildings, vehicles and machinery which do have physical substance.

Creditors on the balance sheet have been categorized into those payable within one year and those payable after more than one year. These categories of creditors replace the categories current liabilities and long-term liabilities which we encountered in the context of internal company accounts.

8.3 CONCLUSION

Published company accounts are more detailed than the simple form of internal company accounts. Published accounts are produced to satisfy the information needs of a large number of user groups. Narrative reports are used to expand upon the information contained in the basic financial statements.

In many jurisdictions, the form and content of published financial statements are subject to a high degree of regulation. In the UK, appendices to the Companies Act 1985 indicate how amounts should be described and disclosed in company balance sheets and profit and loss accounts.

KEY POINTS

1. Users of published company accounts include equity investors, loan creditors, employees, analysts and advisors, the business contact group, the government, and the public.
2. Many large businesses report their results in the form of group accounts.
3. Published annual reports contain narrative reports in addition to the financial statements.
4. Narrative reports include; a chief executive's report, a directors' report, and an auditors' report.
5. The main financial statements are a group profit and loss account, a group balance sheet, a holding company balance sheet, and a group cash flow statement.

NINE

CASH FLOW STATEMENTS

LEARNING OBJECTIVES

After reading this chapter you should:

- Understand the form and content of cash flow statements.
- Be able to prepare simple cash flow statements.

9.1 INTRODUCTION

In this chapter, we will examine the form of a cash flow statement which is presented as a financial accounting statement. Management accountants also refer to cash flow statements. We can distinguish between the two forms of cash flow statement as follows.

Cash flow statements	
Financial accounting	*Management accounting*
Historical cash flows	Historical cash flows and forecasts of future cash flows
Normally prepared for an accounting period of 12 months	Prepared for any period decided upon by management
A summary of cash flows for the whole business	A summary of cash flows for the whole business or for any business sub-unit
A statement prepared for external reporting purposes	A statement prepared for internal reporting purposes
A statement prepared to a prescribed format	A statement prepared to a format decided upon by management

9.2 WHY PRODUCE CASH FLOW STATEMENTS?

Accountants must use considerable judgement in preparing accounting statements. We have seen, in earlier chapters, the problems relating to such things as depreciation, inventory (stock) valuations, and debtors adjustments.

Cash flows are the core transactions in a set of financial statements before any accounting judgements are made. Cash is comparatively easy to define and verify. The requirement to present cash flow statements can be an effective safeguard against the practice of creative accounting where companies deliberately massage their results. Cash flow statements, therefore, provide a valuable information resource for users of accounting statements.

9.3 FINANCIAL REPORTING STANDARD 1 (FRS1): CASH FLOW STATEMENTS

Cash flow statements are a financial reporting requirement in many jurisdictions. We will consider in this chapter the form of cash flow statement required by the UK Standard FRS1 (Revised 1996).

The FRS1 style cash flow statement is a summary of the cash flows of the business during its accounting period. It provides an analysis of the increase or decrease in cash during the period. Cash is defined in the standard as 'cash in hand' and 'deposits repayable on demand' less 'overdrafts repayable on demand'. The term 'repayable on demand' means withdrawal at any time without notice or penalty. 'Cash' includes amounts denominated in foreign currencies. In practice, this means business current accounts and instant access deposit accounts.

9.4 FORMAT OF THE CASH FLOW STATEMENT

FRS1 requires that cash flows be presented in a number of standard headings. These are:

● Operating activities
● Returns on investment and servicing of finance
● Taxation
● Capital expenditure and financial investment
● Acquisitions and disposals
● Equity dividends paid
● Management of liquid resources
● Financing

This sequence should be followed in the presentation of the statement, but if there are no cash flows under a specific heading (for example, acquisitions and disposals), then that heading may be omitted. The basic format of the main cash flow statement is as follows:

Santana Ltd.
Cash flow Statement
For the year ended 31 December 20X1

	£'000s
Operating activities	X
Returns on investment and servicing of finance	X
Taxation	X
Capital expenditure and financial investment	X
Acquisitions and disposals	X
Equity dividends paid	X
Management of liquid resources	X
Financing	X
Increase/(decrease) in cash	X

In addition to the main statement, the standard requires a number of explanatory notes, but, before we deal with these, we need to examine briefly the cash flow headings in the main statement.

Operating Activities

The operating activities of a business are its trading activities. Thus, the operating activities of, say, a book shop would centre around the sale of books.

A business may derive income (and incur expenses) from non-operating activities. For example, income may be derived from investments. It should be clear, therefore, that the presentation of cash flows relating to operating activities enables the reader of the financial statements to appreciate the cash flow effect of core trading activities.

How are cash flows from operating Activities calculated?
FRS1 permits two methods of disclosing these cash flows: the direct method and the indirect method. The starting point for the calculation of cash flows from operating activities depends upon which method is adopted. The direct method is based upon an analysis of cash transactions and the results of this analysis are presented as follows:

	£
Cash received from customers	X
Cash payments to suppliers	(X)
Cash paid to or on behalf of employees	(X)
Other cash payments	(X)
Net cash flow from operating activities	X

This analysis is shown on the fact of the cash flow statement in place of the line 'Operating activities'.

In practice, however, the detailed analysis of cash transactions is a costly exercise, especially in the case of large companies. You will notice that Santana Ltd. has not adopted the direct method. It discloses cash flows from operating activities as a single figure on the face of the cash flow statement. It has adopted the indirect method of presenting its cash flows from operating activities.

In practice, most businesses which fall within the scope of FRS1 use the indirect method. The reason for this is:

1. The expense of a detailed analysis of cash transactions is avoided.
2. FRS1 required that cash flows from operating activities must be reconciled to the profit and loss account. The indirect method is based upon this reconciliation. Thus, even if a business has decided to use the direct method, it would still be required to do most of the work involved in adopting the indirect method.

We will, therefore, concentrate on the indirect method in this chapter.

How are cash flows from operating activities calculated if the indirect method is used?
The basic idea is to take the net profit (before taxation) and adjust it to arrive at cash flows from operating activities. The word 'operating' should not be forgotten. Net profit may reflect investment income and financing charges, and must, therefore, be adjusted to remove these items. Net profit must be turned into operating profit, that is to say, the profit earned from actually engaging in core business activities.

It may be helpful to represent the calculation of cash flows from activities as a sequence of steps in the following way:

Step 1: Calculate operating profit
Imagine that Santana Ltd. has a net profit of £104,000 for the year ended 31 December 20X1 and it has received investment income of £5,000 during the year, and it has paid £1,000 in debenture interest. Operating profit may be calculated as follows:

	£'000s
Net profit for the year	104
Less investment income	(5)
Add debenture interest	1
Operating profit	100

Investment income has been added in to net profit and, therefore, must be deducted to arrive at operating profit. Debenture interest has been deducted as an overhead expense in arriving at net profit and, therefore, must be added back to cancel this deduction to give operating profit. If there are no items such as investment income or debenture interest, net profit is the same as operating profit and Step 1 is not required. Also, in some exercises, operating profit is shown on the face of the profit and loss account.

Step 2: Adjust operating profit to give net operating cash flow
We saw in Chapters 5 and 6 that there are a number of adjustments which must be made in order to calculate an accurate profit figure. These adjustments include stock, depreciation, debtors, creditors, pre-payments and accruals. If we start with profit and remove these adjustments, we will end up with the net cash flow from operating activities. However, we

must make sure that we remove accounting adjustments which have been made at the start and the end of the accounting period. In order to clarify the above points, we need to consider a detailed example.

Example

We need some more information about Santana Ltd. Here is the 20X1 profit and loss account:

Santana Ltd.
Profit & loss account for the year ended 31 December 20X1

	£'000s	£'000s
Sales		520
Less cost of sales		
Opening stock	70	
Purchases	368	
	438	
Closing stock	93	
		345
Gross profit		175
Add investment income		5
		180
Less overhead expenses		
Administration	55	
Depreciation	20	
Debenture interest	1	
		76
Net profit before tax		104
Taxation		25
Profit after tax		79
Ordinary dividends		40
Retained profit for the year		39
Retained profit brought forward		22
Retained profit carried forward		61

Here are the summarized balance sheets for 20X0 and 20X1:

Santana Ltd.

Balance sheet as at 31 December	*20X0*		*20X1*	
	£'000s	£'000s	£'000s	£'000s
Fixed assets:				
Cost	103		194	
Less depreciation	35		55	
	——	68	——	139
Investment in subsidiary company		–		50
Current assets				
Stock	70		93	
Debtors	31		35	
Treasury stock	5		10	
Cash	50		11	
	——		——	
	156		149	
	——		——	
Current liabilities				
Creditors	47		52	
Taxation	29		25	
Dividends	26		40	
	——		——	
	102		117	
	——		——	
		54		32
		——		——
Net assets		122		221
		——		——
Capital and reserves				
Ordinary share capital		90		160
profit and loss account		22		61
Loans: 10% debentures		10		–
		——		——
		122		221
		——		——

We want to turn the operating profit into a cash flow. One way to do this would be to take each of the profit and loss account items in turn and calculate cash flows on an item-by-item basis using 'T' accounts. ('T' accounts are introduced in Chapter 3 if you require further information.) For example, if we take sales, we could calculate the cash flow for sales during 20X1 as follows:

Sales account

	£'000s		£'000s
Balance 1.1X1	31		
		Balance 31.12.X1	35

The opening and closing balances on this account are the debtors figures taken from the balance sheets for 20X0 and 20X1. If we now insert the profit and loss account figure of sales into the 'T' account:

Sales account

	£'000s		£'000s
Balance 1.1X1	31	Balancing figure	
Profit and loss		= Cash flow	516
account	520	Balance 31.12.X1	35
	551		551

The balancing figure is the cash flow in respect of sales. We could, however, do the above calculation much more simply:

Calculation of sales cash flow

	£'000s
Sales	520
Less increase in debtors during 20X1	
(35 − 31)	(4)
Cash flow	516

Instead of going to the trouble of writing out 'T' accounts, we could adjust the profit and loss account items by the movement (the increase or the decrease) in accounting adjustments during the year. We could then take another short cut by starting with operating profit instead of sales. In this way, we can remove all the accounting adjustments very quickly.

Step 2 can now be shown in more detail:

	£'000s	£'000s
Operating profit		100
Less increase in debtors	4	
increase in stock (93 – 70)	23	
	—	(27)
Add increase in creditors	5	
depreciation	20	
	—	25
Cash flow from operating activities		98

Step 2 is a reconciliation between operating profit and the cash flow from operating activities. This reconciliation is one of the explanatory notes required by FRS1 and is, therefore, part of most cash flow assessment exercises. The reconciliation also gives us our first figure for the face of the cash flow statement, so we can start to complete it.

Santana Ltd.
Cash flow statement
For the year ended 31 December 20X1

	£'000s
Operating activities	98

Before we move on to the other cash flows, we need to derive a general set of rules for reconciling operating profit to net operating cash flow. These are that we should do:

1. Calculate operating profit if this is not given.
2. Compare the balance sheets at the start and end of the period.
3. Deduct increases in current asset items (excluding cash, bank, and deposit accounts).
4. Deduct decreases in current liability items except taxation, dividends, and bank overdrafts.
5. Deduct non-cash items in the profit and loss account such as a profit on sale of fixed assets or a decrease in the doubtful debts provision.
6. Add decreases in current asset items (excluding cash, bank, and deposit accounts).
7. Add increases in current liability items except taxation, dividends, and bank overdraft.
8. Add any non-cash expenses in the profit and loss account, e.g. depreciation, loss on sale of fixed assets or increase in the doubtful debts provision.

Another way of representing these general rules is as follows:

Rules for reconciling operating profit to net cash flow from operating activities

			£	£
Net profit before tax				X
Deduct investment income				(X)
Add interest payments and other financing charges				X
				X
Operating profit				X
Deduct: Increase in stock	Information	X		
Increase in debtors	from	X		
Increase in pre-payments	the	X		
Decrease in creditors	balance	X		
Decrease in accruals	sheet	X		
(not those relating to tax and dividends)				
Profit on sale of Fixed assets	Information from profit	X		
Decrease in doubtful Debt provision	and loss account	X		
		—	(X)	
			X	
Add: Decrease in stock	Information	X		
Decrease in debtors	from	X		
Decrease in pre-payments	the	X		
Increase in creditors	balance	X		
Increase in accruals	sheet	X		
(not those relating to tax and dividends)				
Depreciation charge	Information	X		
Loss on sale of fixed assets	from the	X		
Increase in doubtful Debts provision	profit and loss	X		
Bad debts written off	account	X		
		—	X	
Net cash flow from operating activities				X

Returns on investment and servicing of finance

These cash flows are much easier to calculate than the cash flows relating to operating activities. Returns on investment are cash flows that result from the ownership of an investment, and comprise items such as dividends received and interest received. Returns on investment are, therefore, a cash inflow, but this part of the cash flow statement also requires the disclosure of cash outflows in respect of the servicing of finance. This heading includes items such as interest payments and payments of non-equity dividends such as preference dividends.

In the case of Santana Ltd., most of the cash flows relating to returns on investment and servicing of finance can be taken directly from the profit and loss account. Thus, we have investment income of £5,000 and debenture interest paid of £1,000. We now have our second cash flow heading, so the statement now shows:

Santana Ltd.
Cash flow statement
For the year ended 31 December 20X1

	£'000s	£'000s
Operating activities		98
Returns on investment and servicing of finance		
Investment income	5	
Interest paid	(1)	
	—	4

Taxation

The cash flow in respect of taxation may be calculated using a 'T' account:

Taxation

	£'000s		£'000s
Balancing figure = Cash flow	29	Balance 1.1X1 (from 20X0 balance sheet)	29
Balance 31.12.X1	25	Profit and loss account	25
	—		—
	54		54
	—		—

An alternative method of calculating the taxation cash flow is to consider the method used to reconcile the operating profit to the operating cash flow. In this case, we can start with the profit and loss account figure of taxation and adjust it for the movement in taxation creditors during the period. Taxation will always appear as a creditor on the balance sheet at this introductory level.

	£'000s
Taxation charge in the profit and loss account	(25)
Less decrease in taxation creditors during 20X1 (29 − 25)	(4)
Cash flow	(29)

Note that the profit and loss figure is a taxation charge and, therefore, a negative number in this calculation. The tax payment is a cash outflow.

The statement now reads:

Santana Ltd.
Cash flow Statement
For the year ended 31 December 20X1

	£'000s	£'000s
Operating activities		98
Returns on investment and servicing of finance		
Investment income	5	
Interest paid	(1)	
	–	4
Taxation		
Corporation tax paid		(29)

Capital expenditure and financial investment

The cash flows under this heading are those relating to the acquisition or disposal of fixed assets or financial investments. Therefore, there may be cash outflows related to the purchase of new assets or financial investments. Note that the term 'financial investment' is used. This excludes the purchase or sale of interests in other businesses.

Cash inflows can arise when assets and financial investments are sold. In the case of Santana Ltd., we will assume that there has been no sale of assets. We can calculate the cash outflow from the purchase of fixed assets very simply by preparing a 'T' account:

Fixed assets at cost

	£'000s		£'000s
Balance 1.1.X1	103		
Balancing figure	91		
= cash flow		Balance 31.12.X1	194
	194		194

Notice that the account is headed 'Fixed assets at cost'. We ignore depreciation as it is an accounting adjustment and not a cash flow. An alternative to the 'T' account would be to deduct the year end figure from the opening figure.

The cash flow statement now reads:

Santana Ltd.
Cash flow statement
For the year ended 31 December 20X1

	£'000s	£'000s
Operating activities		98
Returns on investment and servicing of finance		
Investment income	5	
Interest paid	(1)	
	—	4
Taxation		
Corporation tax paid		(29)
Capital expenditure and financial investment		
Purchase of fixed assets		(91)

More complex situations: the sale of assets or investments

Fixed asset sales, in particular, can make the calculation of cash inflows and outflows more complex. We could have been told that Santana Ltd. had sold some assets during 20X1. Let us assume that assets costing £20,000 with an accumulated depreciation of £5,000 had been sold during the year and that the profit and loss account disclosed a loss on sale of assets of £4,000. We now need to use this information to calculate two things:

1. The cash inflow from the sale of assets.
2. The cash outflow in respect of the purchase of assets.

We can calculate the cash inflow by reconstructing the fixed asset disposal account:

Fixed asset disposal account

	£'000s		£'000s
Cost of assets		Accumulated depreciation	
Sold	20	to date of sale	5
		Profit and loss account	
		− loss on sale	4
		Balancing figure	
		= Cash inflow	11
	——		——
	20		20
	——		——

The cash outflow is now calculated as follows:

Fixed assets at cost

	£'000s		£'000s
Balance 1.1.X1	103	Cost of assets sold	20
Balancing figure			
= cash outflow	111		
(representing		Balance 31.1.X1	194
assets purchased)	——		——
	214		214
	——		——

As an alternative to 'T' accounts, the following schedules may be used:

1.   Fixed asset disposal cash flow

	£'000s
Cost of assets sold	20
Less accumulated depreciation to	
date of sale	(5)
	——
Net book value at date of sale	15
Add profit on sale in profit and loss account	
OR	
Less loss on sale in profit and loss account	(4)
	——
Cash inflow from sale of asset	11
	——

2.   Fixed asset purchase cash flow

	£'000s
Fixed assets at cost 1.1.X1	103
Less cost of assets sold	(20)
	——
Cost of unsold assets 1.1.X1	83
Less fixed assets at cost 31.12.X1	194
	——
Cash outflow—purchase of assets	(111)
	——

Acquistions and disposals

These cash flows relate to the purchase or sale of subsidiary companies, associated companies or joint ventures. These cash flows are similar to the purchase and sale of fixed assets, except that assets under this heading comprise interests in other businesses. In practice, the disclosure of information in respect of the acquisition and disposal can be quite complex. In this chapter, we will ignore these complications and deal with the cash flows from the purchase and sale of business interests as if additional disclosure of information was not required.

During the year ended 31 December 20X1, Santana Ltd. purchased an interest in a subsidiary company for £50,000. This is shown on the cash flow statement under the heading 'Acquisitions and disposals'; thus the statement now reads:

Santana Ltd.
Cash flow statement
For the year ended 31 December 20X1

	£'000s	£'000s
Operating activities		98
Returns on investment and servicing of finance		
Investment income	5	
Interest paid	(1)	
	—	4
Taxation		
Corporation tax paid		(29)
Capital expenditure and financial investment		
Purchase of fixed assets		(91)
Acquisitions and disposals		
Purchase of interest in subsidiary		
Undertaking		(50)

Equity dividends paid

These are dividends paid to the ordinary or equity shareholders of the company. The amount of the cash flow can be calculated using a 'T' account. In the case of Santana Ltd. the opening balance in the account will be the current liability for dividends in the 20X0 balance sheet. If we then include the 20X1 profit and loss account charge for dividends, the balancing figure in the 'T' account must be the cash outflow.

Dividends paid

	£'000s		£'000s
Balancing figure = cash flow	26	Balance 1.1X1	26
		Profit and loss account	40
Balance 31.12.X1	40		
	66		66

The alternative calculation would be:

	£'000s
profit and loss account charge ordinary dividend	(40)
Add increase in dividend creditors (26 − 40)	14
Cash flow	(26)

The statement now reads:

Santana Ltd.
Cash flow statement
For the year ended 31 December 20X1

	£'000s	£'000s
Operating activities		98
Returns on investment and servicing of finance		
Investment income	5	
Interest paid	(1)	
	—	4
Taxation		
Corporation tax paid		(29)
Capital expenditure and financial investment		
Purchase of fixed assets		(91)
Acquisitions and disposals		
Purchase of interest in subsidiary		
Undertaking		(50)
Equity dividend paid		(26)

Management of liquid resources

FRS1 defines 'liquid resources' as current asset investments held as readily disposable stores of value.

This heading deals with cash flows relating to the investment of cash in short-term deposit accounts and in short-term financial investments. Many businesses operate what is known as a treasury function where surplus cash is invested and withdrawn on a daily basis. Short-term deposit accounts are those deposit accounts which do not fall within the definition of cash because they are not repayable on demand without penalty. Short-term investments are defined as those which are easily purchased and sold in an active market.

A popular form of short-term investment in this context is government securities (such as treasury stock) or corporate bonds.

In the case of Santana Ltd., let us assume that in the year ended 31 December 20X1 £5,000 worth of treasury stock was sold and £10,000 worth of treasury stock was purchased. The cash flow statement is now:

Santana Ltd.
Cash flow statement
For the year ended 31 December 20X1

	£'000s	£'000s
Operating activities		98
Returns on investment and servicing of finance		
Investment income	5	
Interest paid	(1)	
	—	4
Taxation		
Corporation tax paid		(29)
Capital expenditure and financial investment		
Purchase of fixed assets		(91)
Acquisitions and disposals		
Purchase of interest in subsidiary		
Undertaking		(50)
Equity dividend paid		(26)
Management of liquid resources		
Purchase of treasury stock	(10)	
Sale of treasury stock	5	
	—	(5)

Financing

We are now left with the final category of cash flows. These are cash flows related not to the servicing of finance, but with changes in the capital used to finance the business. Cash inflows in this area will include receipts from the issue of new shares and debentures. Cash outflows will include repayments of long-term borrowing and the redemption of preference share capital.

In the case of Santana Ltd., it should be quite clear from a comparison of the balance sheets at 20X0 and 20X1 what the cash flows are in respect of financing. The ordinary share capital has increased to £160,000 from £90,000 and debentures have decreased by £10,000. We are now in a position to complete the main body of the cash flow statement.

Santana Ltd.
Cash flow statement
For the year ended 31 December 20X1

	£'000s	£'000s
Operating activities		98
Returns on investment and servicing of finance		
Investment income	5	
Interest paid	(1)	
	—	4
Taxation		
Corporation tax paid		(29)
Capital expenditure and financial investment		
Purchase of fixed assets		(91)
Acquisitions and disposals		
Purchase of interest in subsidiary		
Undertaking		(50)
Equity dividend paid		(26)
Management of liquid resources		
Purchase of treasury stock	(10)	
Sale of treasury stock	5	
	—	(5)
Financing		
Issue of ordinary shares	70	
Redemption of debentures	(10)	
	—	60
Decrease in cash flow		(39)

( ) = cash outflow

9.5 NOTES TO THE CASH FLOW STATEMENTS

Additional information to assist reader comprehension is given in notes to the cash flow statement. These are:

1. A reconciliation between operating profit and net cash flow from operating activities.
2. A reconciliation of net cash flow movement to movement in net debt.
3. Analysis of changes in net debt.
4. Analysis of changes in financing.

In addition to the above notes, additional disclosures are required in respect of items under the heading of 'Acquisitions and disposals'. We will not deal with these disclosures in this introductory text.

Reconciliation of operating profit

This is merely a restatement of Step 2 in the calculation of cash flow from operating activities.

Reconciliation of operating profit to net cash inflow from operating activities

	£'000s
Operating profit	100
Increase in debtors	(4)
Increase in stock	(23)
Increase in creditors	5
Depreciation charge	20
Net cash inflow from operating activities	98

Reconciliation of movement in net debt

The original version of FRS1, which was issued in September 1991, required that the increase or decrease in cash at the foot of the cash flow statement be reconciled to cash balances on the balance sheet. The revised standard requires additional information to be disclosed.

Net debt is defined as 'borrowings less cash and liquid resources'. Borrowings are long-term loans such as the debenture stock on the 20X0 balance sheet of Santana Ltd. Cash is cash in hand and deposits repayable on demand, and liquid resources can be defined as current asset investments held as readily disposable stores of value.

What this means is that the revised standard has moved beyond a mere consideration of cash balances on the balance sheet. Net debt will normally comprise of the following items:

Cash balances (as defined above)
Overdrafts
Long-term loans and debentures
Government stock (e.g. treasury stock)
Corporate bonds
7-day deposit accounts

The relevant note for the Santana Ltd. cash flow statement is as follows:

Reconciliation of net cash flow movement to movement in net debt

	£'000s
Decrease in cash in the period	(39)
Cash outflow from decrease in debt	10
Cash outflow from increase in liquid resources	5
Change in net debt	(24)
Net funds at 1.1.X1	45
Net funds at 31.12.X1	21

Note that where net debt is positive, it is described as net funds in the above reconciliation. The appendices to FRS1 suggest that the title of this note should still refer to 'Net Debt' even where there are in fact net funds.

On the face of the main cash flow statement, cash outflows are shown in brackets. The above statement is not a cash flow statement, it is a reconciliation. It starts with the increase or decrease in cash in the period, and removes those cash flows which are related to components of net debt. Thus, the cash outflows for the decrease in debt (the redemption of the debentures) and the increase in liquid resources are added back to the cash decrease. They are, in effect, cancelled out, leaving a figure which is the movement in net debt in the period.

Analysis of change in net debt

This next note is an analysis of the figures of net debt:

	At 1.1.X1 £'000s	Movement £'000s	At 31.12.X1 £'000s
Cash	50	(39)	11
Debt:			
10% debentures	(10)	10	–
Current asset Investments:			
Treasury stock	5	5	10
	45	(24)	21

Thus, instead of merely reconciling the increase (or decrease) in cash in the period to balance sheet cash balances, FRS1 gives a wider picture of the cash resources available to the business.

Analysis of changes in financing

The final note is an analysis of the changes in financing. It reconciles the amounts on the main cash flow statement with the opening and closing balances of ordinary shares and debentures.

Analysis of changes in financing during the year

	Ordinary Shares £'000s	10% Debentures £'000s
Balances at 1.1.X1	90	10
Cash inflow	70	
Cash outflow		(10)
Balances at 31.12.X1	160	–

9.6 CONCLUSION

One way of thinking about the cash flow statement is that it is a restatement of the balance sheet and the profit and loss account in another format. The preparation of cash flow statements can appear to be very complex, but in fact they are the result of a number of relatively simple calculations. A suggested method for dealing with assessment questions in this area is to deal with the simplest calculations first, as this will build confidence and provide guidelines for the calculation of the rest of the statement. A suitable strategy is as follows:

1. Draft out the main statement.
2. Calculate the cash flows in respect of:
    (a) Returns on investment and servicing of finance
    (b) Taxation
    (c) Equity dividends paid
    (d) Management of liquid resources
3. Start with note (3), the analysis of net debt. The difference between the opening and closing cash balances will be the number to insert at the foot of the main statement.
4. Go on to produce note (2), the reconciliation of the net cash flow movement to changes in net debt.
5. Produce the analysis of changes in financing note and insert the cash flows in the main statement.
6. Deal with the capital expenditure and acquisitions and disposals cash flow.
7. Produce note (1) the reconciliation of operating profit to operating cash flow and complete the main statement.

It is likely that very few marks will be given for balancing the cash flow statement. It is, therefore, possible to score the majority of marks available in a cash flow assessment exercise, without actually balancing the main statement. It is suggested that the main mark-earning areas in cash flow statements are as follows:

1. Displaying an understanding of the nature and purpose of the cash flow statement and its components.
2. Reconciling the net cash flow movements to changes in net debt.
3. Reconciling operating profit to operating cash flows.

KEY POINTS

1. This chapter is concerned with cash flow statements which are prepared for financial accounting purposes.
2. Financial Reporting Standard No 1 (FRS1) requires that cash flow statements should be prepared using the following headings:

- Operating activities
- Returns on investment and servicing of finance
- Taxation
- Capital expenditure and financial investment
- Acquisitions and disposals

- Equity dividends paid
- Management of liquid resources
- Financing

3. FRS1 permits the use of the direct or the indirect method in the preparation of cash flow statements. The indirect method is the one most widely used in practice and is the method used in this chapter.
4. The following notes are required to the cash flow statement in accordance with FRS1:
   (a) A reconciliation between operating profit and net cash flow from operating activities.
   (b) A reconciliation of net cash flow movement to movement in net debt.
   (c) Analysis of changes in net debt.
   (d) Analysis of changes in financing.

QUESTIONS

9.1 Briefly describe how cash flows are classified in a cash flow statement.

9.2 You have been approached by your friend, Martin, who is contemplating buying shares in a large public company. He is particularly confused by the cash flow statement, and he asks you what is the point of having a cash flow statement and a profit and loss account in an annual report. Write a letter to him explaining the nature and purpose of the cash flow statement.

9.3 Calculate the net cash flow from operating activities using the following information:

	£'000s
Depreciation charge for the year	1,798
Increase in creditors	468
Operating profit	12,044
Increase in stocks	388
Increase in debtors	144

9.4 During the year ended 30 September 20X9, Torvenas Ltd. made a net profit before tax of £135,315 and an analysis of the overhead expenses in the profit and loss account revealed the following:

	£
Selling and distribution expenses	78,780
Loss on sale of fixed asset	1,485
Depreciation	12,000
Interest paid	1,800

Interest received during the year amounted to £840. Analysis of the balance sheet of the company for 20X8 and 20X9 revealed the following working capital movements:

	30.9.X8 £	30.9.X9 £
Stock	41,900	44,810
Debtors	90,615	91,695
Treasury stock	3,750	10,500
Cash at bank	630	13,335
Creditors	17,535	21,045

You are required to calculate the net cash flow from operating activities.

9.5 Extracts of the balance sheet of Nanonics Ltd. for 20X1 and 20X2:

	31.12.X1 £	31.12.X2 £
Treasury stock	3,000	8,400
Cash at bank	504	10,668
Bank overdraft	(21,408)	–
Debentures	(16,992)	(15,144)

The 20X2 cash flow statement revealed an increase in cash during the period of £31,572. You are required to:

1. Analyse the change in net debt during 20X2.
2. Reconcile the net cash flow movement to movement in net debt.

9.6 Using the following information, analyse the change in net debt for Pico Ltd. in respect of the year ended 31 October 20X5.

	31.10.X4 £	31.10.X5 £
Long-term loans	203,904	181,728
Bank overdraft	256,896	100,800
Cash at bank	128,016	6,048
Treasury stock	36,000	–

9.7 Explain why FRS1 (Revised 1996) requires businesses to provide a reconciliation between the movement in cash in a period and the movement in net debt in a period.

9.8 The following information relates to the results of Prime Ltd. You are required to prepare the company's cash flow statement for the year ended 31 December 20X8.

Prime Ltd.
Profit and loss account
for the year ended 31 December 20X8 (extract)

	£'000s	£'000s
Gross profit		49,459
Interest received		168
		49,627
Less overhead expenses		
Administrative expenses	15,756	
Distribution costs	3,751	
Loss on sale of fixed assets	297	
Depreciation	2,400	
Interest paid	360	
		22,564
Net profit before tax		27,063
Taxation		8,327
Profit after tax		18,736
Less ordinary dividend		7,614
Retained profit for the year		11,122
Retained profit brought forward		15,325
Retained profit carried forward		26,447

Prime Ltd.
Balance sheet as at 31 December 20X7 and 20X8

	20X7		20X8	
	£'000s	£'000s	£'000s	£'000s
Fixed assets		34,624		36,502
Current assets				
Stock	8,380		8,962	
Debtors	18,123		18,339	
Treasury stock	750		2,100	
Cash at bank	126		2,667	
	27,379		32,068	
Current liabilities				
Creditors	3,507		4,209	
Bank overdraft	5,352		–	
Corporation tax	8,766		8,327	
Proposed dividend	7,251		7,614	
	24,876		20,150	
Net current assets		2,503		11,918
Net assets		37,127		48,420
Share capital				
£1 ordinary shares		17,554		18,187
Reserves				
Profit and loss account		15,325		26,447
Long-term liabilities				
Debenture stock		4,248		3,786
		37,127		48,420

Notes

1. During the year a number of fixed assets were sold. The aggregate cost and accumulated depreciation values were as follows:

	£'000s
Cost	1,058
Accumulated depreciation	635

2. Receipts from the sale of treasury bills amounted to £600,000 during the year and purchases of treasury bills amounted to £1.95m.

9.9 The following information is a summary of the results of Arvanitis Ltd. for the year ended 31 may 20X5:

	£'000s
Net profit before tax	263
Taxation	88
	175
Proposed dividend	140
Retained profit for year	35

Balance sheet summaries:

	31.5.X4		31.5.X5	
	£'000s	£'000s	£'000s	£'000s
Fixed assets				
Cost		1,400		1,725
Accumulated depreciation		350		630
		1,050		1,095
Investment		–		200
Current assets				
Stock	175		315	
Debtors	245		175	
7 day deposit account	5		3	
Bank	30		4	
	455		497	
Current liabilities				
Creditors	157		192	
Taxation	63		88	
Dividends	123		140	
	343		420	
		112		77
		1,162		1,372
Ordinary shares		700		700
Profit and loss account		462		497
8% debentures		–		175
		1,162		1,372

Notes

1. There were no sales of fixed assets during the year.
2. The debentures were issued on 1 June 20X4, and debenture interest was paid on 30 November 20X4 and 31 May 20X5.
3. During the year, Arvanitis Ltd. purchased an 80% stake in Format Ltd. for cash.

You are required to prepare the cash flow statement of Arvanitis Ltd. for the year ended 31 May 20X5.

9.10 Using the following information, prepare a cash flow statement for NHH Group Plc for the year ended 31 December 20X6.

1. Extract from cash transactions analysis:

	£'000s
Preference dividend paid	225
Purchase of tangible fixed assets	1,756
Interest received	254
Interest paid	1,148
Taxation paid	1,444
Sale of plant and machinery	1,324
Sale of business	2,104
Purchase of subsidiary undertaking	9,110
Purchase of interest in joint venture	1,905
Ordinary dividend paid	1,303
Purchase of government securities	2,500
Sale of government securities	2,150
Sale of corporate bonds	600

2. Financing and working capital movements:

	31.12.X5 £'000s	31.12.X6 £'000s
Ordinary shares	10,000	10,300
Debentures	9,781	10,954
Stock	2,000	8,454
Debtors	1,000	2,887
Cash in hand	118	268
Overdraft	1,264	4,789
7 day deposits	200	100
Government securities	3,000	3,350
Corporate bonds	1,200	600
Creditors	4,208	9,500

3. The depreciation charge for the year was £1,744,000.
4. The operating profit for 20X6 was £9,316,000.
5. Assume there are no profits or losses made on the sale of fixed assets or on the sale of the subsidiary business.
6. No cash balances were acquired in respect of the purchase of the subsidiary undertaking.

TEN

INTERPRETING FINANCIAL STATEMENTS

LEARNING OBJECTIVES

After reading this chapter you should:

- Be aware of the problems that arise in the interpretation of financial statements.
- Understand the basic techniques of financial statement analysis.
- Be able to produce simple reports which present the results of financial statement analysis.

10.1 INTRODUCTION

This is the final chapter in the financial accounting section of this book. We have seen in earlier chapters how source data are introduced into accounting systems, how accounting information is processed, and how accounting statements are prepared.

When we come to interpret a set of accounts, we are starting with the finished product and we are asking: what do these accounts mean? Another way to express this idea is to ask: what is the story being told by the accounting statements?

In Chapter 8 we identified a number of user groups:

1. The equity investor group.
2. The loan creditor group.
3. The employee group.
4. The analyst advisor group.
5. The business contact group.
6. The government.
7. The public.

To this we can add another user group; the internal management group. This comprises, departmental, divisional, company, and group managers and directors. We will distinguish this group from the employee group by describing employees as those persons without habitual access to internal financial accounting statements.

Each of the above user groups may seek to interpret the information contained in accounting statements and each group will have different levels of accounting knowledge. However, the important point here is that each group will have a different reason for analysing financial statements.

The equity investor group will be mainly interested in the security of their investment, the rate of return on the investment, and future prospects for the enterprise. The loan creditor, on the other hand, will be interested in the maintenance of interest payments and loan repayments.

In general terms, interpreters of accounting reports should try to place the contents of such reports in a framework. This framework will vary from user to user, but some common elements can be identified. These are:

1. What are the objectives of the analysis?
   We must establish; who wants the information and why do they want it? For example, an analyst may wish to consider a company as a possible takeover target on behalf of a client or employees may wish to examine company accounts in order to support a pay claim.
2. What information is required?
   The analyst may consider the efficiency of asset utilization and cost control in a company. Employees may consider company profitability and directors' pay and benefits. It is clear that the information required by interpreters of accounts will be determined by the objectives of the analysis.
3. Where is the information to be found?
   An analysis of company performance should normally take into consideration information derived from the economic, political, and technological environment in addition to information derived from financial statements.
4. What factors may distort the financial analysis?
   Accounting policy changes or the inconsistent application of accounting treatments may distort the story being told by accounting numbers. Other factors include; inflation, regulatory changes, and the practice of creative accounting techniques. In fact, many interpreters of accounts try to correct for such distortions.

10.2 REPORTING THE RESULTS OF ANALYSIS

Fundamental to most exercises in financial statement analysis is the requirement to produce a report. The following points represent guidelines for producing interpretive reports based on accounting statements. Numerical analysis is a feature of these reports, and a useful tactic for dealing with these calculations is to present the results of the ratios, percentages, and other statistics as an appendix. The main body of the report can then be used to explain the results of the analysis. A suggested format for the report is set out below.

Report format

Header
Identify the subject of the report, the person or group to whom it is addressed, the author, and the date of the report. In an examination or assessment situation, you may have to make up some of this information if it is not given in the question.

Introduction

This section contains comments which set out the scope of the report and mentions that detailed information is provided in an appendix.

Analysis

This will comprise a number of sections and the exact content will be determined by the requirements of the question. For example, you may be asked to comment on profitability and the efficient utilization of assets. A profitability and an asset utilization section would be appropriate here, and each of these sections would contain an explanation of your understanding of factors relevant to these matters.

Other questions may ask you to consider a company from the point of view of shareholders, loan creditors, and internal management. In this case, your report should contain a section devoted to each of these user groups.

Advice and recommendations

The hardest part of an interpretation exercise is to provide advice and recommendations to the reader. A useful technique to adopt here is to step back from the detail of the report and remind yourself of the report's objectives and the needs of the reader. Then it is a question of stating the simplest and most obvious advice first. This may allow you to provide more detailed advice. For example, your analysis may indicate that a company is suffering from declining profitability. The simplest and most obvious advice is to increase profitability. You should then consider how profitability could be increased. The obvious answer is by increasing revenues and by decreasing costs. If the particular revenues and costs of the company are examined, you may be able to suggest that revenues could be increased by:

1. Reducing selling prices to increase demand.
2. Differential pricing to exploit different market segments.
3. Allowing customers extended credit terms.

In addition, you may be able to suggest that costs are reduced by:

1. Introducing tighter cost controls.
2. Obtaining better terms from suppliers.
3. The elimination of wastage.

The above points serve to indicate the thought processes required in order to deal with this part of an interpretation exercise rather than the presentation of a definitive answer. In many such exercises there is no 'correct' answer. The students that tend to obtain the top marks in such exercises, are the ones who can provide the best answers in the advice and recommendation section of the report. It is suggested that 'best' in this context means the provision of reasoned arguments that display evidence of rational thought.

Conclusion

The concluding section of the report may be used to summarize the main points of the analysis and the key recommendations. In addition it may be useful to indicate the limitations of the analysis. We will return to this point at the end of the chapter.

10.3 TECHNIQUES OF INTERPRETATION

In this section, we will look at methods of interpretation in general terms before focusing on the most widely used technique in this area of the accounting syllabus, namely ratio analysis.

The following techniques may be used to interpret a set of financial statements:

1. *Reading*
Published financial accounts contain a great deal of information. It has been suggested that accounts should be read backwards. This is because the notes to the annual report can allow the reader to compare information concerning different aspects of business performance. For example, a comparison between interest paid and loan capital may indicate whether or not company borrowings have been omitted from the balance sheet. The accounting policies note should indicate changes to accounting policies which may materially affect published results.

2. *Vertical analysis*
This involves taking the numbers shown in the profit and loss account and balance sheet, and expressing these numbers as percentages. The profit and loss amounts are expressed as a percentage of sales, and the balance sheet amounts are expressed as a percentage of the balance sheet totals.

Example
Vertical analysis

Craddock Plc
Profit and loss account for for the year ended
30 November 20X1

	£'000s	%
Sales	17,250	100.0
Cost of sales	(7,200)	(41.7)
Gross profit	10,050	58.3
Overhead expenses	(4,950)	(28.7)
Profit before tax	5,100	29.6
Taxation	(1,650)	(9.6)
Profit after tax	3,450	20.0
Dividends	(300)	(1.7)
Retained profit	3,150	18.3

Craddock Plc
Balance sheet at 30 November 20X1

	£'000s	%
Fixed assets (NBV)	3,000	31.0
Current assets		
Stock	1,950	20.2
Debtors	10,500	108.5
Cash and bank	75	0.8
	12,525	129.5
Current liabilities		
Creditors	(3,900)	(40.3)
Taxation	(1,650)	(17.1)
Dividends	(300)	(3.1)
	(5,850)	(60.5)
Net assets	9,675	100.0

	£'000s	%
Capital and reserves		
Share capital	3,000	31.0
Profit and loss account	6,675	69.0
	9,675	100.0

This method can be used to compare the performance of companies of different sizes. In effect, it reduces the results of different businesses to a set of common values
which aids comparison.

3. *Horizontal analysis*
This method compares business results over time by indicating percentage changes between corresponding amounts in different periods.

Example
Horizontal analysis

Craddock Plc
Profit and loss account for the year ended
30 November

	20X1	20X2	% Change
	£'000s	£'000s	
Sales	17,250	19,837	+15.0
Cost of sales	(7,200)	(8,250)	+14.6
Gross profit	10,050	11,587	+15.3
Overhead expenses	(4,950)	(5,197)	+ 5.0
Profit before tax	5,100	6,390	+25.3
Taxation	(1,650)	(1,815)	+10.0
Profit after tax	3,450	4,575	+32.6
Dividends	(300)	(330)	+10.0
Retained profit	3,150	4,245	+34.8

In this example, the balance sheet analysis has not been shown due to space limitations. However, the above example should indicate that this type of analysis is particularly useful in highlighting areas where a more detailed analysis is required. For example, we may have expected overhead expenses not to increase as these costs are not expected to vary in response to increases in sales; therefore, a detailed analysis of overhead expenses may be required. Another question to ask is; why has the taxation charge increased by 10.0% when the profit before tax has increased by 25.3%? Thus, the elements of the taxation charge could be the subject of enquiry.

4. *Trend analysis*
In trend analysis, monetary amounts can be converted to index numbers and the results of several years trading for a company can be examined. The technique is often applied to the five year financial summaries which are included in many annual reports.

Example
Trend analysis
Part of the five year financial summary from the 20X6 annual report of Theocraties Plc shows the following information.

Theocraties Plc
Five year financial summary—year ended 31 March

	20X2	20X3	20X4	20X5	20X6
	£m	£m	£m	£m	£m
Sales	13,337	13,242	13,675	13,893	14,446
Operating profit	3,370	2,403	2,982	2,663	3,100

Representing these amounts as index numbers gives the following results:

	20X2	20X3	20X4	20X5	20X6
Sales	100	99	103	104	108
Operating profit	100	71	88	79	92

The 20X2 amounts are given a value of 100 and subsequent years are related to that base. The 20X3 index value for sales is calculated as $13,242/13,337 \times 100$.

The trend of the results over the period is immediately apparent. The value of sales dipped slightly in 20X2, but has now recovered. However, operating profit has yet to regain its 20X2 peak and does not show the same consistent growth pattern as sales. A more extensive examination of the results of the company over the period would be needed before any useful conclusions can be drawn about its performance.

5. *Ratio analysis*

For many people, ratio analysis is synonymous with the interpretation of accounts, and most examination and assessment questions in this area of the financial accounting syllabus require an understanding of the technique.

Ratio analysis is a systematic method of examining accounting statements which is based upon the calculation of a number of ratios and statistics. We will look at this technique by considering the categories of information it is possible to obtain from a set of accounts. These categories are: profitability, liquidity, efficiency, and investment. In the next section we will look at each of these categories in some detail.

10.4 PROFITABILITY

The assessment of the profitability of a business is a major factor in most interpretive exercises. We must begin an assessment of profitability by putting it into perspective. This perspective is achieved by a consideration of the resources used to earn profit. For an individual, a deposit account at a bank represents the resource used to earn profit in the form of interest payments. For a business, the resources used to earn profit are the assets and liabilities shown on the balance sheet. Another way of describing the assets and liabilities of a business is to consider how business ownership is represented on the balance sheet. It is represented by capital in the form of a capital account for unincorporated businesses, and share capital and reserves in the case of companies (however, in this chapter we will consider companies only). Thus, to put the profits of a business into perspective, we can compare profit earned with the capital employed in the business.

Return on capital employed (ROCE)

This ratio relates profit to the capital used in generating that profit. The basic formula for the calculation of ROCE is:

$$\frac{\text{Profit}}{\text{Capital employed}} \times 100 = X\%$$

The problem with this basic formula is that it does not define profit or capital employed. In fact, there is no agreed definition of these terms for the ROCE calculation which means that when ROCE is calculated we must take particular care in defining our terms.

Let us consider the term profit first. Some ROCE calculations use operating profit, but for the purposes of this chapter we will consider net profit, only. However, net profit can be described in a number of ways. It can be stated before tax or after tax, and for more detailed analysis it can be presented as:

1. Net profit before interest and taxation or
2. Net profit after taxation and preference dividend.

One of the main principles of the interpretation of accounts is to compare like with like. Net profit before interest and taxation is the profit earned before payments are made to loan creditors and to shareholders. It is also like an individual's gross pay before tax is paid.

It would be logical, therefore, to calculate ROCE in this context by comparing net profit before interest and taxation with a corresponding figure of capital employed. This would be: ordinary share capital, preference share capital, reserves (such as the profit and loss account), and loan capital (such as debentures). We may not be interested in the gross return to the providers of finance of the business if we are ordinary shareholders. In this case, we will want a calculation of ROCE which reflects our interests. Therefore our profit figure should be the amount of profit that is potentially available to the ordinary shareholders. That is the net profit after tax and preference dividend. The corresponding figure of capital employed for this profit should be: ordinary shares and reserves.

Example

A summary of the results of Zhivago Plc is shown below. It should be noted that all sales and purchases are on credit terms and credit purchases during 20X1 amounted to £3,500,000.

Zhivago Plc
Profit and loss account for the year ended
31 December

	20X1 £'000s	20X2 £'000s
Sales	8,625	9,918
Cost of sales	(3,600)	(4,125)
Gross profit	5,025	5,793
Overhead expenses	(2,475)	(2,599)
Profit before tax	2,550	3,194
Taxation	(825)	(907)
Profit after tax	1,725	2,287
Dividends:		
Ordinary	(90)	(105)
Preference	(60)	(60)
Retained profit	1,575	2,122

Zhivago Plc
Balance sheet (extract) at 31 December

	20X1 £'000s	20X2 £'000s
Capital and reserves		
Share capital:		
Ordinary shares	2,400	2,400
Preference shares	1,200	1,200
Reserves:		
Profit and loss account	8,010	10,132
Loan capital:		
£600,000 × 8%		
Debentures	600	600
	12,210	14,332

The calculation of ROCE is as follows:

1. Using profit before interest and tax.

(a) $\text{ROCE} = \dfrac{\text{Profit before interest and tax}}{\text{Ordinary and preference shares + Reserves} + \text{Loan capital}} \times 100$

(b) Profit before interest and tax

	20X1 £'000s	20X2 £'000s
Net profit before tax	2,550	3,194
Interest £600,000 × 8%	48	48
	2,598	3,242

Interest is deducted in arriving at profit before tax, it must therefore be added to arrive at profit before interest.

(c) Return on capital employed

20X1	20X2
$\dfrac{2{,}598}{12{,}210} \times 100 = 21.3\%$	$\dfrac{3{,}242}{14{,}332} \times 100 = 22.6\%$

2. Using profit after tax and preference dividend.

(a) $\text{ROCE} = \dfrac{\text{Profit after tax and preference dividend}}{\text{Ordinary shares + Reserves}} \times 100$

(b) Profit calculation

	20X1 £'000s	20X2 £'000s
Net profit after tax	1,725	2,287
Preference dividend	(60)	(60)
	1,665	2,227

The preference dividend is not deducted in arriving at profit after tax, it must therefore be deducted to arrive at profit after the preference dividend.

(c) Return on capital employed

20X1	*20X2*

$$\frac{1,665}{10,410} \times 100 = 16.0\% \qquad \frac{2,227}{12,532} \times 100 = 17.8\%$$

In an introductory accounting course, a variety of methods of calculating ROCE are likely to be acceptable, unless the examination or assessment question tells you otherwise. The important points are to indicate how you have calculated ROCE and to compare like with like. Strictly speaking, in the calculation of ROCE for Zhivago Plc above we have not compared like with like. We have compared a profit which is earned during a period with a value of capital employed at the end of a period. We should therefore use a figure of average capital employed in the calculation and, in the absence of better information, we can add together the opening and closing values for capital employed and divide by two. Thus, for 20X2, the value of average capital employed (ordinary shares + reserves) is:

	£'000s
Capital employed at 1 January 20X2	10,410
+ capital employed at 31 December 20X2	12,532
	22,972

Average capital employed (22,972 ×1/2) = 11,471

This gives ROCE for 20X2:

2,227/11,471 × 100 = 19.4%

The information is not available to calculate the corresponding figure for 20X1.

Gross profit percentage

This is a much simpler calculation than ROCE. It is gross profit expressed as a percentage of sales. There should be a consistency in the gross profit percentage over time and a consistency between similar businesses. This is because gross profit is generally considered to be sales minus the cost of sales. The cost of sales calculation (opening stock + purchases − closing stock) represents the major costs which vary with sales. It is for this reason that auditors and the tax authorities often use the gross profit percentage as a method of checking the accuracy of profit calculations.

In terms of interpreting a set of accounts in an academic context, we need to consider the factors that may cause a gross profit percentage to change over time. One very obvious reason for a change in gross profit percentage is a reduction in selling prices. This will reduce the value of sales relative to the cost of sales, and therefore manifest itself as a reduction in gross profit and a reduction in the gross profit percentage.

The basic calculation is as follows:

$$\text{Gross profit percentage} = \frac{\text{Gross profit}}{\text{Sales}} \times 100$$

We can calculate the gross profit percentage for Zhivago Plc as follows:

	20X1		20X2	
	£'000s		£'000s	
Gross profit	5,025		5,793	
		$\times 100 = 58.3\%$		$\times 100 = 58.4\%$
Sales	8,625		9,918	

The gross profit percentage appears to be consistent over time, although we should examine more than two periods to confirm this. It is unlikely that we would want to probe any further into these calculations unless information was provided to suggest that Zhivago Plc's gross profit percentage differed materially from the industry average, or it was stated that the relationship between sales and cost of sales had changed during 20X2.

Net profit percentage

This is another simple calculation and is net profit (before tax) expressed as a percentage of sales.

In the case of Zhivago Plc, the calculation may be shown as follows:

	20X1		20X2	
	£'000s		£'000s	
Net profit	2,550		3,194	
		$\times 100 = 29.6\%$		$\times 100 = 32.2\%$
Sales	8,625		9,918	

This is an extremely healthy net profit percentage and, in fact, we should expect to see a small rise in the net profit percentage over time, providing that there are no fluctuations in gross profit. The reason for this is that net profit is after charging overhead expenses. Thus, a rise in the net profit percentage is indicative of good control of overheads. The converse is also true in that a fall in the net profit percentage which is not attributable to movements in gross profit indicates poor control of overheads. This interpretation must be made with care because it is often the case that businesses incur short-term expenditures such as advertising and credit control costs in order to boost sales.

10.5 LIQUIDITY

Zhivago Plc is clearly a profitable company, but this is not the whole story. It is possible that the company could go out of business by expanding too fast and running out of resources as a consequence. The resources we are interested in are known as working capital which are the items shown under current assets and current liabilities on the balance sheet.

The concept of liquidity may be described as indicating how quickly an asset may be turned into cash. If we think of current assets, stock has the least liquidity because it must be processed and sold by the company before any cash is received. Debtors are more liquid than stock because a sale has been made and we expect to receive cash for debtors before we receive cash for stock. Current liabilities, on the other hand, represent a drain on liquid resources as these creditors must be paid.

Before we can calculate any more ratios, we need some more information about Zhivago Plc. Here is the other half of the 20X1 balance sheet.

Zhivago Plc
Balance sheet at 31 December 20X1

	£'000s
Fixed assets (NBV)	8,000
Current assets	
Stock	2,340
Debtors	2,600
Cash and bank	1,429
	6,369
Current liabilities	
Creditors	(1,184)
Taxation	(825)
Dividends	(150)
	(2,159)
Net assets	12,210

There are two main ratios which are normally calculated to assess the liquidity of a business. These are the current ratio and the acid test ratio.

Current ratio

This is calculated by dividing current assets by current liabilities:

$$\text{Current ratio} = \frac{\text{Current assets}}{\text{Current liabilities}}$$

Thus, for Zhivago Plc the current ratio for 20X1 is:

$$\frac{6,369}{2,159} = 2.9{:}1$$

The relationship between current assets and current liabilities is, by convention, expressed as a ratio where current liabilities are given a value of one. The above calculation shows that the company's current assets are 2.9 times greater than its current liabilities in 20X1. We will consider how this ratio might be interpreted when we have calculated the second liquidity ratio.

The acid test ratio

This is similar to the current ratio except that stock is deducted from current assets:

$$\text{Acid test ratio} = \frac{\text{Current assets} - \text{stock}}{\text{Current liabilities}}$$

Thus, for Zhivago Plc the acid test ratio for 20X1 is:

$$\frac{6,369 - 2,340}{2,159} = 1.9:1$$

Current assets minus stock are 1.9 times current liabilities.

Are these results good or bad? This is a difficult question to answer for the following reasons:

1. We have only calculated the liquidity ratios for the day of 31 December 20X1. Our results may not be indicative of the true liquidity position of the company.
2. We need to compare our results with a meaningful standard in order to arrive at an assessment of liquidity.

A comparison of the December 20X1 liquidity ratios with the results of other periods will give us an indication of the trend of liquidity in Zhivago Plc, but a much better indication may be gained by comparison with the industry norm. In the past, many textbooks have suggested that a current ratio of 2:1 and an acid test ratio of 1:1 indicated that a business enjoyed a healthy degree of liquidity. In practice, different types of industry differ in their rates of cash collection. A chain of supermarkets that receives cash every day can operate with much lower liquidity ratios than a construction company. This statement is probably not much help to a student faced with an assessment exercise so we need to derive some general rules for the interpretation of liquidity ratios. Firstly, current assets should exceed current liabilities since excessive current liabilities are a clear indication of a liquidity problem. Secondly, we can look at other evidence to determine the liquidity position of the business. We can make an assessment of how long it is likely to be before stock and debtors are turned into cash. This can be done by comparing stock and debtors to cost of sales and sales, respectively (we will look at this in more detail in the next section). Finally, it should be noted that liquidity ratios can be too high as well as too low. High liquidity ratios may indicate that stock levels are too high for the volume of trade and there is a danger that the stock will be unsaleable. In addition, the existence of high liquidity ratios may indicate that debtors are too high and there is a danger of excessive bad debts.

10.6 EFFICIENCY

We will consider a business to be efficient when there is evidence of the effective management of assets and liabilities. Evidence of effective management of assets and liabilities can be found by:

1. Measuring the productivity of assets by comparing asset values with sales revenue.
2. Measuring how many times stock is replenished during the period.
3. Measuring how long it takes for cash to be received from debtors.
4. Measuring how long it takes for creditors to be paid.

We will look at these measurements in turn.

Asset turnover

The productivity of the assets of a business can be examined by calculating:

1. *Net asset turnover*
   The formula for this is:

$$\frac{\text{Sales}}{\text{Net assets}} = \text{X times}$$

For Zhivago Plc, the net asset turnover at 31 December 20X1 is:

$$\frac{8,625}{12,210} = 0.7 \text{ times}$$

Thus, for every £1 of net assets, sales of £0.7 were generated.

2. *Fixed asset turnover*
   The formula for this is:

$$\frac{\text{Sales}}{\text{Fixed assets}} = \text{X times}$$

For Zhivago Plc, the fixed asset turnover at 31 December 20X1 is:

$$\frac{8,625}{8,000} = 1.1 \text{ times}$$

Thus, for every £1 of fixed assets, sales of £1.1 were generated.

3. *Working capital turnover (Net current asset turnover)*
   The formula for this is:

$$\frac{\text{Sales}}{\text{Working capital}} = \text{X times}$$

For Zhivago Plc, the working capital turnover at 31 December 20X1 is:

$$\frac{8{,}625}{6{,}369 - 2{,}159} = 2.0 \text{ times}$$

Thus, for every £1 of working capital, £2 of sales were generated.

All of the above calculations of asset utilization need to be compared to the results of previous periods and industry norms. In addition, the need to compare like with like means that a more accurate picture of asset utilization may be obtained if it is possible to derive average values for net assets, fixed assets, and working capital.

We have looked at asset utilization starting with net assets, moving on to fixed assets, and then examining working capital. The next logical step in the analysis is to look at the components of working capital. In practical terms, this means examining stocks, debtors, and creditors.

Stock turnover

This measures how quickly stock is being utilized and the interpretation of this ratio is clearly dependent upon the type of business activity being undertaken. Suppliers of perishable products, such as florists, will have a high level of stock turnover. In other words, they need to replenish their stock on a daily basis. Manufacturers of commercial aircraft are in a quite different position. They will have a very low level of stock turnover and will replenish their stock at intervals of several months or longer, depending on trading conditions.

The industry norm is therefore an extremely important concept in the context of stock turnover. The basic calculation is:

$$\text{Stock turnover} = \frac{\text{Cost of sales}}{\text{Stock}} = \text{X times}$$

For Zhivago Plc, the stock turnover for 20X1 is:

$$\frac{3{,}600}{2{,}340} = 1.5 \text{ times}$$

If it is possible to calculate an average stock figure, this should be used in the calculation. A crude measure of average stock is; opening stock + closing stock × 1/2.

Debtor collection period

The prompt collection of debts is a very important indicator of efficiency and the debtor collection period measures the time taken to collect payments from debtors. The calculation is as follows:

$$\text{Debtor collection period} = \frac{\text{Debtors}}{\text{Credit sales}} \times 365 = \text{X days}$$

For Zhivago Plc, the debtor collection period for 20X1 is:

$$\frac{2,600}{8,625} \times 365 = 110 \text{ days}$$

In order to match like with like, we should match debtors (average debtors if possible) with credit sales. If no other information is available in an assessment situation, it is advisable to indicate that an assumption has been made that all sales are credit sales.

Most businesses ask that customers settle their debts within 30 days; however, the UK seems to suffer from particularly slow-paying debtors and it is not unusual for debtor collection periods of up to 90 days to occur. In many other jurisdictions, and particularly in parts of the USA, there are legal requirements which force debtors to pay within 30 days of the invoice date.

The debtor collection period may need to be interpreted in the context of the incidence of bad debts because some businesses find that the offer of extended periods of credit to customers is an effective way of maintaining or increasing sales. This is particularly the case in furniture and electrical goods retailing.

Creditor payment period

This is similar to the debtor collection period and measures the time taken by the business to pay its creditors. The basic calculation is:

$$\text{Creditor payment period} = \frac{\text{Creditors}}{\text{Credit purchases}} \times 365 = \text{X days}$$

As in the case of the debtor collection period, cash transactions must be excluded from the profit and loss account figure of purchases. Where the purchases figure is not available, an approximation of the creditor payment period may be obtained by using the cost of sales figure.

In the case of Zhivago Plc, the creditor payment period for 20X1 is:

$$\frac{1,184}{3,500} \times 365 = 123.5 \text{ days}$$

NB The figure of credit purchases is given at the start of the Zhivago Plc example above.

10.7 INVESTMENT

Investment ratios indicate the health of the business from the point of view of the investor. This involves a consideration of the way in which the business is financed, its ability to pay interest charges, and dividends, and, in addition, the relationship between returns to shareholders and the market price of the company shares. We will consider each of these areas in turn.

Gearing ratio

Gearing is a technical term which describes the relationship between equity capital such as ordinary shares and debt capital such as debentures and other long-term loans. A company is said to be highly geared if it has a large amount of debt capital relative to equity capital.

The use of loans to finance a business has both advantages and disadvantages. The interest paid on loans is a charge against profit, it appears as an overhead expense in the profit and loss account and, most importantly, it is an allowable expense in the calculation of business tax liabilities. Therefore, tax relief is given in respect of loan interest and this makes the financing of debt capital cheaper than the financing of equity capital. A disadvantage of debt is that interest payments must be made even when trading conditions become difficult. In a recession, for example, a company can suspend dividend payments to the ordinary shareholders, but it cannot suspend interest payments.

A highly geared company can display lower than average profitability in times of recession and higher than average profitability in favourable trading conditions.

The gearing ratio is similar to ROCE in that there are a number of definitions of the elements in the calculation. The general form of the formula is:

$$\text{Gearing ratio} = \frac{\text{Debt capital}}{\text{Debt capital} + \text{Equity capital}} \times 100$$

The gearing ratio is sometimes called the debt/equity ratio. We will define the terms debt and equity as follows:

Debt capital = long-term loans, debentures, and preference shares.

Equity capital = ordinary share capital + reserves

For Zhivago Plc, the gearing ratio for 20X1 is:

$$\frac{600 + 1,200}{12,210} \times 100 = 14.7\%$$

Interest cover

The gearing ratio must be interpreted in the light of prevailing economic conditions. However, additional information in respect of the ability of a company to utilize debt capital can be given by calculating interest cover. This relates interest payments to net profit before interest and taxation.

$$\text{Interest cover} = \frac{\text{Net profit before interest and taxation}}{\text{Interest charge}} = \text{X times}$$

The relevant calculation for Zhivago Plc for 20X1 is:

$$\frac{2,550 + 48}{48} = 54.1 \text{ times}$$

It is clear that Zhivago Plc could afford to pay its current interest charges 54 times over.

Earnings per share

This relates profit to the number of ordinary shares and therefore gives profit a context from the ordinary shareholder's viewpoint. The basic calculation is:

$$\text{Earnings per share} = \frac{\text{Net profit after tax and preference dividend}}{\text{Number of ordinary shares in issue}} = \text{Xp}$$

The relevant calculation for Zhivago Plc for 20X1 is:

$$\frac{1,725 - 60}{2,400} = 69.3\text{p per share}$$

We will assume that the balance sheet figure for ordinary shares is in respect of £1 ordinary shares.

Price/earnings (p/e) ratio

This ratio utilizes the earnings per share calculation and compares it with the market price of the share. If we assume that the market value of the ordinary shares in Zhivago Plc is £3.50 on 31 December 20X1, the ratio is:

$$\text{Price/earnings ratio} = \frac{\text{Market price per share}}{\text{Earnings per share}} = \text{X years}$$

$$\frac{350}{69.3} = 5 \text{ years}$$

This indicates that the investor will take five years to recover the cost of his or her investment at the current rate of dividend. The p/e ratio can be compared to the ratios of other companies in the same industry or with the historical record of the same company. There are occasions where a high p/e ratio can indicate that a share is particularly in demand due to market estimations of future earnings.

Dividend cover

This is similar in concept to interest cover and is calculated as:

$$\text{Dividend cover} = \frac{\text{Net profit after tax and preference dividend}}{\text{Paid and proposed ordinary dividends}} = \text{X times}$$

The relevant calculation for Zhivago Plc for 20X1 is:

$$\frac{1,725-60}{90} = 18.5 \text{ times}$$

Zhivago could therefore afford to pay 18.5 times the current rate ordinary dividend.

Dividend yield

This calculation presents dividends as a return on the market value of the company shares. The basic calculation is:

$$\text{Dividend yield} = \frac{\text{Ordinary dividend per share}}{\text{Market price per ordinary share}} \times 100$$

The relevant calculation for Zhivago Plc for 20X1 is

$$\frac{90/2,400}{3.50} \times 100 = 1.1\%$$

10.8 LIMITATIONS OF RATIO ANALYSIS

One of the dangers of a technique like ratio analysis is that it provides answers which have the appearance of certainty. This means that users of ratio analysis and readers of reports which employ the technique need to be reminded of its limitations. These limitations may be stated as follows;

1. The results of ratio analysis do not on their own form a suitable basis for decision making. Ratios need to be compared to some yardstick. This can take the form of some pre-determined target ratios or historical results of a particular company or its industrial group.
2. Careful attention must be paid to defining the terms used to calculate ratios as there is considerable variation in their calculation.
3. Inflation may have a considerable distorting effect on the comparison of ratios over time or between industries.
4. Accounting policy choices by different companies can affect comparability. For example, companies may differ widely in their policies in respect of stock valuation, depreciation, research and development, and goodwill.
5. Historical results may not be an accurate guide to the future.

10.9 CONCLUSION

The interpretation of financial accounts is one of the most difficult areas of the accounting syllabus. One of the major problems at an introductory level is that there is often no 'right' answer to assessment exercises. In practice, it is possible to look beyond the financial statements to the real-world environment of the business in order to find evidence to support the results of an interpretation exercise. In an academic context, this is much more difficult. Key features of high-scoring answers to an academic interpretation exercise are:

1. Clear indications as to how ratios have been calculated.
2. A professional style of report writing.
3. A coherent set of statements supported by evidence from the numerical analysis.

KEY POINTS

1. The following techniques may be used to interpret a set of financial statements: reading, vertical analysis, horizontal analysis, trend analysis, and ratio analysis.
2. Ratio analysis is a systematic method of examining accounting statements.
3. Ratios and statistics may be calculated in order to consider the following categories; profitability, liquidity, efficiency, and investment.
4. There are a number of limitations to ratio analysis: a suitable basis for comparison must

be established, careful attention must be paid to defining terms, and ratios can be distorted by inflation and accounting policy choices.

QUESTIONS

10.1 Using the summarized accounts of Miklos Ltd. below, calculate the following ratios:

Return on capital employed
Gross profit percentage
Net profit percentage
Current ratio
Acid test ratio
Fixed asset turnover
Debtor collection period
Capital gearing

Miklos Ltd.
Profit and loss account for the year ended 31 March 20X5

	£'000s
Sales	3,000
Cost of sales	1,500
	1,500
Overhead expenses	1,250
Debenture interest	25
Profit before tax	225
Taxation	75
Profit after tax	150
Dividends	100
Retained profit for the year	50

Miklos Ltd.
Balance sheet as at 31 March 20X5

	£'000s	£'000s	£'000s
Fixed assets (NBV)			1,712
Current assets			
Stock		188	
Debtors		500	
		688	
Less current liabilities			
Creditors	400		
Bank overdraft	25		
Taxation	75		
Proposed dividend	100		
	—	600	
		—	88
			1,800
Capital and reserves			
Ordinary shares			1,500
Profit and loss account			50
			1,550
Long-term loans			
10% debentures			250
			1,800

10.2 The directors of Harvest Plc are proposing to pay a dividend of 35p per share for the year ended 31 August 20X8. The market price for shares at this date was £1.75. The capital of the company comprises 1 million £1 ordinary shares and the net profit after taxation for 20X8 was £500,000. Calculate:

> Earnings per share
> Price/earnings ratio
> Dividend yield
> Dividend cover

10.3 Calculate the return on capital employed and the capital gearing ratio for Janeway Ltd. based on the following information:

Year ended 31 March 20X4

	£'000s
Profit before tax	385
Capital and reserves	
Ordinary shares of £1 each	420
15% Preference shares of £1 each	70
Share premium account	140
Profit and loss account	1,400
Shareholders' funds	2,030
10% debentures	700
	2,730

10.4 You are presented with the following information in respect of Johnstone Ltd.:

Johnstone Ltd.
Profit and loss accounts for the two years ended
30 September 20X7

	20X6 £'000s	20X7 £'000s
Sales	729,450	875,850
Operating profit	25,857	31,005
Interest payable	2,976	2,976
Profit before tax	22,881	28,029
Taxation	8,601	10,539
Profit after tax	14,280	17,490
Dividends	3,360	3,600
Retained profit for the year	10,920	13,890
Retained profit brought forward	35,310	46,230
Retained profit carried forward	46,230	60,120

Johnstone Ltd.
Balance sheets as at 30 September

	20X6		20X7	
	£'000s	£'000s	£'000s	£'000s
Fixed assets (NBV)		7,493		19,050
Current assets				
Stock	60,217		75,682	
Debtors	60,315		65,055	
Cash at bank	18,138		8,685	
	138,670		149,422	
Current liabilities				
Creditors	48,906		55,845	
Taxation	3,710		4,890	
Proposed dividend	2,677		2,977	
	55,293		63,712	
Net current assets		83,377		85,710
Net assets		90,870		104,760
Capital and reserves				
Ordinary shares of 25p		14,880		14,880
profit and loss account		46,230		60,120
Shareholders' funds		61,110		75,000
Long-term loans				
10% debentures		29,760		29,760
		90,870		104,760

You are required to:

1. Identify two ratios which are of particular significance for each of the following user groups:

   (a) shareholders;
   (a) trade creditors;
   (a) the management of Johnstone Ltd.

2. Calculate the ratios you have identified for each of the above user groups.
3. Comment on the changes between 20X6 and 20X7 in the performance of Johnstone Ltd.

10.5 Hector Gladstone is an international businessman. He wishes to acquire a UK-based machine tools manufacturing company. Two companies have been identified as potential acquisitions and summaries of their latest financial statements are given below:

Profit and Loss Accounts for the year ended 30 April 20X7

	Solo Ltd. £'000s	Mio Ltd. £'000s
Sales	7,880	4,480
Opening stock	1,200	1,160
Materials	2,040	1,088
Closing stock	(1,240)	(1,120)
Labour	1,280	1,000
Factory overheads	1,640	888
Depreciation	280	160
Selling and admin expenses	992	600
Interest	280	80
Profit before tax	1,408	624
Taxation	520	200
Profit after tax	888	424

Balance sheets at 30 April 20X7

	Solo Ltd. £'000s	£'000s	Mio Ltd. £'000s	£'000s
Fixed assets (NBV)		6,120		3,280
Current assets				
Stock	1,240		1,120	
Debtors	1,360		3,160	
Bank	400		360	
	3,000		4,640	
Current liabilities				
Creditors	1,880		2,400	
Other creditors	1,040		1,000	
	2,920		3,400	
Net current assets		80		1,240
Net assets		6,200		4,520
Share capital		3,600		3,520
profit and loss account		840		440
		4,440		3,960
Long-term Loans				
Debentures		1,760		560
		6,200		4,520

Prepare a report for Hector which assesses the financial performance and position of Solo Ltd. and Mio Ltd. State any assumptions you make and any limitations in your analysis.

10.6 You are the accountant at Zork Plc. This is a diversified trading group with over 50 subsidiary companies. You are required to prepare a report for the board of Zork Plc on the performance of two subsidiary companies, Bryzzen Plc and Calleva Plc. A summary of the latest accounts of both companies is set out below:

Year ended 31 March 20X5

	Bryzzen Plc £'000s	Calleva Plc £'000s
Sales	7,010	12,294
Manufacturing costs:		
Direct labour	962	1,248
Materials	2,760	5,202
Depreciation	544	900
Plant hire	84	254
Factory overheads	488	760
Selling and admin expenses	720	1,050
Interest	120	560
	5,678	9,974
Profit before tax	1,332	2,320
Taxation	610	820
Retained profit	722	1,500

	£'000s	£'000s
Fixed assets (NBV)	5,270	7,938
Current assets	6,390	4,700
Current liabilities	4,036	3,364
Ordinary shares and reserves	6,624	5,274
Loan capital	1,000	4,000
	000 employees	
Average number of employees	190	238

Bryzzen Plc and Calleva Plc manufacture office furniture. In April 20X5, MOFTA (Manufacturers of Office Furniture Trade Association) produced a report indicating that the average results achieved by companies in the industry were as follows:

Pre-tax return on capital employed	19%
Net profit percentage	21%
Asset turnover	0.9 times
Current ratio	1.7:1
Capital gearing	
(fixed interest capital/total capital)	28%
Value added per employee	£23,500

Your report should compare the results of Bryzzen Plc and Calleva Plc with each other, and with the information produced by MOFTA. Include in your report the limitations of using ratios as an analysis technique.

ELEVEN

THE MANAGEMENT ACCOUNTING PERSPECTIVE

LEARNING OBJECTIVES

After reading this chapter you should:

- Understand the essential difference between management accounting and financial accounting.
- Understand the role of management accounting in decision making.
- Identify the kinds of decisions for which management accounting can be useful.

There are many ideas about the nature and purpose of accounting. The American Accounting Association in their statement of Basic Accounting Theory (1996) defines accounting as:

> '... the process of identifying, measuring and communicating financial information about an entity to permit informed judgements and decisions by users of the information.'

There are many elements of this definition which are applicable to management accounting, but for a more comprehensive definition we need to turn to the *Oxford Dictionary of Accounting* (1995). This gives us a great deal more information about the nature of management accounting.

> 'The techniques used to collect, process and present financial and quantitative data within an organization to enable effective scorekeeping, cost control, planning, pricing and decision making to take place.'

The scope of the information sources used by management accountants is indicated by the use of the words 'financial and quantitative data'. Management accounting goes beyond the financial information in the accounting system and considers information relating to the operational activities of the business. This will include information regarding; grades of material used, production processes, time taken to complete specific tasks, technical specifications, and physical dimensions.

In addition to collecting information from outside the accounting system, the management accountant collects information in respect of different time periods than his financial accounting counterpart. Financial accountants focus mainly on the past and report economic events after they have occurred. Management accountants collect information about the past and the present. They also produce estimates about what is likely to happen in the future.

Financial accountants tend to concern themselves with the annual results of the business as a whole. Management accountants can concern themselves with any period relevant to the information needs of management. In practice, there is a monthly reporting cycle for much of the reports produced by management accountants, but in cases such as the evaluation of alternative investment projects, the period over which accounting measurements are made can stretch over several years.

In this context, the annual reporting convention of financial accounting may not reflect the longer term nature of business activity. In the case of a new business, money that is expended initially to develop the business, may not result in profits being earned until two, three or possibly more annual accounting periods have expired.

A further difference between the two accounting disciplines is that financial accounting reports the results of the business as a whole, whereas management accounting additionally reports the results of business sub-units. These can be divisions of a large company, regional groupings, individual branches of a retail chain, or departments and departmental groups within an organization. In fact, it is possible to produce management accounting reports about any organizational unit, from the business as a whole, down to individual assets or individual employees.

Management accounting reports can be tailored to the needs of the recipient. The manager of a production department may, for example, receive a monthly report which contains considerable detail about the costs and revenues in his or her department. The managing director of the same organization is likely to receive a less detailed summary report about the costs and revenues of all departments.

Another feature of management accounting reports is the relative absence of regulation of their form and content. There are no Companies Acts, accounting standards or stock exchange rules that apply to such reports. It is, however, normal practice for large companies to set exacting specifications for the form and content of their management accounting reports.

The users of management accounting reports are within an organization. This can be contrasted with the financial accounting practice of reporting mainly to external user groups.

The following chart summarizes the main differences between financial accounting and management accounting.

11.1 A COMPARISON BETWEEN FINANCIAL ACCOUNTING AND MANAGEMENT ACCOUNTING

1. Main sources of information

Financial accounting
- Historical data from the accounting system

Management accounting
- Historical and current data from the accounting system

- Estimates of future costs and revenues
- Non financial quantitative information:
  production schedules
  technical specifications
  physical dimensions

2. Main reporting periods

Financial accounting

- Accounting year

Management accounting

- Any period determined by management

3. Main focus of reports

Financial accounting

- Business as a whole

Management accounting

- Sub-divisions of the business
  Divisions
  Regions
  Departments
  Product lines
  Input units
  Output units
  Assets
  Individuals

4. Regulation of reports

Financial accounting

- Accounting standards
- Companies Acts
- Stock exchange rules

Management accounting

- Internal management group
  (no external regulation of
  form and content of report)

5. Users of accounting information

Financial accounting

- Equity investor group
- Loan creditor group
- Employee group
- Analyst/adviser group
- Government
- Public
- Internal management group

Management accounting

- Internal management group

11.2   THE MAIN TASKS OF THE MANAGEMENT ACCOUNTANT

We will consider the main tasks of the management accountant under the following headings:

1. The measurement of costs and revenues.
2. The collection, processing, and presentation of information for decision making.
3. The collection, processing, and presentation of information for planning and control.

These tasks are in fact linked as the measurement of costs and revenues is a requirement for both decision making, and planning and control. For the moment, however, we will consider the tasks in isolation.

11.3 MEASUREMENT OF COSTS AND REVENUES

The classification of costs and revenues is a task common to both branches of accounting. In financial accounting, the structure of the profit and loss account and the balance sheet largely dictates the nature and extent of such classification.

In management accounting, costs and revenues are analysed in more detail. This is because the measurement of costs and revenues is an important source of information which management needs in order to control and co-ordinate the business effectively. We will look at this in more detail in the next chapter. There is, however, an important management accounting task related to the measurement of costs, which is also extremely important to the financial accountant. The accuracy of the valuation of stocks of raw materials and other inventories is a key determinant of the accuracy of financial accounting profit.

In the following example, the original closing stock valuation of £2,500 was found to be inaccurate and has been reduced to the correct figure of £1,850. This reduction in the stock valuation of £650 has caused the gross profit to be reduced by the same amount.

Example

Toby Ltd.
Profit and loss account (extract) for the year ended 30 June 20X1

	Original stock valuation		Revised stock valuation	
	£'000's	£'000s	£'000s	£'000s
Sales		7,500		7,500
Less costs of sales:				
Opening stock	2,000		2,000	
Purchases	4,750		4,750	
	6,750		6,750	
Closing stock	2,500		1,850	
		4,250		4,900
Gross profit		3,250		2,600

In financial accounting exercises such as those presented in earlier chapters, it is normal for stock valuations to be given on the trial balance and in the notes to the trial balance. In reality, the computation of these numbers can be a complex and time-consuming process.

A typical business may hold stocks of raw materials, stocks of partly finished goods, and stocks of finished goods. Thus, in addition to the purchase price of materials, the management accountant needs to establish:

1. The costs of storage, security and maintenance of stocks.
2. Labour and other manufacturing costs which have been expended in respect of partly finished and finished goods.
3. Non-manufacturing overhead costs which have been expended in respect of stocks.

In certain circumstances, it may even be appropriate to include a proportion of profits in the valuation of particular categories of partly finished or finished stocks. This is particularly the case in the construction industry where businesses may have large inventories of partly completed and completed construction projects.

11.4 INFORMATION FOR DECISION MAKING

Management accountants have developed a number of useful techniques to assist in decision making. A key concept in the development of such techniques is the notion of relevant information. That is to say, information which is relevant to a particular decision. Relevant information may include management accounting information and other information such as design considerations, and employee and customer perceptions.

It is important to realize that management accounting numbers should be used to support the decision-making process, rather than dominate it. In practice, people are strongly influenced by accounting numbers. This is because numbers give an appearance of certainty. Therefore, we will continually need to remind ourselves that management accounting reports are only part of the story when it comes to the often difficult task of decision making. Most introductory management accounting syllabuses tend to concentrate on particular types of decisions. These are short-term pricing and output decisions, and longer-term capital investment decisions.

11.5 INFORMATION FOR PLANNING AND CONTROL

Management accountants can assist the planning and control process by producing plans which express business activities in monetary terms. These plans are essentially forecasts of future events, and have an important function of communicating and co-ordinating the objectives of organizations.

A budget is an example of a plan expressed in monetary terms. It is a forecast of the future costs and revenues of an organization and its sub-units.

In some industries, particularly in manufacturing, it is useful to calculate very detailed estimates of future costs and revenues. This is known in accounting jargon as 'standard costing'. This technique allows organizations to monitor operational processes in considerable detail.

One of the key concepts in budgeting and standard costing is the idea of responsibility accounting. This is based upon the idea of sub-dividing an organization into a number of responsibility centres where a named individual is assigned responsibility for the costs and/or revenues associated with a particular business sub-unit.

KEY POINTS

1. Management accounting is concerned with the presentation of information to assist the internal management group.

2. Management accounting uses historical and current financial and quantitative data, together with estimates of data relating to future events.
3. The main focus of management accounting reports is on the business as a whole, and defined sub-units such as divisions, departments, and product lines.
4. The main tasks of the management accountant are:
    (a) The measurement of costs and revenues.
    (b) The presentation of information for decision making.
    (c) The presentation of information for planning and control.

TWELVE

THE CLASSIFICATION OF COSTS

LEARNING OBJECTIVES

After reading this chapter you should:

- Understand the rationale behind cost classification.
- Be able to undertake basic cost classification tasks in respect of the calculation of unit cost.

12.1 INTRODUCTION

This chapter will introduce one of the main building blocks of management accounting: the classification of costs. In addition, we will consider how cost classification principles can be employed to enable the unit cost of products or services to be calculated.

12.2 WHY CLASSIFY COSTS?

In financial accounting, costs (and revenues) are classified into various categories to enable meaningful financial statements to be constructed. In management accounting, the main focus of activity is in providing the internal management group with information which can be used to make decisions, in order to control the business on a day-to-day basis.

12.3 HOW ARE COSTS CLASSIFIED?

This depends upon the objective of a particular cost classification exercise. In practice, such objectives will include:

1. A profitability assessment of an organizational sub-unit, a unit of product or a unit of service.
2. Valuation of period end inventories of raw materials, partly finished goods, and finished goods.
3. The provision of information to support a pricing decision.
4. The assessment of future costs in the short term and the longer term.

12.4 THE CALCULATION OF UNIT COST: AN EXERCISE IN COST CLASSIFICATION

There are a number of different ways of classifying costs. In this chapter, we will look at one method of classifying costs. We will start with some definitions and then move on to build up a numerical example. The definitions are:

Cost unit   This is a unit of production or service for which the management accountant wishes to establish the costs incurred. This may be the final item produced, such as a computer, or it may be the cost of a sub-assembly such as a circuit board. In the case of services, the cost unit may be the cost of transporting a passenger for a mile, a kilometre, or some other defined distance.

Cost centre   This is a larger scale of measurement than a cost unit. A cost centre is an organizational sub-unit for which costs are collected. We will consider a cost centre as a department in a typical manufacturing business. Cost centres can be sub-divided into production costs centres which are involved in making a product, and service cost centres which provide a service to the production cost centres.

Example

Cost centres in a typical manufacturing organization:

Production cost centre	*Service cost centre*
● Preparation	● Warehouse
● Machining	● Canteen
● Assembly	● Maintenance
● Inspection	

Direct costs   Costs which can be directly and economically identified with a unit of production or service, for example, raw materials.

Indirect costs   Costs which cannot be directly identified with a unit of product or service, for example, lubricating oil or supervisor's wages.

Cost classification for unit costs requires that costs are broken down into two categories:

1. Direct costs.
2. Indirect costs.

Direct costs

These costs are comparatively easy to identify. They are the costs which can be traced to particular cost units. They can be broken down into elements such as:

Direct materials: these are the costs of the materials which can be identified with a unit of output. For example, timber or steel.

Direct labour costs: these are the costs of the employees used to make a product or provide a service. For example, time taken to assemble one unit.

Direct expenses: these are expenses that have been incurred as a result of making a product or providing a service. For example, hire of special equipment.

Indirect costs

These costs cannot be traced economically to a particular unit of product or service. They can also be broken down into elements such as:

Indirect material costs: these will include lubricants and cleaning materials, but the category can also include small value items such as nails or screws which could, in theory be identified with particular units of product or service, but which would result in an inefficient use of accounting or administrative personnel.

Indirect labour costs: these will include costs such as a supervisor's salary.

Indirect expenses: these might include costs such as rent of property, building insurances, and depreciation.

12.5 THE CALCULATION OF UNIT COSTS

We will examine the process of calculating unit costs in general terms and then consider problem areas, such as cost estimation, and service centres.

The process of calculating the cost of a unit of product or service can be stated very simply as:

1. The collection of direct costs on a unit basis.
2. The allocation of indirect costs to departmental cost centres.
3. The apportionment of indirect costs to departmental cost centres.
4. The absorption of departmental indirect costs into cost units.

12.6 STAGE 1

The calculation of unit direct costs

Costs which are classified as direct costs are those which can be identified easily and economically with a cost unit. If we consider a simple manufactured product, such as an office desk, we can identify the following categories of cost as direct costs:

> Raw materials:
> > Wood for the working surface.
> > Tubular steel for the frame.
> > Screws.
> Labour:
> > Material preparation.
> > Assembly and finishing.

We need to consider this list again. Wood and tubular steel are the most expensive of the raw materials. It is clearly necessary to include these costs in direct materials costs. The screws could be identified with each unit of production, but as the screws are relatively low-value items, it would not be cost effective in administrative time and effort to go to the trouble of treating these as direct costs. We can, therefore, remove screws from the list of direct costs and treat them as indirect costs.

In practice, raw materials are delivered in bulk, and placed in a warehouse. They are then issued to the appropriate production department when they are required. One problem that arises due to this procedure is that suppliers' prices may change and goods which enter a warehouse at different times may be physically identical. A number of methods have been established in order to deal with this problem. These are:

1. First in–first out (FIFO)
This is a very common method of establishing the cost of materials used in production. The method is based upon the idea that materials issued by the warehouse to a production department are valued at the price paid for the oldest materials in the warehouse. Thus, the accountant will:

1. Charge materials issued to production at the price paid for the oldest materials in the warehouse.
2. When the oldest materials in the warehouse have been issued, subsequent issues will be priced at the next oldest price. When these have been issued, the next oldest price is used.

Example

Genesis Ltd. is a manufacturer of office furniture. The following is part of the company's stock records for January 20X5:

Stock records January 20X5				Materials Type: WPO407		
	Receipts into warehouse			Issues to production		
Date	Units	Price £	Value £	Units	Price £	Value £
4.1.X5	200	17	3,400			
10.1.X5	300	18	5,400			
15.1.X5				250		
20.1.X5	100	20	2,000			
31.1.X5				300		

Tarquin Tuffnell is responsible for working out the costs to be charged to the production department. Using the FIFO method, he works out the cost of the issues on the 15th and 31st January as follows:

Date	Quantity issued to production	Price	Value £
15.1.X5	250	200 @ 17	3,400
		50 @ 18	900
			——
			4,300
			——
31.1.X5	300	250 @ 18	4,500
		50 @ 20	1,000
			——
			5,500
			——

2. Last in–first out (LIFO)
The LIFO method uses the latest prices to value issues to production.

Example

The LIFO method of costing direct materials.
Tarquin has changed his mind about the FIFO method and now wants to use the LIFO method. He now prices his January 20X5 issues as follows:

Date	Quantity issued to production	Price	Value £
15.1.X5	250	250 @ 18	4,500
			——
31.1.X5	300	100 @ 20	2,000
		50 @ 18	900
		150 @ 17	2,550
			——
			5,450
			——

3. Average value
This method values stock issues at an average price.

Example

The average value method of costing direct materials.
   Tarquin has decided to dispense with the tedious arithmetic of FIFO and LIFO and adopts the average value method. The value of the January 20X5 issues is now recorded on the stock records in the following way:

Genesis Ltd.

Stock records   Material type: WPO407
January 20X5

| Date | Units | Receipts into warehouse | | Issues to production | | | |
		Price £	Value £	Ave price £	Unit	Price £	Value £
4.1.X5	200	17	3,400	17			
10.1.X5	300	18	5,400				
	500		8,800	17.6*			
15.1.X5	(250)		(4,400)	——	250	17.6	4,400
20.1.X5	100	20	2,000				
	350		6,400	18.29**			
31.1.X5	(300)		(5,487)	——	300	18.29	5,487
	50		913				

*£8,800 divided by 500 units = 17.6 average price
**£6,400 divided by 350 units = 18.29 average price

The average price in each case is used to value issues to production.

Which method to use?

The choice of method needs to be determined in the light of particular circumstances. The FIFO method must be used when calculating stocks for financial accounting purposes in the UK. It would, therefore, seem logical to use FIFO for management accounting purposes. However, the LIFO method has the advantage that current rather than historic prices are charged to production. The average value method is the simplest to calculate and reduces the fluctuations caused by changing prices.

Direct labour

The cost of direct labour is normally allocated to cost units on the basis of time spent.

Example

Julian, Sandy, and Shirley each work in the production departments of Genesis Ltd. There are three departments: material preparation, cutting, and assembly. Julian is paid £6 per hour, Sandy is paid £7 per hour and Shirley is paid £8 per hour. The time they spend producing one unit of product XYZ is as follows:

	Hours	Department
Julian	2	Material preparation
Sandy	3	Cutting
Shirley	0.5	Assembly

The direct labour costs for a unit XYZ is:

	Hours	Rate per Hour £	Total £
Julian	2	6	12.00
Sandy	3	7	21.00
Shirley	0.5	8	4.00
			37.00
Additional employment costs @ 25%			9.25
			46.25

The additional employment costs relate to such things as pension fund contributions, holiday pay, and administration costs. In fact, we could make the calculation simpler by adding these costs to the hourly pay of the employees:

	Hours	Rate per hour £	Total £
Julian	2	7.50	15.00
Sandy	3	8.75	26.25
Shirley	0.5	10.00	5.00
			46.25

Direct expenses

These expenses are less common than materials and labour because it is not normally possible to identify economically direct expenses with cost units. We will assume that Genesis Ltd. does not have any of the kind of expenses which fall into this category.

12.7 STAGE 2

The allocation of indirect costs to departmental cost centres

We will concentrate upon Genesis Ltd.'s three production departments: material preparation, cutting, and assembly. We will ignore non-production departments for the time being. Depreciation of equipment is an indirect cost which must be allocated or apportioned to a cost centre. The equipment used by Genesis Ltd. is as follows:

	Department	Annual depreciation
		£'000s
Fork lift trucks	Material prep	20
Cutting machines	Cutting	100
Power tools	Assembly	10

In addition, each department has a supervisor: Fred, Ginger and Rupert. They each cost the company £22,500 per annum in salary and associated costs.

We can easily identify each of these overhead costs with a particular department. We can, therefore, prepare an overhead analysis sheet to allocate these overheads:

Genesis Ltd.
Overhead analysis sheet

	Total	Materials preparation	Cutting	Assembly
	£'000s	£'000s	£'000s	£'000s
Depreciation	130	20	100	10
Supervisor	67.5	22.5	22.5	22.5

12.8 STAGE 3

The apportionment of indirect costs to departmental cost centres

This is possibly the most difficult part of the unit cost calculation. It is not possible in many cases to determine economically the amount of overhead expenses which can be identified with each departmental cost centre. In fact, many items of overhead expenditure are incurred for the benefit of a number of cost centres. To solve this problem, we must examine each item of overhead in turn and establish a suitable basis to apportion overhead costs to cost centres. There can be no hard and fast rules about dividing indirect costs between departments. Several alternative methods could be used and each of them could provide an acceptable solution.

Example

Genesis Ltd. has the following categories of overhead costs:

	Suitable apportionment basis
Light, heat	Floor area/volume
Depreciation of property	Floor area/volume
Rates	Floor area/volume
Insurance	Value of items
Works canteen	Number of employees

A method of apportionment should be chosen that provides a reasonable measure of the resources used by each department. It would be inappropriate to apportion machinery insurance costs on the basis of the number of employees in each department, as the overhead is related to the value of the machinery in each department.

12.9 STAGE 4

The absorption of departmental indirect costs into cost units

Once indirect costs have been established at a cost centre level, we need to find a suitable basis to bring these costs down to cost unit level. We need to calculate what is known as an overhead absorption rate for each cost centre. There are a number of ways this could be done.

The basic calculation is:

$$\frac{\text{Cost centre indirect costs}}{\text{Absorption basis}}$$

In practice, the choice of absorption basis is related to the amount of time a product unit spends in each department. Widely used absorption bases are, therefore, direct labour hours or machine hours. The choice of absorption base should be guided by the activities undertaken in a departmental cost centre. Thus, if a department utilizes a high proportion of direct labour hours, these will represent a suitable absorption base, whereas if a department utilizes a high proportion of machine hours, these will represent a suitable absorption base.

Example

Brand X Ltd. has three production departments: A, B and C. An overhead analysis sheet has been prepared which provides the following totals for indirect costs:

	Total	Departments		
		A	B	C
Indirect costs (£'000s)	960	160	320	480

In departments A and B, no machining is undertaken, whereas department C is essentially a machining department.

The number of labour and machine hours utilized by Brand X Ltd. in each of its departments is as follows:

Department	Direct labour hours £000's	Machine hours £000's
A	80	–
B	40	–
C	10	80

Overhead absorption rates can now be calculated for each department as follows:

	Department		
	A	*B*	*C*
Indirect costs £'000s	160	320	480
Direct labour hours	80	40	
Direct machine hours			80

Overhead absorption rate:

Department A	160/80 = £2 per direct labour hour
Department B	320/40 = £8 per direct labour hour
Department C	480/80 = £6 per machine hour

We might have used direct labour hours as an absorption basis in department C, but we would have calculated a less accurate absorption rate as the main reason for indirect costs being incurred in department C is the use of machine hours.

Indirect costs are then charged to cost units on the basis of the time that particular units spend in each department. If we assume that product Alpha is manufactured in the following way:

Department	*Time spent manufacturing one unit of product alpha*
A	10 hours
B	6 hours
C	5 hours

The calculation of unit indirect cost is as follows:

Department	*Hours*	*Overhead absorption rate* £	*Indirect cost* £
A	10	2	20
B	6	8	48
C	5	6	30
			98

The total indirect cost of £98 is then added to the total direct costs to arrive at total unit cost.

Detailed example

Robotech is a business that manufactures a range of scientific instruments. Kim Harris, the management accountant, has been asked to calculate the unit cost of a new product called Microtek 5 which will be manufactured in January 20X5.

The business has three departments, all of which are concerned with manufacturing. These are machining, assembly, and finishing. Kim has already calculated that the direct costs for each unit of Microtek 5 are:

	£
Direct materials	31
Direct labour:	
14 hours @ £7.50 per hour	105
Direct expenses	2

The time spent manufacturing one unit of Microtek 5 is: Machining 6 hours, Assembly 6 hours and Finishing 2 hours.

The following information for the year to 31 December 20X5 is also relevant:

	£'000s
Power	102
Light and heat	10
Depreciation of machinery	7
Rent and rates	25
Administrative expenses	63

102000
40000

	Machining	*Assembly*	*Finishing*
Indirect materials			
(£000's)	15	4	8
Direct labour hours	12,000	8,000	16,000
Machine hours	40,000	5,000	6,000
Number of employees	6	4	8
Floor area (sq metres)	1,000	600	400
Value of Machinery (£)	20,000	5,000	3,000

Kim knows there are four tasks to complete, so she writes down the tasks and then considers how to set out the calculations she will need to make in order to complete these tasks.

Task	*Procedure*
• Collect direct costs on unit basis.	• Open up a working called 'Microtek 5 unit cost calculation' and enter the direct costs.
• Allocate indirect costs to cost centres.	• Open up a working called an 'overhead analysis sheet' and enter the indirect costs.
• Apportion indirect costs to cost centres.	• Enter the costs on the overhead analysis sheet.
• Absorption of indirect costs into cost units.	• Use the information from the overhead analysis sheet to calculate overhead absorption rates and indirect unit costs for each cost centre and enter onto the unit cost calculation.

Robotech: overhead analysis sheet for the year ended 31 December 20X5

Cost	Basis	Total £'000s	Machining £'000s	Assembly £'000s	Finishing £'000s
Indirect					
materials	Allocation	27	15	4	8
Power	Machine hrs	102	80	10	12
Light, heat	Sq metres	10	5	3	2
Depreciation	machine value	7	5	1.25	0.75
Rent and rates	Sq metres	25	12.5	7.5	5
Admin expenses	No. of employees	63	21	14	28
		234	138.5	39.75	55.75

Absorption basis:

direct labour hours ('000s hours)			12	8	16
Overhead absorption rates			£11.50	£5.00	£3.50

Microtek 5: unit cost calculation

January 20X5	£
Direct materials	31
Direct labour: 14 hours @ £7.50 per hour	105
Direct expenses	2
	138
Indirect costs:	
Machining: 6 hours @ £11.50	69
Assembly: 6 hours @ £ 5.00	30
Finishing: 2 hours @ £ 3.50	7
Unit cost	244

Service departments

Service departments are departments that are not directly engaged in production, but which do incur a proportion of indirect costs. A maintenance department is a good example of a service department. Costs are incurred in this department, and these costs must ultimately be borne by the production departments. Thus, the production departments incur their own indirect costs as well as a proportion of the costs of the service departments.

To deal with this problem we need to:

1. Include the service departments in the analysis of overheads.
2. Re-apportion the total service department costs to the production departments.

The basis for the re-apportionment of service department costs should be decided upon after an assessment of the amount of service department resources consumed by each production department.

Example

Larsen Ltd. has five departmental cost centres; three of these are production departments and two are departments which provide services to the production departments. An overhead analysis sheet for Larsen Ltd. shows the following indirect costs:

	Departments				
	Production			Service	
	1	2	3	4	5
	£	£	£	£	£
Total indirect costs	19,000	10,000	5,000	2,500	1,500

Larsen Ltd.'s management accountant has examined how each production department utilizes the service departments. Suitable bases for the re-apportionment of these costs are then calculated. These are as follows:

	Production department		
	1	2	3
Bases for re-apportionment of service department costs:			
Department 4	50%	30%	20%
Department 5	10%	20%	70%

The service department costs can now be re-apportioned as follows:

	Departments				
	1	2	3	4	5
	£	£	£	£	£
Total indirect costs	19,000	10,000	5,000	2,500	1,500
Re-apportionment of service department costs:					
Department 4	1,250	750	500	(2,500)	
Department 5	150	300	1,050		(1,500)
	20,400	11,050	6,550		

Overhead absorption rates are then calculated in the normal way.

KEY POINTS

1. Cost classification is one of the main building blocks of management accounting.
2. Cost classification for the calculation of unit costs requires that costs are broken down into two categories: direct costs and indirect costs.
3. The process of calculating unit costs is:
   (a) Calculate direct costs per unit
   (b) Allocate indirect costs to cost centres
   (c) Apportion indirect costs to cost centres
   (d) Re-apportion service department costs

(e) Calculate overhead absorption rates for each cost centre
(f) Calculate indirect costs per unit and add to direct costs

QUESTIONS

12.1 Apportion the following overhead expenses based upon the information given below:

	£
Rent	20,529
Depreciation of machinery	900
Rates	5,176
Canteen expenses	384
Machinery power	4,335

	Department		
	1	*2*	*3*
Horse power of machinery	6,500	250	3,125
Value of machinery £'000s	4	2	3
Number of labour hours	2,000	2,800	700
Floor space occupied (m²)	900	700	400
Number of machine hours	4,000	720	1,800
Number of employees	25	30	9

12.2 The finance director of CS Ltd. has asked your advice about suitable methods of allocating or apportioning overhead costs for the purpose of producing an overhead analysis sheet. The cost classifications are as follows:

> Telephone
> Depreciation of machinery
> Rent and rates
> Factory power
> Heat and light
> Indirect wages
> Canteen expenses

You are required to set out your advice in a memo to the finance director.

12.3 Shadowlands Ltd. is a clothing manufacturer. You are required to group the costs listed below into the following classifications. Each cost is intended to belong to only one classification:

> Classifications:
> > Direct materials
> > Direct labour
> > Direct expenses
> > Indirect materials
> > Indirect expenses

Costs:

Telephone charges
Wages of machinists
Lubricant for sewing machines
Cost of fabric
Royalty payable on number of units of
  product ZX produced

12.4 Perelandra Ltd. is a manufacturing company with three production departments. The following information is relevant for the year ended 31 December 20X2:

	Machining	Department Assembly	Finishing
	£	£	£
Direct wages	704,940	1,037,700	403,575
Indirect wages & salaries	361,062	716,910	269,100

Overhead expenses:

	£
Rent	38,056,500
Rates	10,352,700
Heat and light	2,956,050
Machinery power	8,671,800
Depreciation	1,800,000
Canteen expenses	768,000

Other information:

	Machining	Assembly	Finishing
Number of machine hours	400,000	72,000	180,000
Number of labour hours	200,000	280,000	70,000
Value of machinery £'000s	750	90	360
Horse power of machinery	13,000	500	6,500
Floor space occupied (m²)	1,800	1,400	800
Number of employees	50	60	18

You are required to:

1. Prepare Perelandra Ltd.'s overhead analysis sheet for 20X2
2. Calculate appropriate overhead absorption rates for each department.

12.5 You are the management accountant of Roundup Ltd. Using the following information, work out the unit cost of product 507 Alpha.

Direct material costs per unit of 507 Alpha   £800

	Department		
	A	B	C
Hourly direct wage costs £	7	5	8
Overhead absorption rate			
£ per labour hour	75	70	80
Number of labour hours			
spent in manufacturing			
507 Alpha	40	60	15

12.6 Lewis Ltd. manufactures products for use in industrial air-conditioning installations. The company employs 50 people in the production departments and, in addition, there are five managers who oversee the production process. Using the following information, work out the unit cost of contract WPO 2751.

	Department		
	X	Y	Z
Direct labour hours	100,000	60,000	40,000
Direct wage costs (£)	772,000	420,000	200,000
Number of direct workers	25	15	10
Floor area (m²)	5,000	4,000	1,000
Plant and equipment cost (£)	340,000	280,000	180,000
Repairs and maintenance costs (£)	84,000	20,000	20,000

Overhead costs	£	Basis of apportionment
Depreciation	80,000	Cost of plant and equipment
Consumable supplies	18,000	Direct labour hours
Wage-related costs	174,000	12.5% of direct wage costs
Indirect labour	180,000	Direct labour hours
Canteen expenses	60,000	No. of direct workers
Rates and insurance	52,000	Floor area

Contract WPO 2751	Direct material costs:	£1,600
	Direct labour hours:	X − 30 hours
		Y − 10 hours
		Z − 5 hours

12.7 Bascombe Ltd. has three production cost centres and two service cost centres which provide benefits for each of the production cost centres. An overhead analysis for the year ended 30 September 20X8 produced the following results:

	Cost centres				
	Production			Service	
	1	2	3	4	5
Allocated and apportioned costs (£000's)	90	70	320	120	68

The estimated benefit provided by each service cost centre is as follows:

	Department number	
	4	5
Department number		
1	25%	30%
2	20%	40%
3	45%	30%
4	–	–
5	10%	–

You are required to re-apportion the service department overhead costs.

12.8 An engineering business manufactures process control machines to customer order. It has three production departments and two service departments. Budgeted overhead costs for the coming year are as follows:

	£
Rent and rates	6,400
Machine insurance	3,000
Telephone	1,600
Depreciation	9,000
Production supervisor's salary	12,000
Heating and lighting	3,200
	35,200

The following information is relevant:

	Departments				
	Production			Service	
	A	B	C	X	Y
Floor area (m²)	1,500	900	300	300	200
Machine value (£'000s)	12	5	4	2	1
Direct labour hours	1,600	900	500		
Labour rates per hour (£)	3.80	3.50	3.40	3.00	3.00
Allocated overheads (£'000s)	1.40	0.85	0.60	0.40	0.30
Bases of apportionment of service dept costs:					
Dept X	50%	25%	25%		
Dept Y	20%	30%	50%		

Required
1. Calculate overhead absorption rates for each production department.
2. Calculate the total costs of the following machines:

	Machine 123	Machine 124
Direct material	£77	£54
Direct labour	20 hrs Dept A	16 hrs Dept A
	12 hrs Dept B	10 hrs Dept B
	10 hrs Dept C	14 hrs Dept C

3. If the firm requires a profit of 25% on selling price, calculate the selling prices of both the above machines.

12.9 XLS Ltd. has estimated the following costs and related data for the year ended 31 December 20X9:

			Departments		
			Production		Service
Costs		A	B	C	D
(£'000s)	Total	A	B	C	D
Direct wages	388	120	64	144	60
Indirect wages	48	20	12	16	–
Direct materials	188	160	20	8	–
Indirect materials	94	30	8	16	40
Power	204				
Light and heat	20				
Depreciation	14				
Rent and rates	50				
Personnel	126				
Other information:					
Direct labour					
hours ('000s)	84	24	16	32	12
Machine hours ('000s)	102	80	10	12	–
Employees	42	12	8	16	6
Floor area (m²)	4,000	2,000	800	600	600
Value of fixed					
assets (£'000s)	70	40	16	6	8

The service department is expected to spend 60% of its time working for Department A, with the remainder of the time being shared equally between the other departments.

Required
1. An overhead analysis sheet for the year ended 31 December 20X9.
2. Appropriate overhead absorption rates for each of the production departments.
3. A cost estimate for the following product which will be produced in January 20X9:

		Department	
	A	B	C
Direct materials (£)	5,000	800	400
Direct labour hours	1,600	700	280
Machine hours	2,800	200	160

THIRTEEN

TECHNIQUES FOR SHORT-TERM DECISIONS

LEARNING OBJECTIVES

After reading this chapter you should:

- Understand how costs may be classified to support short-term decision making.
- Be able to produce a variable costing statement.
- Understand how contribution is used in short-term decision making.
- Be able to deal with basic limiting factor problems and shutdown decisions.

13.1 INTRODUCTION

In the previous chapter, we considered how management accountants classify costs in order to calculate the cost of a unit of product or service. In this chapter, we will examine how management accountants can employ a different method of cost classification which will provide financial information to support short-term decision making.

13.2 WHAT ARE SHORT-TERM DECISIONS?

We will define short term as being a period of up to one year. The kind of decisions made by businesses in the short-term are:

1. Pricing and output decisions, i.e. how many units will be produced and what price will be charged for these units.
2. Resource allocation decisions, i.e. to discontinue production of a product, or to allocate labour, materials or some other resource to one product rather than another.

13.3 A COST CLASSIFICATION METHOD TO SUPPORT SHORT-TERM DECISIONS

In order to provide information to support short-term decision making, costs may be classified into the following categories:

1. *Fixed costs*

   There are costs that are unaffected by fluctuations in the level of output. In a manufacturing context, a good example of a fixed cost would be the cost of renting a factory. At any output level, the factory rent would remain unchanged.

   It should be remembered that we are dealing with a short-term decision horizon here and that the definition of a fixed cost should be expanded to 'costs unaffected by fluctuations in output in the short term'.

   It should be obvious that if a factory continued to produce zero output, it would not be economically rational to incur rental costs in the longer term.

2. *Variable costs*

   These are costs that vary in proportion to the level of output. Thus, for a taxi driver, the cost of fuel is a variable cost which varies directly with the number of miles driven.

It should be emphasized at this point that we are now classifying costs using a different classification to that employed in the previous chapter. This is because we are seeking to use financial information for a different purpose. Thus, the choice of method of cost classification should be seen as being dependent upon the objective of the accounting exercise. The implication of this is that the same cost may be classified differently as accounting objectives change. Material costs may be classified as direct or indirect costs if the objective of an accounting analysis is to calculate unit costs. Those same costs could be classified as variable costs if the objective of the analysis is to support short-term decisions.

13.4 SOME TERMINOLOGY

Accountants, as we have seen, can never agree upon the terms used to describe particular accounting practices or techniques. In the area of management accounting related to supporting short-term decision making, the following terms are often used interchangeably:

1. Variable costing
2. Marginal costing

Variable costing and marginal costing are two names for the same method of cost classification. The essence of the method is that:

1. Costs are divided into the categories 'variable' costs and 'fixed' costs.
2. Variable costs are deducted from sales revenue to calculate contribution.
3. Fixed costs are deducted from contribution in order to calculate profit (or loss).

In this text, we will describe the method as variable costing.

Contribution is so called because it is a contribution to fixed costs. It is a very useful calculation and it is particularly important in the context of decision making. This is because contribution:

1. is quick and easy to calculate;
2. can be used to compare the relative profitability of products or business segments;
3. can be used to determine output levels necessary to cover total costs (this is known as the break-even level of output);

4. can be used to assist in resource allocation decisions where output is restricted by a limiting factor such as the availability of labour, materials, or some other resource.

However, before we examine some of the more advanced aspects of decision making using variable costs, we must consider a simple introductory example.

Example: a basic variable costing statement

Gladstone Ltd. manufactures and sells a single product. There are no opening and closing stocks. Tara, the management accountant, has analysed costs for October 20X5. She has determined that variable costs will be £12 per unit, selling price will be £20 per units and fixed costs for the month will be £90,000.

Required
Construct a variable costing statement to show contribution and profit for October 20X5 if the production is: (a) 10,000 units or (b) 20,000 units.

Answer

	10,000 units	*20,000 units*
	£'000s	*£'000s*
Sales revenue (£20 per unit)	200	400
Variable costs (£12 per unit)	120	240
Contribution	80	160
Fixed costs	90	90
Profit/(loss)	(10)	70

A production level of 10,000 units appears to be undesirable as this will result in a loss. With information about variable and fixed costs, Tara could make a number of extremely useful calculations which could allow her to examine the effects of changes in costs, revenues, and output levels on profitability.

Example: decision making using a variable costing statement

The marketing manager of Gladstone Ltd. has given Tara the following information in respect of October 20X5:

1. At a selling price of £20 per unit, it would be possible to sell 20,000 units.
2. If the price per unit were to be reduced by 10%, it would be possible to sell 25,000 units.
3. If the price remained at £20 per unit, it is estimated that by spending £5,000 on advertising the units sold would increase to 22,000 units.

Required
Construct a variable costing statement to show the effect on profitability of the above situations.

Answer

	Option A Selling price £20	Option B Reduce selling price by 10%	Option C Increase fixed costs by £5,000
Units	20,000	25,000	22,000
	£'000s	£'000s	£'000s
Sales revenue	400	450*	440**
Variable costs			
(£12 per unit)	240	300	264
Contribution	160	150	176
Fixed costs	90	90	95
Profit	70	60	81

*25,000 × £18.
**22,000 × £20.

It would seem from the above analysis that option C would be preferred.

13.5 USING CONTRIBUTION IN DECISION MAKING

Contribution is beginning to emerge as an effective tool in providing financial information to support pricing and output decisions at Gladstone Ltd.

Given a selling price of £20 per unit, variable costs of £12 per unit and fixed costs of £90,000, we can extend the analysis to provide other useful information.

13.6 PROFITABILITY AT VARIOUS OUTPUT LEVELS

A quick method of calculating profitability at various output levels is to calculate contribution per unit and multiply this by units of output.

Example

Gladstone Ltd.
Contribution per unit

	£
Sales revenue	20
Variable costs	12
Contribution	8

Profitability for the following output levels can then be calculated as follows:

Output levels	30,000 units	40,000 units
	£'000s	£'000s
Contribution £8 per unit	240	320
Fixed costs	90	90
Profit	150	230

The contribution per unit could also be expressed as a percentage of sales. This is known as the profit/volume ratio or PV ratio.

Gladstone Ltd.
Profit/volume ratio

$$\frac{\text{Contribution}}{\text{Sales revenue}} \times 100 = \frac{8}{20} \times 100 = 40\%$$

The PV ratio is useful because it allows contribution to be calculated for any given level of sales. Thus, if Gladstone Ltd. decides that it requires sales revenue of £500,000 in October 20X5, the results can be easily calculated.

	£'000s
Contribution (£500,000 × 40%)	200
Fixed costs	90
Profit	110

13.7 COVERING COSTS: THE BREAK-EVEN LEVEL OF OUTPUT

The break-even level of output is where there is no profit or no loss because sales revenue is exactly equal to the costs incurred. For planning purposes, it is very important to know how many units of production or service must be sold to cover costs. In addition, knowledge of the break-even point allows managers to discover a number of other useful pieces of information. Consider the following example:

Example: calculation of break-even point

In December 20X8, Palmerston Ltd. expect to sell 10,000 units of their product at £16 per unit. It has been determined that variable costs are £10 per unit and fixed costs for the month amount to £42,000.

Required
Calculate the break-even level of output.

Answer

Palmerston Ltd.
Break-even analysis

Fixed costs
_____

Contribution per unit

		£
Fixed costs		42,000
		___
Contribution per units:		£
Selling price		16
Variable costs		10
		__
		6
		__

The break-even point is therefore:

$$\frac{42,000}{6} = 7,000 \text{ units}$$

In fact, there are a number of ways of calculating the break-even point. If we consider that the break-even point is where there is no profit and no loss, the break-even level of output must occur where total contribution equals fixed costs. We can prove this by producing a variable costing statement for Palmerston Ltd. for December 20X8.

Palmerston Ltd.
Variable costing statement
December 20X8

	7,000 units
	£
Sales revenue (£16 per unit)	112,000
Variable cost (£10 per unit)	70,000
	_____
Contribution	42,000
Fixed costs	42,000
	_____
Profit/(loss)	nil
	_____

In addition, an alternative way of expressing the break-even point is in terms of sales revenue.

Palmerston Ltd.
Break-even sales revenue

$$\frac{\text{Contribution}}{\text{PV ratio}}$$

Contribution (and fixed costs) = £42,000

PV ratio:

$$\frac{\text{Contribution per unit}}{\text{Selling price per unit}} \times 100 = \frac{6}{16} \times 100 = 37.5\%$$

Therefore, break-even sales revenue is:

$$\frac{42,000}{37.5\%} = £112,000$$

Thus, Palmerston Ltd. can be advised that in December 20X8 their break-even level of sales will be £112,000 and their break-even level of output will be 7,000 units. Management accountants must produce information which will be comprehensible to non-financial managers. Therefore, the management accountant of Palmerston Ltd. may decide that expressing the break-even point for December 20X8, in terms of sales revenue, may be appropriate in discussions with the sales manager, whereas the production manager may prefer a measure expressed in terms of units of output.

13.8 EXTENDING BREAK-EVEN ANALYSIS: TARGET PROFIT AND THE MARGIN OF SAFETY

The break-even point represents zero profit. It is quite a simple task to extend the analysis to determine levels of output and sales in terms of target profit. In the case of Palmerston Ltd., the directors may decide that the company should make a profit of £18,000 in December 20X8. The output levels for this profit may be calculated as follows:

1. *In terms of units of output:*

$$\frac{\text{Fixed costs plus Target profit}}{\text{Contribution per unit}}$$

$$\frac{42,000 + 18,000}{6} = 10,000 \text{ units}$$

2. *In terms of sales revenue:*

Break-even total contribution plus target profit
(or fixed costs)

PV ratio

$$\frac{42,000 + 18,000}{37.5\%} = £160,000$$

The margin of safety is a way of expressing the difference between the expected or budgeted level of sales or output and the break-even point.

Palmerston Ltd.
Margin of Safety

1. *Units of output:*
Expected output less break-even output

10,000 units $-$ 7,000 units

= 3,000 units or 30% of expected output

2. *Sales revenue:*
Expected sales less break-even sales

160,000 $-$ 112,000

= 48,000 or 30% of expected sales

13.9 PRICING DECISIONS AND BREAK-EVEN ANALYSIS

We have seen that at the break-even point all costs are covered by sales revenue. Another way of looking at this is to consider that once the break-even point has been reached, fixed costs have been paid for. This means that businesses may have a certain flexibility in pricing decisions for special orders once the break-even point has been reached.

Example: pricing decisions above the break-even point

Major Ltd. produce a single product which normally sells for £25 per unit. Variable costs are £15 per unit and fixed costs for April 20X9 amount to £35,000. Sales for April 20X9 are expected to be 4,000 units. However, the company has recently received an order from Ashdown Ltd. for 1,500 units. This is a special one-off order as Ashdown Ltd. normally uses another supplier. The managing director of Ashdown Ltd. refuses to pay the full retail price of £25 per unit and insists he will only pay £16.50 per unit.

Required
Advise Major Ltd. whether or not the company should accept the offer from Ashdown Ltd.

Answer
In order to advise Major Ltd. of the correct course of action, we must first calculate the break-even point and then consider the effect on the profitability of Major Ltd. of accepting the contract with Ashdown Ltd.

Major Ltd.
Break-even Point

$$\frac{\text{Fixed costs}}{\underset{\text{per unit}}{\text{Contribution}}} = \frac{35,000}{25 - 15} = 3,500 \text{ units}$$

The company expects to sell 4,000 units in April 20X9; therefore, the fixed costs of £35,000 will be covered.

Ashdown contract:	£
Selling price per unit	16.50
Variable cost per unit	15.00
Contribution	1.50

As the fixed costs have been covered by the normal level of sales, the company should accept the contract from Ashdown Ltd. as it makes a positive contribution to the profit of Major Ltd. in April 20X9:

Major Ltd.
Profit statement April 20X9

	£
Contribution from normal sales	
4,000 × £10	40,000
Contribution from Ashdown contract	
1,500 × £1.50	2,250
Total Contribution	42,250
Fixed costs	35,000
Profit	7,250

Above the break-even point, unit selling prices may be reduced to any level above variable cost without an adverse effect on overall profits.

13.10 GRAPHICAL METHODS OF BREAK-EVEN ANALYSIS

In some cases, it may be appropriate to set out the relationships between costs, profit, and output in the form of a graph. A typical break-even chart is shown in Figure 13.1.

The vertical axis of the chart indicates costs and revenues. Fixed costs do not vary with output, so the fixed cost line is parallel to the horizontal axis at all levels of output. The total cost line comprises both fixed and variable costs. At zero output, total cost will be equal to fixed costs, but as output increases, total costs will be increased by variable costs. The sales revenue line starts at the origin. At zero output, there is zero sales

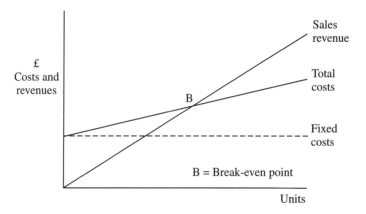

Figure 13.1   Example: the layout of a break-even chart

revenue. The sales revenue line increases as output increases and ends at the level of expected sales.

Notice that the break-even point is where the sales revenue line cuts the total costs line. This is where sales revenue equals total costs and zero profit or loss is made. The cost and sales revenue lines all end at the level of expected output. The margin of safety is, therefore, indicated by the distance between the expected output level and the break-even point.

All the lines on the graph are straight. This indicates one of the basic assumptions of break-even analysis. It is assumed that the relationship between costs and revenues will be constant over the range of output being analyzed. Thus, if a business has an expected output of 1,000 units and variable costs are 50% of sales revenue, it is assumed that variable costs will remain at 50% of sales revenue at any output level up to 1,000 units.

The break-even chart shown above is not the only method of presenting information about costs, revenues, and output. Two commonly used alternatives are the contribution chart and the profit volume chart.

The shaded area in Figure 13.2 shows contribution for each level of output.
The profit volume line starts at a point on the vertical axis equal to zero production. At this

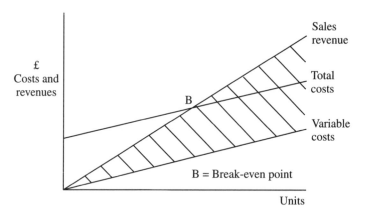

Figure 13.2   Exampe: layout of a contribution chart

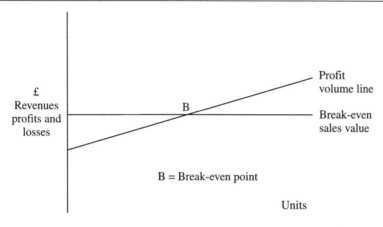

Figure 13.3   Example: the layout of a proft volume chart

point, the firm is suffering a loss equal to fixed costs. One way of interpreting the profit volume line is to say that it represents the amount of profit or loss incurred by the firm at any given level of output within the expected output range.

Graphical methods of break-even analysis are a useful way of augmenting the numerical calculations. They are particularly useful in displaying the relationship between variables over a narrow range of output.

Example

Lambo Ltd. manufactures and sells a single product. It has a variable cost of £4 per unit. Fixed costs per period are £30,000, and an analysis of market conditions indicates the following range of unit selling prices and expected sales volumes:

Selling price per unit £	Expected sales volume units
8.80	7,500
8.00	10,000

Required

1. Calculate:
   (a) The budgeted profit at each possible selling price
   (b) The break-even point
   (c) The margin of safety.
2. Advise Lambo Ltd. which selling price to choose.
3. Draw a break-even chart using the chosen selling price.

Answer

Lambo Ltd.

Budgeted profit	Selling prices per unit	
	£8.80	£8.00
	£	£
Fixed costs	30,000	30,000
Variable costs at expected sales volumes:		
7,500 × 4	30,000	
10,000 × 4		40,000
Total costs	60,000	70,000
Sales revenue at expected sales volumes:		
7,500 × 8.80	66,000	
10,000 × 8.00		80,000
Budgeted profit	6,000	10,000
Break-even points:		
Fixed costs	30,000	30,000
Contribution per unit (selling price—variable cost)		
8.80 − 4.00	4.80	
8.00 − 4.00		4.00
Break-even points—units	6,250	7,500

Margin of Safety:

	Selling prices per unit	
	£8.80	£8.00
	Units	Units
Break-even point	6,250	7,500
Expected sales	7,500	10,000
Margin of safety	1,250	2,500

Margin of safety as a percentage of expected sales:

$$\frac{1{,}250}{7{,}500} \times 100 = 16.7\%$$

$$\frac{2{,}500}{10{,}000} \times 100 = 25\%$$

Advice to Lambo Ltd.

A unit selling price of £8 per unit provides a higher expected profit and a wider margin of safety. Given a choice of the two prices, it would appear that £8 per unit is the preferred

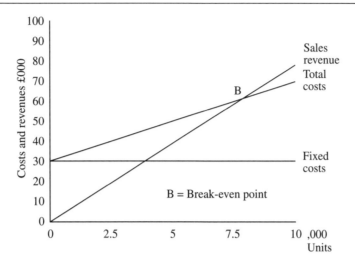

Figure 13.4   Lambo Ltd.: break-even chart with selling price of £8.00 per unit

option. The company may wish to consider other price levels as it appears that a reduction of selling price from £8.80 to £8.00 per unit (9%) will result in sales increasing from 7,500 units to 10,000 units (33.3%).

We have seen that the ability to classify costs into fixed and variable elements can provide information to support short-term decisions. We will now extend the analysis a little further and consider two problem areas which are commonly dealt with in this part of the introductory management accounting syllabus. These are limiting factor problems and shutdown decisions.

13.11 LIMITING FACTOR PROBLEMS

Most businesses are faced with constraints. Anything which limits the activity of a business is termed a 'limiting factor'. Examples of such factors include sales demand, labour shortages, material shortages, and manufacturing capacity. In this section we will consider how contribution analysis can be used to deal with simple limiting factor problems.

When a business is faced with a limiting factor, it may be possible to calculate the contribution per unit of limiting factor in order to allocate resources effectively. An underlying assumption of the analysis of limiting factor problems is profit maximization. Thus, resources should be allocated in order to maximize profit.

Example: limiting factor problem

Diablo Ltd. makes two products. The following information is given in respect of the month of January 20X8:

	Products	
	X	Y
	£	£
Direct materials per unit	2	6
Direct labour per unit at £6 per hour	12	6
Variable overhead per unit	2	2
	16	14
Selling price per unit (£)	28	22
Sales demand in units	6,000	10,000

In January 20X8, fixed costs will be £40,000 and direct labour hours available will be limited to 16,000 hours.

Required
Produce a production budget for Diablo Ltd. for January 20X8 which will maximize profit.

Answer

	Products	
	X	Y
Contribution per unit	£	£
Sales revenue	28	22
Less variable costs	16	14
Contribution	12	8

Without a limitation in direct labour hours, Diablo Ltd. should produce as much of product X as it is possible to sell, as the unit contribution of product X is 50% higher than product Y.

However, since labour hours has been identified as the limiting factor, it is necessary to calculate the unit contribution per limiting factor, as follows:

	Products	
	X	Y
Number of labour hours required per unit: $\dfrac{\text{Unit labour cost}}{\text{Labour rate per hour}}$		
12/6	2	
6/6		1
Contribution per labour hour: $\dfrac{\text{Contribution per unit}}{\text{Labour hours per unit}}$		
12/2	£6	
8/1		£8

Now we can see that where labour hours are limited to 16,000 hours, it would be sensible to manufacture as many units of product Y as possible as this represents a more efficient use of the scarce resource.

Diablo Ltd.
Production budget
January 20X8

	No. of units produced	No. of hours required	No. of hours remaining	£
Available hours			16,000	
Product Y	10,000	10,000	6,000	
Contribution:				
10,000 hrs × £8				80,000
Product X	3,000*	6,000	–	
Contribution:				
6,000 hrs × £6				36,000
				116,000
Fixed costs				40,000
Profit				76,000

*6,000 hours will only allow a production of 3,000 units of product X.

If we did not calculate contribution per labour hour, we would not be able to maximize profit on the basis of contribution per unit. We can prove this with the following calculation:

Diablo Ltd.
Production budget based on product unit contribution
January 20X8

	No. of units produced	No. of hours required	No. of hours remaining	£
Available hours			16,000	
Product X	6,000	12,000	4,000	
Contribution:				
6,000 units × £12				72,000
Product Y	4,000	4,000	–	
Contribution:				
4,000 units × £8				32,000
				104,000
Fixed costs				40,000
Profit				64,000

13.12 SHUTDOWN DECISIONS

These decisions are about whether or not to close down a segment of business activity. The segment may be a factory, a department or a product line. In practice, it is likely that shutdown decisions will involve a number of long-term considerations. However, we will look at such decisions from a short-term perspective only. This means that the main criterion we will use in considering the financial aspects of a shutdown decision is contribution.

Example: a shutdown decision

Espada Ltd. produces four products. The budget for the year ended 31 December 20X9 is as follows:

Products	A £	B £	C £	D £	Total £
Direct materials	10,000	12,000	8,000	16,000	46,000
Direct labour	8,000	16,000	12,000	8,000	44,000
Variable overhead	2,000	4,000	3,000	2,000	11,000
	20,000	32,000	23,000	26,000	101,000
Sales	40,000	30,000	28,000	40,000	138,000
Contribution	20,000	(2,000)	5,000	14,000	37,000
Fixed costs	12,000	8,000	8,000	4,000	32,000
Profit/(loss)	8,000	(10,000)	(3,000)	10,000	5,000

Required
Advise Espada Ltd. whether or not it should produce all four products in 20X9.

Answer
Advice to Espada Ltd.:
If production decisions are considered from a short-term financial perspective, the company should:

1. Cease production of product B. Contribution is negative as the revenue earned does not cover variable costs.
2. Cease production of product C only if fixed costs of £5,000 or more can be saved. As the analysis assumes fixed costs will not change in the short-term, product C should continue in production providing it makes a positive contribution.

Espada Ltd.
Production budget
for the year ended 31 December 20X9

Products	A	C	D	Total
	£	£	£	£
Contribution	20,000	5,000	14,000	39,000
Fixed costs				32,000
				———
Profit				7,000
				———

13.13 DECISION MAKING USING VARIABLE COSTING TECHNIQUES

There are a number of limitations in the techniques we have considered in this chapter. These are:

1. We are making decisions based on short-term factors only in respect of a limited range of output.
2. We assume that it is possible to break down costs into fixed and variable elements.
3. We assume that fixed costs will remain constant.
4. We assume that the relationship between costs and revenues will remain constant, i.e. selling price per unit will remain constant despite increases in volume, and that variable costs per unit will not reflect bulk purchase discounts.
5. We have assumed that units of production and units sold are the same. We have, therefore, ignored movements in raw materials and other inventories.
6. In break-even analysis, we examined the variable costs and revenues in respect of a single product or a constant product mix. We have, therefore, ignored the effects on profitability of changes in contribution caused by changes in the relative proportions of products sold.

Example: the effect of product mix changes on profitability
Mycroft Ltd. produces two products. The unit contribution earned from each of the products is as follows:

	Products	
	P	Q
Contribution per unit	£8	£4

During 20X2, the company expects to sell 10,000 units: 5,000 units of product P and 5,000 units of product Q. The budgeted contribution is therefore:

		£
Product P	5,000 × £8	40,000
Q	5,000 × £4	20,000
		———
Total contribution		60,000
		———

During 20X2, 10,000 units were in fact sold, but only 3,000 units of product P and 7,000 units of product Q. The actual contribution is, therefore:

			£
Product	P	3,000 × £8	24,000
	Q	7,000 × £4	28,000
			52,000

7. We have assumed that firms have the single objective of short-term profit maximization.

13.14 NUMBERS IN CONTEXT: QUALITATIVE FACTORS IN DECISION MAKING

Variable costing methods employ a number of quantitative techniques which express the results of analysis in the form of accounting numbers. This can tend to obscure other factors relevant to the decision-making process which cannot be quantified easily in numerical form. These qualitative factors can include the following:

1. Customer loyalty.
2. Perceptions of quality.
3. Staff morale.
4. Competitors' reactions.
5. Product design.

KEY POINTS

1. Short-term decisions are those related to a period of up to one year.
2. The kind of decisions made by businesses in the short term are: pricing and output decisions, and resource allocation decisions.
3. In order to support short-term decisions, costs may be classified into fixed costs and variable costs.
4. Review the format of a variable costing statement.
5. Contribution equals fixed costs minus variable costs.
6. Variable costing techniques can be used to calculate profitability at various output levels, output at target profit levels, and break even points.
7. Variable costing techniques can also be used to deal with limiting factor problems and shutdown decisions.

QUESTIONS

13.1 Wood Ltd. produces a single product. An analysis of the company's costs for June 20X6 is as follows:

	£'000s
Direct wages	40
Direct materials	90
Manufacturing overheads	10
Non-manufacturing overheads	25
	£
Sales revenue per unit	20

Required

Construct a variable costing statement to show contribution and profit for June 20X6 on the basis that production is: (a) 15,000 units; (b) 30,000 units. Assume that non-manufacturing overheads are fixed costs and that the cost analysis above is based upon an output of 10,000 units.

13.2 Drury Ltd. normally earns a contribution of 20% of sales. In the year to 31 December 20X4, fixed costs are expected to be £600,000. The selling price of the company's single product is £200 per unit.

Required

1. Calculate the number of units that the company needs to sell to break even.
2. Calculate the number of units the company needs to sell to make a profit of £400,000.

13.3 Pendrill Plc has produced the following information about its trading results in respect of the year ended 31 December 20X3.

Units sold	4m
Selling price per unit	£0.25
Profit volume ratio	40%
Net profit per unit	£0.05

Required

1. Calculate the break-even point in terms of sales revenue for 20X3.
2. If fixed costs increase by 50% in the year to 31 December 20X4 (but the profit volume ratio remains at 40%), how many units must be sold to break even?

13.4 Weetman Ltd. has produced the following statement in respect of July 20X7:

Output	50,000 units
	£'000s
Sales revenue	500
Variable costs	350
Contribution	150
Fixed costs	120
Profit	30

The directors of the company are considering the following mutually exclusive options:

1. Reduce selling price per unit by 10%. It is estimated that this will increase demand by 20%.
2. Increase the quality of the product by using higher grade materials. This will increase variable costs by £1.50 per unit.
3. Increase spending on promotion and distribution. This will increase fixed costs by £40,000 per month. It is estimated that this will increase sales by more than 30%.

Required
Advise the directors which option should be adopted.

13.5 Acre Ltd. manufactures only three products. An analysis of the costs and revenues of these products for the year ended 30 June 20X8 is as follows:

Product	A	B	C	Total
	£'000s	£'000s	£'000s	£'000s
Sales	100	80	120	300
Variable costs	60	50	70	180
Contribution	40	30	50	120
Fixed costs	34	36	40	110
Profit/(loss)	6	(6)	10	10

Acre Ltd. is considering whether or not to cease production and sales of product B. A detailed analysis of fixed costs has revealed that £10,000 of the fixed costs charged against product B would be saved if the product were discontinued.

Required
Advise Acre Ltd. whether or not it should discontinue the production and sale of product B.

13.6 Brittan Plc produces three products. The following information is given in respect of June 20X1:

	Product		
	X	Y	Z
	£	£	£
Direct materials per unit	16	31	12
Direct labour per unit			
at £12 per hour	24	36	12
Variable overheads			
per unit	10	10	10
Selling price per unit	100	110	70
Sales demand in units	10,000	10,000	15,000

In June 20X1, fixed costs will be £900,000 and direct labour hours will be limited to 47,000 hours.

Required
Assuming that Brittan Plc wishes to maximize its profit, calculate:

1. The number of units of each product that should be manufactured in June 20X1.
2. The total number of labour hours to be spent manufacturing each product.
3. The maximum profit that can be earned by the company in June 20X1.

13.7 Berry Plc is a highly successful retailer of watches and costume jewellery. The products are sold in retail outlets in department stores, airports, and in selected hotel foyers. The products are presented in standard display cases, each of which occupies 80 square metres of space. There are five product ranges. At each retail outlet space is at a premium and either one or two display cases can be devoted to each range. Retail outlets cannot contain more than seven display cases.

The company has recently completed an extensive analysis of the performance of the product ranges in its retail outlets. The main results of this analysis are as follows:

Range	Sales per display case per week		Profit volume ratio
	1 Case	2 Cases	
	£	£	%
Classic	3,375	3,125	20
Elegance	1,750	1,575	40
Sport	2,400	2,300	25
Continental	3,200	2,600	25
Hi Tech	1,667	1,700	30

Required
For each product range, calculate:

1. The contribution earned from one display case.
2. The incremental contribution earned from the second display case.

Use this information to determine the optimal allocation of shop space, clearly stating your assumptions.

13.8 Glautier Ltd. operates a chain of retail stores. The company is considering a special sales promotion campaign in order to increase sales of the product Theta. The product is currently being sold at £5.60 per unit and average weekly sales are 4,800 units. At a selling price of £5.60 per unit, the company earns a contribution of £2.52. It is proposed to reduce the selling price of the product by 20% during the four-week sales promotion period. It is expected that average weekly sales will increase by a factor of 2.5 during this period. In addition, it is expected that the additional fixed costs of running the promotion will be £2,700 per week and that variable costs will be unchanged.

Required

Calculate the weekly sales volume that would be required in order for the promotion to break even and advise the company whether or not it should undertake the promotional campaign.

Your answer should also indicate if there are any other factors which should be considered before the company makes a final decision in respect of the promotion.

FOURTEEN

PLANNING AND CONTROL 1: BUDGETING

LEARNING OBJECTIVES

After reading this chapter you should:

- Understand the budget preparation process.
- Understand how budgets are used to provide control information.
- Be able to prepare simple budget statements.

In this chapter we will consider the use of management accounting techniques for planning and control purposes. We will examine how budgets are prepared and how a budgetary control system is established.

A key element in planning and control is the construction of targets for the results of business activity. In order to be successful, a business must attempt to look into the future. It must make plans in respect of revenues, expenses, assets, liabilities, and cash flows. A budget can be defined as a plan which is quantified mainly in monetary terms. It provides a focus for organizational activities. It assists in coordinating those activities and it facilitates control.

14.1 ADVANTAGES OF BUDGET PREPARATION

The advantages to an organization of preparing a budget are as follows:

1. *Managers are encouraged to consider organizational objectives*
   The preparation of a budget encourages managers to shift their focus from the day-to-day operational activities of the business and to consider fundamental questions such as: what is the corporate mission? and what has the business been set up to do?

   Many students new to management accounting might be forgiven for thinking that the objective of a business is short-term profit maximization because this objective is implicit in many basic accounting techniques. In practice, however, a business is likely to have a number of objectives. These could include product development, increases in market share, technological innovation, and the maintenance of quality.

The budget preparation process encourages managers to select appropriate objectives for the business.

2. *Budget preparation encourages planning*
This is closely related to the agreement of corporate objectives. Once objectives have been established, the next logical step is to plan resource allocations so that objectives can be achieved.

3. *The communication of business plans*
The budget process requires managers to plan levels of output (and associated costs and revenues) for each sub-unit of the business. Accounting numbers can form a useful basis for communicating the results of business activity across disciplinary boundaries. Senior managers, for example, may not need to know the technical aspects of production. Thus, the use of output measures, costs, and revenues is a convenient shorthand for the technical complexity of organizational activity.

4. *The co-ordination of activity*
The adoption of a sales budget which exceeds production capacity or a production budget which does not take into account the availability of labour and material resources would result in wasteful expenditures of time, effort and resources. The budget process requires business sub-units to co-ordinate their activities.

5. *The maintenance of control*
A key concept in the control of business activity is responsibility accounting. In essence, this means that named individuals are made responsible for designated business sub-units. There are three main types of responsibility centre: a cost centre, a profit centre, and an investment centre. In the case of a cost centre, an individual is made responsible for costs. In the case of a profit centre, the responsibility extends to costs and revenues, while in the case of an investment centre the responsibility includes costs, revenues, and capital expenditure.
The budget preparation process provides a framework for the establishment of a system of responsibility accounting. Control is achieved by comparing budgetary targets with actual results. We will examine this point in more detail later in the chapter.

14.2 THE BUDGET PREPARATION PROCESS

Budgets are normally prepared for a period of one year. In practice, the year is broken down into twelve (monthly) or thirteen (four weekly) control periods. We will consider a simplified example of the budget preparation process using information in respect of Ariodante Ltd. for the year ended 31 March 20X8. The company produces two products and is organized into four departments: sales, production, purchasing, and administration. Each department is controlled by a manager. These departmental managers have produced cost and revenue estimates for the year ended 31 March 20X8. The completed budget will take the form of a budgeted profit and loss account, balance sheet, and cash flow schedule. Note that as this is a management accounting exercise, we will not be producing an FRS1 style financial accounting cash flow statement, the budgeted cash flow schedule is entirely different.

Before we examine the budget preparation process in detail, we need some more information about Ariodante Ltd. Here is the balance sheet at the start of the period:

Ariodante Ltd.
Balance sheet as at 1 April 20X7

	£	£
Fixed assets (net book value)		
Land and buildings		90,000
Plant and machinery		224,000
		314,000
Current assets		
Stock: Raw materials	30,600	
Finished goods	94,400	
Debtors	39,000	
Cash at bank	8,600	
	172,600	
Current liabilities		
Creditors	13,600	
		159,000
		473,000
Share capital		300,000
Profit and loss account		173,000
		473,000

No new fixed assets will be purchased in the year ended 31 March 20X8. In addition, we will ignore taxation and the payment of dividends.

14.3 STAGES IN THE BUDGET PREPARATION PROCESS

Essentially, the budget preparation process involves the preparation of a number of sub-unit budgets which are then amalgamated into the budgeted profit and loss account, balance sheet, and cash flow schedule. The stages are as follows:

1. *Identification of the principal budget factor*
This is the factor that restricts the activities of the business. In the case of Ariodante Ltd., the principal budget factor is sales demand. In other businesses, the principal budget factor could be the availability of materials, labour or some other resource. The key point is that once the factor has been identified, all the elements of the completed budget must reflect this factor. Thus, if the principal budget factor is sales demand, it would be pointless for the production manager to produce budget estimates based upon an output exceeding sales demand.

2. *Preparation of the sales budget*

Sales demand is the principal budget factor for Ariodante Ltd. This will be the first sub-unit budget that is produced. The sales manager has produced the following estimates for the year ended 31 March 20X8.

	Product	
	A	*B*
Estimated demand (units)	9,000	8,000
Estimated selling price per unit	£64	£88

The sales budget is therefore:

Product	*Demand in units*	*Selling price per unit*	*Sales value*
		£	£
A	9,000	64	576,000
B	8,000	88	704,000
			1,280,000

3. *Preparation of the production budget*

Once the sales budget has been produced, the next logical step for Ariodante Ltd. is to deal with the production budget as this is where most of the company's costs will be incurred. The production manager has produced the following schedule of quantities and cost estimates in respect of the year ended 31 March 20X8:

	Product	
	A	*B*
Closing stock of finished goods at 31 March 20X8 (Units)	800	2,400
Opening stock of finished goods at 1 April 20X7 (Units)	1,800	400
Unit cost of opening stock	£40	£56
Raw material content of each unit of product:		
Material 1 (kg)	3	1
Material 2 (kg)	4	8
Material 1 costs £3 per kg and material 2 costs £2 per kg.		
Production time for each unit:		
Machining time (hours)	0.5	0.8
Assembly time (hours)	0.4	0.6
Direct labour hours per unit (hours)	12	8
Direct labour wage rate per hour	£3.20	£3.20
Production overheads:	£	
Machining	84,000	
Assembly	36,800	

These are to be absorbed on the basis of machine hours and the overheads include a depreciation charge of £40,000.

The production budget can now be prepared. This will give us the total cost of production. However, the production budget is a little more complicated than the sales budget because we have to work out the number of units to be produced and the cost of the resources we will use to produce those units.

We can break down the production budget into a number of steps, as follows:

(a) *Units to be produced*

	Product	
	A	B
	units	units
Sales demand per sales budget	9,000	8,000
Less: Opening stock of finished goods	1,800	400
Add: Closing stock of finished goods	800	2,400
Number of units to produce	8,000	10,000

Notice that we had to start from sales units and work back to the number of units to produce by *deducting* opening stock and *adding* closing stock. This is the reverse of the cost of sales calculation in financial accounting.

(b) *Number of units of raw material required in production*

	Material 1 kg	Material 2 kg
Product A—production of 8,000 units		
Material 1 3 kg per unit		
8,000 × 3 kg =	24,000	
Material 2 4 kg per unit		
8,000 × 4 kg =		32,000
Product B—production of 10,000 units		
Material 1 1 kg per unit		
10,000 × 1 kg =	10,000	
Material 2 8 kg per unit		
10,000 × 8 kg =		80,000
Raw material required in production	34,000	112,000

(c) *Machine hours required in production*

	Machining hours	Assembly hours
Product A—production of 8,000 units		
Machining 0.5 hours per unit		
8,000 × 0.5 =	4,000	
Assembly 0.4 hours per unit		
8,000 × 0.4 =		3,200
Product B—production of 10,000 units		
Machining 0.8 hours per unit		
10,000 × 0.8 =	8,000	
Assembly 0.6 hours per unit		
10,000 × 0.6 =		6,000
Machine hours required in production	12,000	9,200

(d) *Labour hours required in production and labour costs*

	Product A	Product B
Production units	8,000	10,000
Direct labour hours per unit (hours)	12	8
Labour hours required in production:		
Product A 8,000 × 12	96,000	
Product B 10,000 × 8		80,000
Direct labour wage rate per hour	£3.20	£3.20
Direct labour cost per unit:		
Product A 12 × £3.20	£38.40	
Product B 8 × £3.20		£25.60

(e) *Overhead costs per unit of production*
The overhead costs per unit must be calculated by multiplying the number of machine hours per unit by the overhead absorption rate in machining and assembly. The production manager has given us the number of machine hours per unit, but we need to calculate the overhead absorption rates.

	Machining £	Assembly £
Total overhead costs per production manager	84,000 hours	36,800 hours
Machine hours for production	12,000	9,200
Overhead absorption rate per machine hour (£84,000/12,000)	£7	
(£36,800/9,200)		£4

The production overhead costs per unit are:

	Product A £	Product B £
Product A		
Machining 0.5 hours × £7	3.50	
Assembly 0.4 hours × £4	1.60	
Product B		
Machining 0.8 hours × £7		5.60
Assembly 0.6 hours × £4		2.40
Production overheads per unit	5.10	8.00

(f) Total cost of production

The above information allows us to calculate the total budgeted cost of production.

		Product A £	Product B £
Direct material cost per unit			
Product A			
Material 1 3 kg × £3		9.00	
Material 2 4 kg × £2		8.00	
Product B			
Material 1 1 kg × £3			3.00
Material 2 8 kg × £2			16.00
Direct labour cost per unit (d)		38.40	25.60
Production overhead per unit (e)		5.10	8.00
Production cost per unit		60.50	52.60

Total cost of production

	£
Product A	
8,000 units × £60.50	484,000
Product B	
10,000 units × £52.60	526,000
	1,010,000

4. *Preparation of the purchases budget*
The purchasing department manager has provided the following information:

	Material 1 kg	Material 2 kg
Opening stock of raw materials 1 April 20X7	2,200	12,000
Closing stock of raw materials 31 March 20X8	1,200	2,000

Material 1 costs £3 per kg and material 2 costs £2 per kg.

The raw materials purchases budget can now be prepared. The production budget tells us how many units of raw material will be required during the year ended 31 March 20X8, but we need to work out how many units we need to purchase. We can do this by working backwards from production requirements and adjusting for stocks of raw materials.

	Material 1 kg	Material 2 kg
Per production budget	34,000	112,000
Less:		
Opening stock of raw materials 1 April 20X7	2,200	12,000
Add:		
Closing stock of raw materials 31 March 20X8	1,200	2,000
	33,000	102,000

The cost of the raw materials purchases will be:

	£
Material 1 33,000 units × £3 per unit	99,000
Material 2 102,000 units × £2 per unit	204,000
	303,000

5. *Preparation of the non-production overhead cost budget*
The administration manager has estimated the non-production overheads for the year ended 31 March 20X8 as £60,800. We do not, at this stage, need to look into the administration manager's estimates in any detail.

6. *Preparation of the cash budget*
The administration manager has collected information from the other departmental managers and has produced estimates of cash inflows and outflows for each of the four quarters of the year ended 31 March 20X8.

		Quarterly periods			Total
	1	*2*	*3*	*4*	
	£'000s	£'000s	£'000s	£'000s	£'000s
Receipts:					
Sales	280	400	400	180	1,260
Payments:					
Materials	70	80	100	50	300
Wages	180	120	100	150	550
Other expenses	40	20	20	30	110

7. Co-ordination and revision of budgets

Once the sub-unit budgets have been prepared, the managers of Ariodante Ltd. will meet to review the departmental budgets. They will look for inconsistencies and check the calculations for errors. We will assume that no errors have been found and the departmental budgets are based upon the principal budget factor, which is sales demand. We can now proceed to the final stage.

8. Preparation of the master budget

This is the final agreed budget for the whole organization. In the case of Ariodante Ltd., the master budget is a summary of the departmental budgets, and takes the form of a budgeted profit and loss account, balance sheet, and cash flow schedule.

Ariodante Ltd.
Budgeted profit and loss account
For the year ended 31 March 20X8

Ref		£	£
(2)	Sales revenue		1,280,000
	Less:		
	Cost of sales		
	Opening stock		
(W1)	of finished goods	94,400	
(3f)	Cost of production	1,010,000	
		1,104,400	
	Closing stock		
(W2)	of finished goods	174,640	
			(929,760)
	Non-production overheads		(60,800)
	Budgeted profit for the year		289,440

References are to workings [(W1) etc., below] or to stages in the budget preparation process above.

Ariodante Ltd.
Budgeted cash flow schedule
for the year ended 31 March 20X8

		Quarterly periods				Total
		1	2	3	4	
		£'000s	£'000s	£'000s	£'000s	£'000s
Receipts:						
Sales	[A]	280	400	400	180	1,260
Payments:						
Materials		70	80	100	50	300
Wages		180	120	100	150	550
Other expenses		40	20	20	30	110
	[B]	290	220	220	230	960
Net receipts						
A − B	[C]	(10)	180	180	(50)	300
Opening cash balance	[D]	8.6	(1.4)	178.6	358.6	8.6
Closing cash balance C + D		(1.4)	178.6	358.6	308.6	308.6

Note

The opening cash balance at the beginning of quarter 1 is taken from the balance sheet as at 1 April 20X7. This balance is also inserted in the total column which is a summary of the year.

   The closing cash balance at the end of one quarter becomes the opening cash balance in the next quarter.

Ariodante Ltd.
Budgeted balance sheet as at 31 March 20X8

Ref		£	£
(W3)	Fixed assets (net book value)		274,000
	Current assets		
(W4)	Stocks	182,240	
(W5)	Debtors	59,000	
	Cash (per cash flow schedule)	308,600	
		549,840	
	Current liabilities		
(W6)	Creditors	61,400	
			488,440
			762,440
	Share capital		300,000
(W7)	Profit and loss account		462,440
			762,440

Workings

(W1)	Opening stock of finished goods	£
	Balance sheet as at 1 April 20X7	94,400
(W2)	Closing stock of finished goods	

		Product	
		A	*B*
	Closing stock units	800	2,400
	Unit cost (3f)	£60.50	£52.60

Value of closing stock		£
Product A	800 × £60.50	48,400
Product B	2,400 × £52.60	126,240
		174,640

Note

The production cost per unit calculation (at 3f above) includes the cost of raw materials used in production.

Therefore, in the cost of sales calculation we need only to adjust the total production cost for opening and closing stocks of finished goods.

(W3)   Fixed assets

	£
Net book value per balance sheet as at 1 April 20X7	314,000
Less: depreciation charge for the year included in overheads	40,000
Net book value 31 March 20X8	274,000

(W4)   Stocks

	£
Finished goods (W2)	174,640
Raw materials:	
Material 1 1,200 units × £3	3,600
Material 2 2,000 units × £2	4,000
Balance as at 31 March 20X8	182,240

(W5)   Debtors

	£
Balance per balance sheet as at 1 April 20X7	39,000
Budgeted sales	1,280,000
Less:cash receipts per cash flow schedule	(1,260,000)
Balance as at 31 March 20X8	59,000

(W6)	Creditors		£
	Balance per balance sheet		
	as at 1 April 20X7		13,600
	Budgeted costs in year:		
	Production overheads	(3e)	
	Product A		
	8,000 units × £5.10		40,800
	Product B		
	10,000 units × £8.00		80,000
	Labour costs (3d)		
	Product A		
	8,000 units × £38.40		307,200
	Product B		
	10,000 units × £25.60		256,000
	Raw materials	(4)	303,000
	Non-production		
	overheads	(5)	60,800
			1,061,400
	Less:		
	Depreciation included		
	in overheads		(40,000)
	Cash payments per cash		
	flow schedule		(960,000)
	Balance as at 31 March 20X8		61,400

(W7)	Profit and loss account	£
	Balance per balance sheet	
	as at 1 April 20X7	173,000
	Budgeted profit for year	289,440
Balance as at 31 March 20X8		462,440

Once a budget has been prepared, it can be used as a control mechanism by comparing actual results with budgeted results. We will discuss this in more detail later in the chapter.

14.4 ZERO BASED BUDGETING

The techniques of zero based budgeting (ZBB) provides a useful perspective on the traditional budget preparation process. We saw in the case of Ariodante Ltd. above that each of the departmental managers provided estimates which were used as the basis for the 20X8 budget. In practice, much of the information which is used in budget preparation is merely incremental changes to prior year costs and revenues. Thus, the 20X8 budget for Ariodante Ltd. is the 20X7 budget adjusted for agreed changes to costs and revenues.

This incremental approach to budget preparation has been criticised because it can perpetuate past inefficiencies, for example, expenditures which have been allowed in previous years can continue to be incurred without any detailed value-for-money considerations.

The basic idea of ZBB is that for each cost centre or department the budget for the next period is zero. This means that managers have to justify expenditures which are to be included in the budget. This is, essentially, a forward-looking approach which considers each of the activities of a business as if they are being performed for the first time. Thus, the allocation of resources is not based upon historical precedent.

14.5 THE ZBB BUDGET PREPARATION PROCESS

We will concentrate on the essential differences between the zero based and the traditional budget setting process. The main stages in ZBB are as follows:

1. *Definition of decision packages*
Ariodante Ltd. has taken the traditional approach to budgeting and utilized departmental cost and revenues as the building blocks of the master budget. A decision package is a detailed category of analysis. It identifies and describes a specific activity such as production or sales.

2. *Quantification of decision packages*
A key point here is that specific activities can be considered from a number of perspectives. Alternative methods of getting the same job done can be analysed and activities can be examined in terms of different levels of resource allocation.

ZBB questions the status quo. Managers have to ask some extremely searching questions as they seek to quantify decision packages. These are:

(a) Should a particular activity be carried out?
Managers are required to consider how an activity
benefits the organization.
(b) How should a particular activity be carried out?
If it is decided that an activity is of benefit to the organization, then managers should consider the most efficient way in which it can be carried out.
(c) How much should an activity cost?
This question takes a value-for-money perspective on the resources allocated to the decision package.

3. *Evaluation and ranking of decision packages*
At this stage of the budget setting process, managers meet to arrive at a consensus about the combination of decision packages that will be of most benefit to the organization. It is at this stage that non-beneficial decision packages will be dropped. Resources are then allocated on the basis of the chosen combination of decision packages.

14.6 ADVANTAGES OF ZERO BASED BUDGETING

A key advantage of the zero based approach to budgeting is that it has the potential to allocate resources much more efficiently than the traditional approach. It provides an important psychological impetus to avoid wasteful expenditures. The method is also highly responsive to changes in the business environment and it encourages managers to consider alternative methods of completing tasks.

14.7 DISADVANTAGES OF ZERO BASED BUDGETING

The ZBB approach has not been widely adopted outside North America. The main disadvantage of the method is the time and effort required to define and quantify the decision packages. In fact, the resources required to evaluate alternative operating methods may be beyond the capability of some organizations. Another disadvantage is that both individuals and organizations can be highly resistant to change, and the ZBB method implies fundamental changes to existing operating practices.

The ZBB method is particularly useful in an academic context because it provides a perspective on the strengths and weaknesses of the traditional budget setting process.

14.8 BUDGETARY CONTROL

The use of budgets for control purposes is rooted in the idea of responsibility accounting where named individuals are made responsible for defined sub-units of an organization. Control information is produced by comparing actual costs and revenues with budgeted costs and revenues. The difference between budgeted and actual values is known as a variance. Variances analysis is a process of examining the differences between actual and budgeted amounts. We now need to spend some time considering some of the ideas in variance analysis.

Example: comparing budgeted and actual results

Caesar Ltd. has provided the following information in respect of the results for the month of June 20X2:

	Budgeted results	Actual results	Variance: favourable/ (adverse)
Sales (units)	4,000	6,000	
	£	£	£
Sales revenue	40,000	60,000	20,000
Less expenditures:			
Direct materials	12,000	17,000	(5,000)
Direct labour	8,000	9,000	(1,000)
Maintenance	2,000	2,800	(800)
Depreciation	4,000	4,400	(400)
Rent and rates	3,000	3,200	(200)
Other costs	7,200	10,000	(2,800)
Total costs	36,200	46,400	–
Profit	3,800	13,600	9,800

A variance is said to be favourable when the actual result exceeds the budgeted result. An adverse or unfavourable variance exists when the actual result falls short of the budgeted result.

At first glance, the results of Caesar Ltd. for June 20X2 look to be encouraging. The sales variance is favourable as is the profit variance. The cost variances are uniformly adverse. This might suggest that if Caesar Ltd. introduced tighter cost controls it would be even more profitable. Unfortunately, the above analysis has ignored one of the fundamental rules of accounting and that is to compare like with like. We have produced a set of variances based upon a fixed budget. A fixed budget is based upon an estimated volume of output and is not adjusted when actual output volumes differ from budgeted output. We need to produce a more accurate set of variances by constructing what is known as a flexible budget. This adjusts variable costs for changes in output volume.

The correct approach to meaningful variance analysis is to:

1. Identify fixed and variable costs, and
2. Produce a flexible budget or, as accountants like to put it, 'flex' the original budget.

14.9 PRODUCING A FLEXIBLE BUDGET

One of the problems in identifying fixed and variable costs is that some costs contain both variable and fixed elements. They are semi-variable costs. In the case of Caesar Ltd., let us assume that we can classify the costs in the following way:

Variable costs	*Semi-variable costs*	*Fixed costs*
Direct materials	Other costs	Depreciation
Direct labour	(we will assume these	Rent and rates
Maintenance	costs comprise a fixed	
	element of £3,200 and	
	a variable element of £1	
	for every unit of output)	

We can now recalculate the variances for June 20X2.

Caesar Ltd.
Results for June 20X2

	Fixed budget	Flexible budget	Actual	Variance F/(A)
Sales (units)	4,000	6,000	6,000	
	£	£	£	£
Sales revenue	40,000	60,000	60,000	–
Less expenditures:				
Direct materials	12,000	18,000	17,000	1,000 F
Direct labour	8,000	12,000	9,000	3,000 F
Maintenance	2,000	3,000	2,800	200 F
Depreciation	4,000	4,000	4,400	(400) A
Rent and rates	3,000	3,000	3,200	(200) A
Other costs	7,200	9,200	10,000	(800) A
Total costs	36,200	49,200	46,400	2,800 F
Profit	3,800	10,800	13,600	2,800 F

The variances have now been calculated by comparing the flexed budget to the actual results. The overall profit variance is still favourable. This is due to the fact that the variable costs were lower than anticipated.

We will develop the idea of using variances to monitor activity in the next chapter.

KEY POINTS

1. A budget is a plan which is quantified mainly in monetary terms.
2. The advantages of preparing budgets are that organizational objectives are considered, planning is encouraged, communication and co-ordination of activities is enhanced, and control may be maintained over revenues and expenditures.
3. Review the budget preparation process.
4. Zero based budgeting considers each of the activities of the business as if they are being performed for the first time. It avoids the traditional incremental approach to budgeting and therefore has the potential to allocate resources with a high degree of efficiency.
5. Budgetary control is maintained by comparing actual results with budgeted targets. This is known as variance analysis.
6. The correct approach to variance analysis is to identify fixed and variable costs, and to produce a flexible budget.

QUESTIONS

14.1 1. What do you understand by the term 'master budget'?
2. Outline and briefly explain the stages in the budget preparation process in a manufacturing business.

14.2 Explain the advantages to an organization of preparing a budget.

14.3 1. What is zero based budgeting?
2. Explain how budgets are prepared using zero based budgeting.

3. What are the advantages and disadvantages of the zero based budgeting technique?

14.4 What do you understand by the term 'flexible budget'?

14.5 1. Explain the concept of responsibility accounting.
2. Describe three types of responsibility centre.

14.6 The marketing director of MacHeath Ltd. has produced the following estimate of sales demand for the year ended 31 December 20X9:

		Product	
	A	B	C
Estimated demand (units)	18,000	16,000	24,000
Estimated selling price per unit (£)	128	176	264

Prepare the sales budget for 20X9.

14.7 Peachum Ltd. produces a single product. The following estimates have been produced in respect of the year ended 30 September 20X7:

Closing stock of finished goods 30.9.X7 (units)	100
Opening stock of finished goods 1.10.X7 (units)	225
Sales demand (units)	1,125
Raw material content per unit of output:	
Material J167 (kg)	3
Material L345 (kg)	4

Calculate how many units of raw material will be required during the year ended 30 September 20X7.

14.8 Using the following information, produce a cash budget for Lockit Ltd. for 6 months ended 31 December 20X6:

	July £'000s	Aug £'000s	Sept £'000s	Oct £'000s	Nov £'000s	Dec £'000s
Receipts						
from customers	120	600	800	400	700	900
Payments:						
Materials	50	200	300	200	500	100
Wages	220	240	250	250	275	290
Overhead expenses	30	25	25	30	35	40

At 1 July 20X6, the balance of cash in hand amounted to £50,000.

14.9 The purchasing manager of Polly Ltd. has produced the following information in respect of the year ended 31 March 20X5:

	Material A kg	Material B kg
Closing stock of raw materials as at 31.3.X5	2,400	4,000
Opening stock of raw materials as at 1.4.X4	4,400	24,000

It has been estimated that the unit cost of raw materials during 20X5 will be:

Material A	£6 per kg
Material B	£4 per kg

The production budget indicates that the material requirements for 20X5 will be:

Material A	68,000 kg
Material B	224,000 kg

Calculate the cost of materials to be included in the purchases budget for Polly Ltd. for the year ended 31 March 20X5.

14.10 The directors of Lucy Ltd. are considering the budget for the year ended 31 August 20X4. They hope that the company will be operating at 85% of capacity during 20X4. The company, which produces a single product, is currently operating at 65% of capacity. This represents an output of 20,000 units and 400,000 direct labour hours worked by 200 production staff.
The flexed budgets for the current year are:

Capacity Level	55% £	65% £	75% £
Direct materials	1,692,400	2,000,000	2,307,600
Direct wages	2,961,700	3,500,000	4,038,300
Production overhead	1,192,340	1,300,000	1,407,660
Non-production overheads	624,620	640,000	655,380
Total costs	6,471,060	7,440,000	8,408,940

The profit in any year is budgeted to be 1/6 of sales.
Assume that production overheads are variable and that non-production overheads contain fixed administrative overheads of £240,000. Current year costs are not expected to increase during 20X4.
Prepare a flexible budget statement for Lucy Ltd. in respect of the year ended 31 August 20X4. Your statement should show both contribution and profit.

PLANNING AND CONTROL 2: STANDARD COSTING

LEARNING OBJECTIVES:

After reading this chapter you should:

- Understand how a standard costing system can be used for budgetary control.
- Be able to calculate simple production cost and sales margin variances.
- Be able to prepare operating statements to report the results of variance analysis.

15.1 STANDARD COSTING

It is often difficult to interpret the kind of variances produced by the comparison of a flexed budget with actual results. The costs and revenues reported are aggregations of accounting data. There may be times when we need to move from the macro level of the flexible budget to the micro level of unit costs and revenues. Standard costs are pre-determined estimates of unit costs. They are budgetary targets at the micro level. Thus, there are standard costs for: a unit of raw material; an hour of direct labour.

These standards can be further subdivided in order to provide useful information for planning and control purposes. In the case of raw materials, for example, the basic variance between the standard cost and the actual cost can be broken down into a price component and a usage component. A materials price variance can be calculated which allows standard and actual unit prices to be compared. This could be a measure of purchasing efficiency. A materials usage variance can be calculated which allows standard and actual quantities to be compared. This could be used as a measure of production efficiency.

The calculation of standard costs is particularly suited to large-scale manufacturing operations where a number of repetitive tasks are undertaken. Before we look at the techniques for calculating variances with standard costs, we need to consider:

1. Why is standard costing used?
2. How are standards set?
3. What are the advantages and disadvantages of standard costing?

15.2 THE USE OF STANDARD COSTING

It is a highly effective budgetary control technique. Standard costing is particularly useful for highlighting deviations from plan. It enables managers to focus on areas of the business that require the most urgent attention.

The detailed knowledge which must be acquired in setting standards assists in the prediction of future costs to be used in decision making.

15.3 SETTING STANDARDS

In practice, standards are set once a year and they are based upon a detailed analysis of the business environment. For example, standards for material costs can be based upon information gathered from pricing discussions with suppliers, availability of discounts, and forecasts of price movements. Standards for material usage can be based upon technical specifications of raw materials, production methods, and finished product specifications.

15.4 ADVANTAGES OF STANDARD COSTING

The advantages of standard costing are:

1. Accurate budgetary targets can be produced. This provides yardsticks for measuring actual costs in considerable detail. The basic level of budgetary control information provided by a flexed budget is magnified by the use of standard costing. Managers can observe cost behaviour down to the level of individual units of resource.
2. The standard setting process requires managers to consider the optimal use of production resources and the most efficient production techniques. The detailed analysis which is required for standard setting provides a framework for the continued re-evaluation of resource allocation and operating methods.
3. Standards are detailed efficiency targets. They promote awareness of efficiency targets that are simple in concept and easy to communicate to non-accounting personnel.
4. A comparatively simple technique which provides timely feedback of control information at all levels in an organization.

15.5 DISADVANTAGES OF STANDARD COSTING

Standard costing is not without disadvantages. A major disadvantage is the time and effort required to set and maintain standards, and to collect and analyse the appropriate actual costs. In many cases, the production of standard cost variance reports can become a mechanical process governed by precedent rather than a continual re-evaluation of the operating environment. It is important that reported variances distinguish between cost behaviour which is controllable by managers and that which is not controllable. It is possible to engender negative motivation in managers who are continually being evaluated on the basis of adverse variances which are outside their control.

Standards are forecasts of future cost behaviour. These may be distorted by external factors such as inflation, exchange rate movements, and regulatory changes. In addition, standards may be distorted by changes in production methods, changes in the relative proportions of materials and other resources used in production, and changes in the quality of production resources.

15.6 USING STANDARD COSTING: BASIC VARIANCE ANALYSIS

An overview of the elements of the basic form of a standard costing variance analysis is given in the figure 15.1.

Standard costing is particularly suited to a manufacturing environment. We will, therefore, pay particular attention to the production cost variances. In order to calculate variances, we need to consider the following example:

ACIS Ltd. has provided the following information in respect of the manufacture of the product Rextrose for April 20X5. ACIS Ltd. does not manufacture any other product. We will assume that production equals sales.

Rextrose: standard costs per unit

		£
Direct materials		
4 kg of material 0597 @ £2 per kg		8.00
2 kg of material 0785 @ £6 per kg		12.00
Direct labour		
6 hours @ £6		36.00
Variable overhead is recovered on the basis of		
direct labour hours at a rate of £4 per hour:		
Variable overhead		
6 hours @ £4		24.00
		────
Standard variable costs per unit		80.00
Standard contribution per unit		80.00
		────
Standard selling price per unit		160.00
		────

ACIS Ltd. uses a variable costing system for management accounting. This means that it does not include fixed costs in determining the unit cost of its product. The fixed costs for April 20X5 are estimated to be £240,000, and these are a mixture of both production and non-production costs. We will assume that there are no variable non-production overheads.

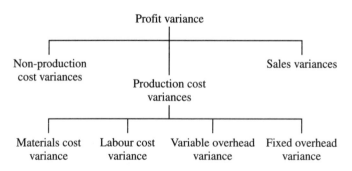

Figure 15.1   Basic variance analysis: The Relationship between variances

ACIS Ltd.
Budgeted results for April 20X5

Sales (units)			5,000
	£	£	£
Sales revenue			
5,000 × £160			800,000
Less expenditures:			
Direct materials			
0597: 20,000 kg @ £2	40,000		
0785: 10,000 kg @ £6	60,000		
		100,000	
Direct labour			
6 × 5,000 @ £6		180,000	
Variable overhead			
6 × 5,000 @ £4		120,000	
			400,000
Contribution			400,000
Fixed costs			240,000
Profit/(loss)			160,000

ACIS Ltd.
Actual results for April 20X5

Sales (units)			4,500
	£	£	£
Sales revenue			
4,500 × £168			756,000
Less expenditures:			
Direct materials			
0597: 19,000 kg @ £2.20	41,800		
0785: 10,100 kg @ £5.60	56,560		
		98,360	
Direct labour			
28,500 hours @ £6.40		182,400	
Variable overhead		104,000	
			384,760
Contribution			371,240
Fixed costs			232,000
Profit/(loss)			139,240

We could use the above information and simply produce a flexed budget which would give us total variances. However, with standard costing information about the product Rextrose, we can examine these total variances in more detail.

15.7 THE CALCULATION OF STANDARD COST VARIANCES

The simplest variances are the production cost variances. We will examine these first. The variances we can calculate are as follows:

Production cost variances

Item	Total variance	Components of total variance	
Materials	Material cost variance	Material price variance	Material usage variance
Labour	Labour cost variance	Labour rate variance	Labour efficiency variance
Variable overheads	Variable overhead Cost variance	Variable overhead expenditure variance	Variable overhead efficiency variance
Fixed overheads	Fixed overhead Cost variance	–	–

We will examine situations where it is possible to calculate the components of a fixed overhead cost variance later in the chapter.

The basic method of calculating a standard cost variance is to compare standard cost with actual cost. Care must be taken in defining the terms used.

Materials variances

The **total variance** is the result we would get from flexing the budget. We compare the standard material cost of the actual output with the actual material cost of those units.

Material type	Standard cost of output units £	Actual cost of output units £	Variance F/(A) £
0597	4,500 units × std cost per unit: 4,500 × £8 36,000	41,800	(5,800)A
0785	4,500 × £12 54,000	56,560	(2,560)A

F = favourable variance
A = adverse variance

The **materials price variance** is that component of the total variance which is attributable to a difference between the standard unit price and the actual unit price of materials. In order to calculate the price variance, we must calculate standard and actual costs in terms of the actual quantity of material used, not the number of output units.

Material type	Standard cost of actual quantity of material used	Actual cost of material used	Variance F/(A)
0597	Std cost of £2 per kg × actual no. of kg used £2 × 19,000 kg 38,000	Actual cost of £2.20 × actual no. of kg used £2.20 × 19,000 kg 41,800	(3,800)A
0785	£6 × 10,100 kg 60,600	£5.60 × 10,100 kg 56,560	4,040 F

In order to calculate the price variance, we have merely restated our standard cost in terms of actual units of material used, rather than units of output.

The **materials usage variance** is that component of the total variance which is attributable to a difference between the standard and the actual quantity of material used in production, multiplied by the standard price.

Material type	Standard cost of standard quantity of material used for actual output	Standard cost of actual quantity of material used	Variance F/(A)
0597	£2 × (4,500 units × 4 kg per unit) £2 × 18,000 kg 36,000	£2 × 19,000 kg 38,000	(2,000) A
0785	£6 × (4,500 units × 2 kg per unit) £6 × 9,000 kg 54,000	£6 × 10,100 kg 60,600	(6,600) A

Note the order in which the calculations are set out. An adverse variance is a negative number, resulting from deducting the second column from the first.

Labour variances

The **total variance** is a comparison between the standard and the actual cost for the actual level of output.

Standard cost	Actual cost	Variance F/(A)
4,500 units × £36 162,000	182,400	(20,400)A

The **labour rate variance** is similar to the materials price variance. It is the component of the total variance which is attributable to the difference between standard and actual unit prices. In this case, the unit price is the hourly wage rate.

Standard cost of actual hours	Actual cost	Variance F/(A)
£6 × 28,500 171,000	182,400	(11,400)A

The **labour efficiency variance** is the difference between the standard hours and the actual hours used in production multiplied by the standard rate.

Standard cost of standard hours for actual output	*Standard cost of actual hours*	*Variance F/(A)*
£6 × (4,500 × 6)		
£6 × 27,000	£6 × 28,500	
162,000	171,000	(9,000)A

Variable overhead variances

The **total variance** is as follows:

Standard cost	*Actual cost*	*Variance F/(A)*
£4 × (4,500 × 6)		
£4 × 27,000		
108,000	104,000	4000 F

The **variable overhead expenditure variance** compares the actual cost with a standard cost, expressed in terms of the absorption base (in this case labour hours), rather than a standard expressed in terms of output units.

Standard cost of actual hours	*Actual cost*	*Variance F/(A)*
£4 × 28,500		
114,000	104,000	10,000 F

The **Variable overhead efficiency variance** compares the standard and actual labour hours (or other absorption base) multiplied by the standard overhead recovery rate.

Standard cost of standard absorption base for actual output	*Standard cost of actual hours*	*Variance F/(A)*
£4 × (4,500 × 6)		
£4 × 27,000	£4 × 28,500	
108,000	114,000	(6,000)A

Fixed overhead variance

ACIS Ltd. uses a variable costing system. It is not possible to sub-divide the fixed overhead cost variance if a variable costing system is being used. This means that the calculation of the fixed overhead variance for ACIS Ltd. for April 20X5 is quite simple to calculate. It is basically an expenditure variance—the difference between the budgeted fixed overhead and the actual fixed overhead.

Standard cost	Actual cost	Variance F/(A)
240,000	232,000	8,000 F

It is useful at this stage to summarize the production cost variances of ACIS Ltd.

ACIS Ltd.
Production cost variances April 20X5

Materials:	Type 0597 £	Type 0785 £	Total £
Materials price variance	(3,800) A	4,040 F	240 F
Materials usage variance	(2,000) A	(6,600) A	(8,600) A
Total materials variance	(5,800) A	(2,560) A	(8,360) A

Labour:			
Labour rate variance			(11,400) A
Labour efficiency variance			(9,000) A
Total labour cost variance			(20,400) A

Variable overheads:			
Variable overhead expenditure variance			10,000 F
Variable overhead efficiency variance			(6,000) A
Total variable overhead cost variance			4,000 F

Fixed overheads:			
Total fixed overhead cost variance			8,000 F

15.8 USING FORMULAE TO CALCULATE PRODUCTION COST VARIANCES

It is sometimes easier to use a formula approach to calculating production cost variances. There is a certain similarity in the calculation of the variance components for materials, labour, and variable overheads. All these variances break down into a price/expenditure element and a usage/efficiency element.

The component variances for production costs are as follows:

Item	Price/expenditure variances	Usage/efficiency variances
Materials	Price	Usage
Labour	Rate	Efficiency
Variable overheads	Expenditure	Efficiency

Price/expenditure variances

A formula which can be used for the calculation of the materials price variance is as follows:

$$(SP—AP) AQ = \text{materials price variance}$$

Where SP = standard price per unit of material
AP = actual price per unit of material
AQ = actual quantity of materials used

If this formula is applied to material type 0597 used by ACIS Ltd. in the production of Rextrose, the result is:

$$(£2 - £2.20) \; 19,000 = (3,800)A$$

The labour rate formula is very similar to the materials price formula. In fact, it is only the terminology used for price and quantity that changes. The price of labour is the labour rate and the expression of quantity for labour is the labour hour. Thus, the formula is:

$$(SR - AR) AH = \text{labour rate variance}$$

Where SR = standard rate per hour
AR = actual rate per hour
AH = actual hours used

The labour rate variance for ACIS Ltd. is therefore:

$$(£6—£6.40) \; 28,500 = (11,400)A$$

The general form of the method of calculating price and expenditure variances is to take the difference between the standard and actual prices and multiply by the quantities used in production.

We could calculate the variable overhead expenditure variance by modifying the basic formula given above. The result would be:

$$(SOAR - AOAR) AH = \text{Variable overhead expenditure variance}$$

Where SOAR = standard overhead absorption rate; for ACIS Ltd. this is £4 per labour hour
AOAR = actual overhead absorption rate; for ACIS Ltd. this can be calculated as:

$$\frac{\text{Actual variable overheads}}{\text{No. of labour Hours used in production}}$$

$$= \frac{104,000}{28,500}$$

$$= £3.65$$

AH = actual hours of absorption base used in production

The variance calculation for ACIS Ltd. would be:

$$(\pounds 4 - \pounds 3.65)\ 28{,}500 = 9975\ F$$
(which can be rounded to 10,000 F)

However, given that the actual overhead absorption rate multiplied by the actual hours used in production is equal to the actual variable overhead cost, we could modify our formula to make the calculation of the variance easier.

$$(\text{SOAR} \times \text{AH}) - \text{actual cost} = \text{variable overhead expenditure variance}$$

For ACIS Ltd., the result would be:

$$\pounds 4 \times 28{,}500 - 104{,}000 = 10{,}000\ F$$

Usage/efficiency variances

We saw above that the general form of the price/expenditure variance is the difference between standard and actual prices multiplied by actual production quantities. The general form of the usage/efficiency variance is the difference between standard and actual quantities multiplied by a standard price.

A formula for the materials usage variance is:

$$(\text{SQ} - \text{AQ})\ \text{SP} = \text{materials usage variance}$$

Where   SQ = standard quantity of materials for actual output volume
         AQ = actual quantity of materials used
         SP   = standard unit price of materials

The materials usage variance for material type 0597 is therefore:

SQ = (4,500 units $\times$ 4kg per unit)   18,000 kg
AQ =   19,000 kg
SP   =   £2 per kg

$$(18{,}000 - 19{,}000)\ \pounds 2 = (2{,}000)\text{A}$$

The labour efficiency variance merely substitutes expressions for labour quantity and labour price into the basic formula:

$$(\text{SH} - \text{AH})\ \text{SR} = \text{labour efficiency variance}$$

Where   SH = standard hours for actual output
         AH = actual hours used
         SR   = standard rate per labour hour

Thus, the labour efficiency variance for ACIS Ltd. is:

$$SH = (4,500 \text{ units} \times 6 \text{ hours per unit}) \qquad 27,000$$
$$AH = \qquad\qquad\qquad\qquad\qquad\qquad\qquad 28,500$$
$$SR = \qquad\qquad\qquad\qquad\qquad\qquad\qquad £6$$

$$(27,000—28,500) £6 = (9,000)A$$

The Variable overhead efficiency variance again requires the substitution of relevant terms into the basic formula.

$$(SH - AH) SOAR = \text{variable overhead efficiency variance}$$

Where SH = standard hour s for actual output of the absorption base; in the case of ACIS Ltd. this is 27,500 labour hours.

AH = actual hours of the absorption base; 28,500 for ACIS Ltd.

SOAR = standard overhead absorption rate; £4 per labour hour for ACIS Ltd.

The variance is:

$$(27,000 - 28,500) £4 = (6,000)A$$

15.9 WHEN SHOULD FORMULAE BE USED TO CALCULATE VARIANCES?

The answer to this depends upon the nature of the assessment exercise and, to some extent, on personal preference. Comparing standard cost with actual cost is a method which can be used to calculate all variances and their components. The formula approach is a short-cut method which is particularly suitable for calculating the components of production cost variances. One advantage of the formula method is that it provides a general form which can be modified for different variances.

15.10 SALES VARIANCES

These are calculated to provide information in respect of the performance of the sales department. Sales variances are calculated on the basis of contribution or profit margins because this method of calculation gives the most meaningful performance measure. The variances that are calculated are as follows.

Sales margin variances

Total sales margin variance
This is calculated in terms of contribution where a variable costing system is used and in terms of profit where an absorption costing system is used. The total sales margin variance for ACIS Ltd. is calculated as follows:

Actual contribution − Budgeted contribution = Total sales margin variance

However, before we calculate the variance, we must calculate an appropriate figure for contribution. The sales department has a responsibility for sales price and sales volume, not manufacturing costs. For this reason, we must calculate the actual contribution by deducting *standard* costs from sales revenue. The calculation of actual contribution for the purpose of calculating the total sales margin variance is:

	£
Actual sales revenue	
4,500 units × £168	756,000
Less standard variable cost	
of sales	
4,500 units × £80	360,000
Actual contribution margin for	396,000
sales variance calculation	

The variance is:

Actual contribution	Budgeted contribution	Variance F/(A)
396,000	400,000	(4,000)A

Sales margin price variance
This isolates the effect of changes in selling prices on the sales margin. It is calculated as follows:

Actual contribution	Standard unit contribution × actual sales volume £80 × 4,500 units	Variance F/(A)
396,000	360,000	36,000 F

Sales margin volume variance
This indicates the effect on sales margin of the difference between budgeted and actual sales volume.

Standard unit contribution × actual sales volume	Budgeted contribution	Variance F/(A)
360,000	400,000	(40,000)A

15.11 VARIANCES AND ABSORPTION COSTING

We mentioned above that ACIS Ltd. used a variable costing system. It could have used an absorption costing system which includes fixed costs in unit costs. The use of an absorption costing system means that standard cost variances are calculated slightly differently in respect of sales variances and fixed overhead variances. Under absorption costing, sales variances are calculated on the basis of profit margin rather than contribution margin. The greatest effect, however, is in the calculation of fixed overhead variances.

Under a variable costing system, we can only calculate an expenditure variance in respect of fixed overheads. When an absorption costing system is used, a fixed overhead absorption rate is calculated which allows unit costs to contain a portion of fixed costs. This means that a further fixed overhead variance can be calculated. This is called the fixed overhead volume variance and is a measure of the difference between actual production and budgeted production. This variance can be further sub-divided into a capacity variance and an efficiency variance. This helps to explain the reasons for a fixed overhead volume variance.

An adverse volume variance may be caused either by a failure to use production resources efficiently or by a failure to use production capacity. Under-use of production capacity may be due to machine breakdowns, material or labour shortages, or merely due to poor production planning.

In this introductory text, it is not proposed to examine this area of standard costing in any more detail, particularly as fixed overhead variances are not particularly useful for control purposes.

15.12 REPORTING THE RESULTS OF VARIANCE ANALYSIS

There are several methods of reporting the results of a variance analysis exercise. Such a report is normally called an operating statement. We will examine two forms of operating statement: one which uses variances to reconcile budgeted profit and actual profit and one which expands on the variances that are reported using flexible budgets.

ACIS Ltd.
Operating statement for April 20X5

	£	£	£
Budgeted profit			160,000
Sales variances:			
Sales margin: Price	36,000 F		
Volume	(40,000)A	(4,000)A	
Cost variances:			
Materials: Price	240 F		
Usage	(8,600)A	(8,360)A	
Labour: Rate	(11,400)A		
Efficiency	(9,000)A	(20,400)A	
Variable overheads:			
Expenditure	10,000 F		
Efficiency	(6,000)A	4,000 F	
Fixed overheads:			
Expenditure		8,000 F	
		———	(20,760)A
Actual profit			139,240

ACIS Ltd.
Operating statement for April 20X5

	Original budget	Flexible budget	Actual	Variance	Price/ exp variance	Usage/ effic variance
Sales revenue	800,000	720,000	756,000	36,000 F	36,000 F	–
Variable costs						
Materials	100,000	90,000	98,360	(8,360)A	240 F	(8,600)A
Labour	180,000	162,000	182,400	(20,400)A	(11,400)A	(9,000)A
Variable						
overheads	120,000	108,000	104,000	4,000 F	10,000 F	(6,000)A
Contribution	400,000	360,000	371,240	11,240 F	34,840 F	(23,600)A
Fixed						
overheads	240,000	240,000	232,000	8,000 F	8,000 F	–
Profit	160,000	120,000	139,240	19,240 F	42,840 F	(23,600)A

Note that there is no sales margin volume variance that is reported because the original budget has been flexed. In practice, the choice of operating statement format will depend on management requirements. The first form of statement highlights the variances and is, therefore, a useful indication of which variances must be investigated in more detail. The second statement gives an overview of the components of cost and revenue. It also neatly illustrates the extended analysis that can be performed with a standard costing system. The two types of statement are not mutually exclusive as different levels of management will have different information requirements.

15.13 INVESTIGATION OF VARIANCES

Variances are calculated and reported in order to provide managers with information to assist in planning and control. Variances, by their nature, are a deviation from a previously agreed plan. It is logical, therefore, that these deviations should be investigated. As a general rule, however, variances should be investigated only when the benefits of the investigation outweigh the costs of the investigation. The investigation of every variance reported in a monthly operating statement is unlikely to be an efficient use of management time or of benefit to the business. The following factors should be borne in mind in deciding whether or not to investigate a variance.

1. *Materiality*
   Is the variance large enough to warrant investigation? This can only be answered by examining the operating environment in particular cases. A variance is clearly material if it has a significant effect on profitability.
2. *Trend*
   The trend of variance movements over a number of reporting periods can indicate a worsening control problem. In addition, an excessive concentration on short-term variance movements may obscure longer term improvements.
3. *Measurement errors*
   We have assumed, so far, that standards are accurate. This is not an assumption that can be relied upon in practice. Standards may be based on out-of-date prices, production methods or material specifications.
4. *Linkage between variances*
   Variances do not exist in isolation. In fact, the root cause of a variance which occurs in one department may originate in another department. For example, an adverse labour efficiency variance may be caused by defective materials.

15.14 INTERPRETING VARIANCES

The correct interpretation of variances depends upon a detailed knowledge of operating conditions. The following table is an indication of why particular variances might have occurred.

Type of variance	Favourable variance	Adverse variance
Materials price Variance	• Additional purchase discount • Price negotiation efficiency	• Price increase • Price negotiation inefficiency • failure to select cheapest supplier
Materials usage variance	• Reduction in wastage • More efficient use of materials	• Excessive wastage • Theft of materials • Less efficient use of materials
Labour rate variance	• Use of lower grade workers	• Wage rate increase • Excessive overtime
Labour efficiency variance	• Increased motivation • Better quality equipment or materials	• Lack of training • Defective materials
Overhead expenditure variance	• Cost savings • More economical use of services	• Cost increases • Change in type of services used
Variable overhead efficiency variance	This variance depends on the efficiency of the use of the absorption base	
Sales price variance	• Efficiency in negotiating with customers	• Adverse market conditions • Competitors' actions
Sales volume	• Marketing efficiency	

The sales variances are difficult to interpret because they
will tend to be interdependent, for example, a change in price
is likely to affect sales volume.

KEY POINTS

1. Standard costs are predetermined estimates of unit costs. They are budgetary targets at the micro level.
2. Standard costing is particularly useful for highlighting deviations from plan.
3. The main standard cost variances are as shown in Figure 15.2.
4. The basic method of calculating a standard cost variance is to compare standard cost with actual cost. Care must be taken in defining the terms used. It is sometimes easier to use formulae to calculate variances.
5. Sales variances are calculated in terms of contribution where a variable costing system is used, and in terms of profit where an absorption costing system is used.
6. Where an absorption costing system is used, a detailed analysis of fixed overhead variances is possible.

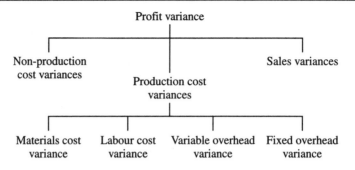

Figure 15.2

QUESTIONS

15.1 The budgeted and actual results of Department S of Wyngarde Ltd. for June 20X1 are as follows:

		Budget Units	Actual Units
Output:	Product A	1,200	1,000
	Product B	800	1,000
		£	£
Costs:	Materials	26,400	26,600
	Direct labour	14,000	16,800
	Machining	19,200	18,900
	Overheads	8,800	8,800
		68,400	71,100

The budget was constructed on the following bases:

	Product	
	A	B
Material required per unit	8 kg	10 kg
Direct labour hours per unit	2 hours	4 hours
Machine hours per unit	1 hour	0.5 hours

Machining costs include a variable element of £4 per machine hour and overhead costs include a variable element of £1 per direct labour hour.

Required
Calculate the production cost variances for June 20X1.

15.2 Cain Ltd. produces product Gamma which is sold in packs of ten. The standard cost of a pack of Gamma is as follows:

Direct materials   2 kg at £2 per kg
Direct labour   2 hours at £4.40 per hour
Variable production
  overheads   £2 per direct labour hour

The company operates a variable costing system.
The actual results for May 20X3 were:

Production   16,400 packs
Direct materials   42,000 kg at £1.96 per kg
Direct labour   31,600 hours costing £126,400
Variable production
  overheads   £28,500

Required
Calculate the production cost variances for May 20X3.

15.3 Calculate the sales variances for Fabbiani Ltd. for November 20X4 using the following information:

	Budget	*Actual*
Sales	200 units	240 units
	£ per unit	£ per unit
Selling price	60	56
Variable cost	40	40
Contribution	20	16

15.4 Using the following information in respect of Jason Ltd. for September 20X2, calculate sales and production cost variances:

	Budget	*Actual*
Output	4,000 units	4,400 units
	£ per unit	£ per unit
Selling price	300	290
Variable costs		
Direct materials		
(14 kg × £10 per kg)	140	
(16 kg × £9 per kg)		144
Direct labour		
(10 hrs × £5 per hr)	50	
(8 hrs × £6 per hr)		48
Variable overheads		
(10 hrs × £6 per hr)	60	

Actual variable overhead cost £130,000.
Jason Ltd. operates a variable costing system.

CAPITAL INVESTMENT APPRAISAL

LEARNING OBJECTIVES

After reading this chapter you should:

- Understand the importance of capital investment appraisal.
- Be able to use capital investment appraisal techniques and explain their role in simple capital investment decisions.
- Understand the advantages and disadvantages of capital investment appraisal techniques.

Capital expenditure decisions are probably the most important decisions that managers have to make. In this chapter, we will examine the main methods used by management accountants to support capital expenditure decisions.

16.1 WHAT ARE CAPITAL EXPENDITURE DECISIONS?

These are decisions relating to the investment of an organization's resources in projects yielding returns over a number of future time periods.

Examples of capital expenditures are:

1. The purchase or replacement of fixed assets such as machinery, equipment, plant, vehicles, and buildings.
2. Research and development projects.
3. The purchase of an interest in another business.
4. Investment in new production facilities.

The importance of capital expenditure decisions is due to the fact that they involve the commitment of substantial resources and, once such decisions are made, they can be extremely difficult to reverse. The investment of resources in a capital expenditure project is a decision which may have long-term effects on an organization's profitability. Capital expenditure involves an outflow of funds in exchange for a stream of benefits in future years. The long-term nature of capital investment projects can make future benefits difficult to quantify. We will simplify our examination of capital expenditure decisions by making the following assumptions:

1. Future benefits will be defined in monetary terms as either cost savings or cash inflows.
2. All cash inflows and outflows during the life of an investment project are known with certainty.
3. The primary objective of an organization is profit maximization.
4. There are no taxes.
5. There is no inflation.

16.2 METHODS USED TO SUPPORT CAPITAL EXPENDITURE DECISIONS

There are two categories of management accounting techniques that we must consider. These are:

1. *Discounted cash flow (DCF) methods*
   The two most commonly used DCF methods are:
   (a) The net present value method.
   (b) The internal rate of return.

2. *Non DCF methods*
   These are:
   (a) Payback.
   (b) The accounting rate of return.

16.3 DISCOUNTED CASH FLOW (DCF) METHODS

A full discussion of the theories underlining the discounted cash flow methods is beyond the scope of this introductory text. We will, therefore, consider how DCF techniques are used in capital investment appraisal, rather than probing the theoretical bases of the techniques.

We need to consider what is meant by the term discounted cash flow. The cash flows used in capital investment appraisal are those relevant to specific projects being considered by managers. These cash flows will typically consist of an initial expenditure followed by cash inflows in future periods. Consider the following example:

Hale Ltd. is considering the purchase of a new machine which will generate a stream of cash inflows during its useful life. The relevant cash flows are:

	£'000s
Cash outflow 31 December 20X0	(2,000)
Cash inflows at 31 December	
20X1	800
20X2	1,500
20X3	1,500

We could simply add up the cash inflows and deduct the cash outflow. However, if we did this we would not (according to DCF theory) be comparing like with like. The DCF method recognizes that money has a time value, so that a receipt of £1 in a year's time is worth less than £1 which is received today. We have decided to ignore inflation, so how can it be that £1 received in one year's time is worth less than £1 which is received today? One way to answer this question is to consider how a business utilizes cash inflows. A business spends money on resources that generate cash inflows and, ultimately, profit. If a business receives £1 today, it can use that money to generate income. If £1 is received in a year's time, the opportunity to generate income is lost for the current year.

16.4 THE DISCOUNT RATE

A measure of the time value of money, suitable for capital investment appraisal, is known as a discount rate. Every business will have an individual discount rate, as the rate represents the opportunity cost of using its capital resources.

In the above example, Hale Ltd. is considering the purchase of a new machine. This investment will utilize financial resources which may have an alternative use. Thus, if Hale Ltd. spends £2m on a new machine, it must forego the benefits of alternative investments. We will assume that the company has a discount rate of 10%. This rate, which is also known as the cost of capital, must be given in assessment exercises. The calculation of discount rates is based upon complex theories in finance that are beyond the scope of introductory management accounting courses.

16.5 DISCOUNT FACTORS

We need to make a further simplifying assumption in our exploration of capital investment appraisal methods. We will assume that a firm's discount rate will not change over the life of a capital investment project.

We will now examine how the discount rate may be used in evaluation of capital expenditure projects. We need to consider the following points:

1. Compounding.
2. Discounting.

Compounding

If we wish to work out the value of an investment at the end of a number of time periods, we could make the following calculations:

1. The value of an investment of £1 at the end of 1 year is equal to:　　　£1 + r%
   where r is the rate of return on the investment.

   Let us assume that r is 10%. The calculation is £1 + 10%. We could express the calculation in a more useful form:

$$£1 \times (1.10) = £1.10$$

2. The value of an investment of £1 at the end of 5 years. The general form of the calculation is:

$$\pounds 1 \times (1 + r)^n$$

If r is 10% the calculation is:

$$\pounds 1 \times (1.10)^5$$
$$= \pounds 1 \times 1.61 = \pounds 1.61$$

Compounding allows us to work out the value of a monetary amount at the end of a number of periods. A compound factor of $(1 + r)^n$ is applied to the initial investment. In this case, r is the rate of return and n the number of years.

Discounting

This is the reverse of compounding. If we wish to work out the present value of a monetary amount which is to be received at the end of a number of time periods, we can calculate a discount factor. The general form of the calculation is:

$$1/(1 + r)^n$$

If we know we will receive £1.61 in five years time and we have an opportunity cost of capital (r) of 10%, the calculation is:

$$\pounds 1.61 \times 1/(1 + r)^n$$
$$= \pounds 1.61 \times 1/(1.10)^5$$
$$= \pounds 1.61 \times 1/1.61$$
$$= \pounds 1.61 \times 0.621$$
$$= \pounds 1$$

16.6 THE NET PRESENT VALUE METHOD

This method uses discount factors to compare project cash flows at a specific time period: the present.

Hale Ltd.
Net present value calculation

Date	Cash flows	Discount factor	Present value
	£'000s		£'000s
31.12.X0	(2,000)	1	(2,000)
31.12.X1	800	0.909	727.2
31.12.X2	1,500	0.826	1,239
31.12.X3	1,500	0.751	1,126.5
Net present value			1,092.7

The net present value is the sum of the present values of the project cash flows. All the cash flows relating to Hale Ltd.'s decision to purchase a new machine have been expressed at a common point in time—31.12.X0. Thus, the discount factor at this date is 1. The discount factors for 20X1 to 20X3 are:

$$
\begin{array}{llll}
20\text{X}1 & 1/(1.10)^1 & = 1/1.10 & = 0.909 \\
20\text{X}2 & 1/(1.10)^2 & = 1/1.21 & = 0.826 \\
20\text{X}3 & 1/(1.10)^3 & = 1/1.331 & = 0.751
\end{array}
$$

The project has a net positive cash flow of £('000s) 1,092.7. It should, therefore, be accepted.

In general terms, the net present value method indicates that a project should be undertaken if it has a positive net present value. If a project has a negative net present value, it should be rejected. If more than one project is being considered, those projects with the largest positive net present value should be undertaken before those projects with a lower net present value.

The cash flows of the Hale Ltd. project occur at the end of each year. This is a simplification which allows us to use discount factors based on years rather than months, thus reducing the complexity of the net present value calculation.

16.7 THE INTERNAL RATE OF RETURN METHOD

The internal rate of return (IRR) of an investment project is the discount rate which results in a net present value of zero. If the internal rate of return of an investment project exceeds the opportunity cost of capital of the business as a whole, then, according to the IRR decision rule, the project should be accepted.

How is the IRR of a project calculated? The computation of the IRR requires the calculation of the net present value of the project.

Example

Bopp Ltd. has an opportunity cost of capital of 10%. The company wishes to invest £10m in building a new factory. The net cash flows are as follows:

Year	£'000s
1	1,400
2	5,000
3	6,000
4	1,000

We could try to work out the internal rate of return by trial and error. However, a slightly better method would be to choose two discount rates, one should result in a low positive net present value and the other should result in a low negative net present value. We can then calculate the internal rate of return using a process known as linear interpolation. A useful starting point for the calculation of IRR is to calculate the net present value using the cost of capital of the business.

Bopp Ltd.
Net preset value of factory project
with a discount rate of 10%

Year	Cash flow	Discount factor	Present value
	£'000s		£'000s
0	(10,000)	1	(10,000)
1	1,400	0.9091	1,273
2	5,000	0.8264	4,132
3	6,000	0.7513	4,508
4	1,000	0.6830	683
Net present value			596

An increase in the discount rate will decrease the net present value. If the discount rate is increased to 15%, the result is as follows:

Bopp Ltd.
Net present value of factory project
with a discount rate 15%

Year	Cash flow	Discount factor	Present value
	£'000s		£'000s
0	(10,000)	1	(10,000)
1	1,400	0.8696	1,217
2	5,000	0.7561	3,781
3	6,000	0.6575	3,945
4	1,000	0.5718	572
Net present value			(485)

We will now summarize the results of our calculations and give these results some general terms in order to indicate how IRR may be calculated.

Discount factor		*General term*
10%	Lower rate	A
15%	Higher rate	B

Net present value		
596	Positive net present value	C
485	Negative net present value (the negative sign is ignored)	D

16.8 LINEAR INTERPOLATION

We can use the following formula to calculate IRR using linear interpolation:

$$IRR = A + \left[\frac{C}{C + D} \times (B - A) \right]$$

where   A =   the lower discount factor
        B =   the higher discount factor
        C =   positive net present value
        D =   negative net present value

The calculation is made easier if the discount percentages are expressed as decimals, thus 10% becomes 0.10.

The IRR for Bopp Ltd.'s factory project is therefore:

$$0.10 + \left[\frac{596}{596 + 485} \times (0.15 - 0.10) \right]$$

$$= 0.10 + (0.551 \times 0.05)$$
$$= 0.10 + 0.0274$$
$$= 0.1275 \text{ or } 12.75\%$$

We can check this by performing another net present value calculation.

Bopp Ltd.
Net present value of factory project
with a discount rate of 12.75%

Year	Cash flow £'000s	Discount factor	Present value £'000s
0	(10,000)	1	(10,000)
1	1,400	0.8869	1,242
2	5,000	0.7866	3,933
3	6,000	0.6977	4,186
4	1,000	0.6188	619
Net present value			(20)

The net present value is not exactly zero because the linear interpolation method provides an approximation of the true IRR. However, the method is accurate enough for decision-making purposes. The factory project has an IRR of 12.75%. This is in excess of the company's cost of capital of 10%, therefore, in the absence of more profitable investment opportunities, the project should be undertaken.

16.9 NON-DCF METHODS
The most commonly used non-DCF methods are the payback method and the accounting rate of return method.

The payback method
This method is essentially a calculation of the period of time taken for a project's cash inflows to pay back the initial investment outlay of the project.

Example
Hubble Ltd. is considering two alternative investment projects for which the following information is given:

		Project	
		A	*B*
Year		£'000s	£'000s
0	Initial cost	(100)	(100)
1	Cash inflows	20	20
2		40	20
3		40	20
4		40	20
5		20	80
6		–	60
7		–	60

The calculation of the payback period is extremely simple. However, difficulty can arise when a payback period is not a whole number of years.

The payback period for project A can be calculated as follows:

Year	*Annual cash flows* £'000s		*Cumulative cash flows* £'000s
0	(100)		(100)
1	20	(100) + 20	(80)
2	40	(80) + 40	(40)
3	40	(40) + 40	0
4	40		
5	20		

Notice that in year 3 the cumulative cash flow is equal to zero. The initial cost has been fully recovered at the end of year 3. We can, therefore, state that project A has a payback period of 3 years.

The payback period for project B is slightly more difficult to calculate because the payback period is not a convenient whole number of years. The calculation of the payback period for project B is as follows:

Year	Annual cash flows £'000s		Cumulative cash flows £'000s
0	(100)		(100)
1	20	(100) + 20	(80)
2	20	(80) + 20	(60)
3	20	(60) + 20	(40)
4	20	(40) + 20	(20)
5	80	(20) + 80	60
6	60		
7	60		

The cumulative cash flow turns from negative to positive during year 5. If we assume that cash is received evenly during year 5, we can calculate the relevant fraction of year 5 as follows:

$$\frac{\text{Cumulative cash flow at end of year 4 (ignoring the minus sign)}}{\text{Actual cash inflow during year 5}} = \frac{20}{80} = 0.25$$

The payback period for project B is, therefore, 4.25 years.

We could state the rules for calculating the payback period in general terms as follows:

Step 1 Calculate the cumulative cash flow for the project including the initial cost of the investment.

Step 2 Stop when the cumulative cash flow reaches zero or becomes a positive number. Read off the number of years on the left-hand scale. We will call this year n.

Step 3 If the cumulative cash flow is zero, the payback period = year n.

Step 4 If the cumulative cash flow is greater than zero, the payback period is:

$$P = \text{year } n - 1 + \frac{\text{Cumulative cash flow year } n - 1}{\text{Actual cash inflow year } n}$$

where P = payback period

$\quad\quad\quad$ year n = year in which cumulative cash flow becomes zero or greater

We can summarize the results of our analysis as follows:

	Project	
	A	B
Payback period (years)	3	4.25

Project A is preferred over project B because it has a shorter payback period.

THE ACCOUNTING RATE OF RETURN METHOD (ARR)

The accounting rate of return method has some similarity to the financial accounting calculation return on capital employed. The basic formula for the calculation of ARR is:

$$ARR = \frac{Profit}{Capital\ employed} \times 100$$

We must define the elements of the formula very carefully as we had to do in the context of ratio analysis.

Profit
We must use an average figure for profit. We are comparing profit that is earned over a number of periods with the capital employed to generate that profit. In general terms, we must use the average annual net profit earned by the project. Therefore, unlike the financial accounting calculation, our figure of profit could be the profits of a business sub-unit. If the investment project was large enough to encompass the whole business (as in the case of building a new factory to replace all existing production facilities), we would use the profit of the business as a whole. However, it may be that we are considering the purchase of equipment for just one department of the business. In this case, the figure of profit to be used is average departmental profit over the life of the project.

Capital employed
In this context, the capital employed is represented by the cost of the assets utilized in the investment project. One measure of capital employed is, therefore, the initial cost of the investment. However, as we are using an average measure for profit, it may be better to compare this with an average measure for capital employed. Therefore, many accountants use a measure of capital employed in the ARR calculation which is the average cost of the assets utilized during the life of the investment project.

How is average investment calculated?
The basic calculation of the average investment used in an ARR calculation is:

$$(Initial\ cost + Residual\ value) \times 0.5$$

This calculation can, at first glance, seem to be incorrect and, in fact, what we should be doing is using the following formula:

$$\frac{Initial\ cost - Residual\ value}{Life\ of\ project}$$

In fact, this formula will give us the annual depreciation charge (assuming that this is calculated on a straight-line basis) for the investment, not the average amount invested.

We need to use some numbers to examine the average investment calculation further. If we consider a project with a cost of £50,000 and a residual (or scrap) value of £10,000, and a life of 4 years, we can make the following calculations:

Year	Cost of investment £	Annual depreciation £	Accumulated depreciation £	Net book value £
1	50,000	10,000	10,000	40,000
2		10,000	20,000	30,000
3		10,000	30,000	20,000
4		10,000	40,000	10,000

The annual depreciation charge is calculated as:

$$\frac{50,000 - 10,000}{4 \text{ years}} = £10,000$$

In the average investment calculation, we conventionally assume that the investment is being depreciated on a straight-line basis. Therefore, half-way through the life of the project the net book value of the investment is £30,000 in the above example. We can find this value very quickly by applying our formula:

$$(\text{Initial cost} + \text{Residual value}) \times 0.5$$

$$(50,000 + 10,000) \times 0.5 = £30,000$$

We can, therefore, restate the basic ARR formula as:

$$ARR = \frac{\text{Average annual profit}}{\text{Initial investment}} \times 100$$

or

$$ARR = \frac{\text{Average annual profit}}{\text{Average investment}} \times 100$$

In this book, we will use the second formula as it can be justified on the grounds that it is a comparison of like terms. However, some textbooks use initial investment as the denominator in the formula.

Example
Christian Ltd. is considering the following projects. Assuming that the company only has the resources to undertake one project, you are required to advise Christian Ltd. which project should be chosen.

	Project	
	A	B
Year	Profit	Profit
	£'000s	£'000s
1	560	420
2	420	280
3	350	210
4	490	350
5	–	700
	1,820	1,960

The initial outlay for each project is £2.1m. The assets purchased for each project will be sold for £980,000 at the end of year 4 or £420,000 at the end of year 5.

Notice that we are given accounting profit rather than cash flow. These are the accounting profits relating to each project. If we base our advice on the calculation of ARR only, Christian Ltd. should undertake the project with the highest ARR. The calculations are as follows:

			Project	
			A	B
			£'000s	£'000s
Average profits:				
A	1,820/4		455	
B	1,960/5			392
Average investment:				
A	(2,100 + 980) × 0.5		1,540	
B	(2,100 + 420) × 0.5			1,260

$$\text{ARR} = \frac{455}{1,540} \times 100 = 29.5\% \text{ (A)} \qquad \frac{392}{1,260} \times 100 = 31\% \text{ (B)}$$

Project B has the highest ARR and should, therefore, be chosen.

At this stage it is convenient to summarize what we know about capital investment appraisal methods and consider the advantages and disadvantages of each method.

16.10 CAPITAL INVESTMENT APPRAISAL METHODS

A. Net present value

Decision rule

Accept the project with the highest positive net present value. Reject projects with negative net present values.

Advantages

1. Takes account of the time value of money.
2. Decision rules are explicit and easy to apply.

3. The discount rate represents the opportunity cost of using capital resources. It, therefore, takes account of alternative uses of these resources.

Disadvantages
1. In practice, there may be considerable difficulty in calculating the cost of capital.
2. The concepts underlining the method may be difficult to justify to non-accountants.

B. Internal rate of return

Decision rule
Accept only those projects with an IRR in excess of the company's cost of capital. Where resources are limited, choose the project or projects with the highest IRR.

Advantages
1. It takes account of the time value of money.
2. Decision rules are explicit and easy to apply.
3. The notion of a percentage return on a project is easy to justify to non-accountants.

Disadvantages
1. It can be difficult to calculate.
2. The use of linear interpolation results in an approximate rate of return only.

C. Payback

Decision rule
Accept the project or projects with the shortest payback period.

Advantages
1. Simple to calculate and use.
2. Useful for ranking projects of equal merit where there are liquidity constraints.
3. Useful where cash flows are difficult to predict due to risk and uncertainty.
4. Concentrates on cash flows early in the project life. Managers have the most confidence in these cash flows as they are the easiest to predict.

Disadvantages
1. Does not take account of cash flows after the payback period.
2. Does not take timing of cash flows into account.
3. Can result in acceptance of a project with a negative net present value.

D. Accounting rate of return

Decision rule
Accept only those projects with a positive ARR. Where resources are limited, choose the project or projects with the highest ARR.

Advantages
1. Simple to calculate and use.
2. Similar concept to the familiar financial accounting calculation of return on capital employed.

Disadvantages
1. Ignores time value of money.
2. Accounting profit may be subject to problems of accounting policy choice. Cash flows are easier to define.
3. There is no guidance as to what is an acceptable rate of return.

16.11 HOW DO WE DECIDE WHICH METHOD TO CHOOSE?

This is a very difficult question and there is no simple answer. Research suggests that the net present value method has considerable support from accountants because it is based upon the notion that capital resources have an opportunity cost and this is reflected in the discount rate. In addition, the NPV method benefits from decision rules which give a clear indication of preferred projects.

Payback and the IRR method are extensively used in practice, and many firms use a combination of investment appraisal techniques rather than relying on a single technique. It should be clear, however, that the complexity of capital investment decisions is difficult, if not impossible, to describe adequately in management accounting terms. The outcome of an investment decision may be that staff morale or customer perceptions of quality are substantially enhanced. Qualitative factors such as these should be considered by managers as they evaluate investment projects. It is important, therefore, to continue to remind ourselves that accounting calculations are only one component in a decision-making process.

KEY POINTS

1. Capital expenditure decisions involve the commitment of substantial resources.
2. Two categories of management accounting techniques for capital investment appraisal are:
   (a) Discounted cash flow (DCF) methods
   (b) Non-DCF methods
3. The two most commonly used DCF methods are the net present value method and the internal rate of return method.
4. The two most commonly used non-DCF methods are payback and the accounting rate of return method.
5. A measure of the time value of money, suitable for capital investment appraisal, is known as the discount rate.
6. The discount rate is also known as the cost of capital and represents the opportunity cost of using capital resources.
7. Cash flow multiplied by a discount factor = present value.
8. Discount factors can be calculated using the general formula $1/(1 + r)^n$

   where r = the discount rate
   n = the number of time periods elapsing before the cash flow occurs

9. Net present value is the sum of the present values of project cash flows.
10. Projects with negative net present values should be rejected. The project with the highest net present value should be accepted.

11. The internal rate of return is the discount rate giving a net present value of zero. Projects with an IRR greater than the firm's cost of capital should be accepted.
12. The IRR can be estimated using linear interpolation. The general formula is:

$$IRR = A + \left[\frac{C}{C + D} \times (B - A) \right]$$

where   A = lower discount rate
         B = higher discount rate
         C = positive NPV
         D = negative NPV

13. The payback period is the length of time taken for a project's cash inflows to pay back the initial investment outlay.
14. Projects with a shorter payback period are preferred over projects with a longer payback period.
15. The accounting rate of return can be calculated as:

$$ARR = \frac{\text{Average annual profit}}{\text{Average investment}} \times 100$$

16. Projects with higher ARRs are preferred to projects with lower ARRs.

QUESTIONS

16.1 Malacandra Ltd. is considering investing £5m in new production facilities. The expected cash inflows from the project are as follows:

Year	Cash inflow £'000s
1	1,600
2	1,700
3	1,660
4	2,400
5	1,400

The company has a cost of capital of 15%. The relevant discount factors are:

Year	Discount factor
1	0.8696
2	0.7561
3	0.6575
4	0.5718
5	0.4972

Required
Calculate the net present value of the above project.

16.2 Meldilorn Ltd. is considering the following capital expenditure projects. However, the company does not have the resources to undertake both projects:

	Project	
	A	*B*
	£	£
Initial cost	400,000	460,000
Expected scrap value of machinery at end of project	20,000	30,000
Expected life of project (years)	5	5
	£	£
Expected cash inflows		
End of year 1	160,000	200,000
2	140,000	140,000
3	130,000	100,000
4	120,000	100,000
5	110,000	100,000

Meldilorn's cost of capital is 18%. The relevant discount factors are:

Year	*Discount factor*
1	0.8475
2	0.7182
3	0.6086
4	0.5158
5	0.4371

Required
Calculate the net present value for each project and advise the company which project to accept.

16.3 Calculate the internal rate of return of the following project:

Year	*Cash outflow* £'000s	*Cash inflows* £'000s
0	2,900	
1		460
2		740
3		1,200
4		840
5		220

Assume that the investing company has a cost of capital of 5%.

16.4 Dr Ransome is the development director of Thulcandra Ltd., an aircraft components producer. He is preparing a capital expenditure bid in respect of the construction of new test facilities. He has asked for your help in preparing the internal rate of return calculation for the project. Using the following cash flows, calculate the internal rate of return of the new test facilities for Dr Ransome. Assume a cost of capital of 15%.

Year	Cash flows £'000s
0	(950)
1	100
2	400
3	450
4	450
5	150

16.5 Calculate the payback period in respect of the following project:

Year	Cash flows £'000s
0	(360)
1	110
2	130
3	190
4	216

16.6 The directors of Perelandra Ltd. insist that the payback method is the best method to use for capital investment appraisal. They refuse to consider any other appraisal method. You are the new management accountant of the company and you have been given the following information about two projects that will be considered at the next board meeting:

	Project cash flows	
Year	A £	B £
0	(2,000)	(20,000)
1	720	4,600
2	576	5,280
3	692	6,080
4	828	7,000
5	996	8,040

Required
1. Calculate the payback period for each project.
2. Assuming that only one of the two projects can be undertaken, advise the directors which project they should undertake.
3. What are the disadvantages of using the payback method?

16.7 Calculate the accounting rate of return in respect of the following project:

Year	Accounting profit £'000s
1	200
2	500
3	500
4	400

Initial outlay	£1m
Project life	4 years

16.8 Explain, with reasons, how you would treat depreciation in a computation for each of the following appraisal techniques:

1. Accounting rate of return
2. Payback
3. Net present value

16.9 Lewis Ltd. is considering three capital expenditure projects. However, the company only has the resources to undertake one of the projects. The cash flows are as follows:

	Alpha	Project Beta	Gamma
Expected life (years)	5	5	4
Cash flows	£'000s	£'000s	£'000s
Year			
0	(800)	(920)	(720)
1	320	400	220
2	280	280	260
3	260	200	380
4	240	200	432
5	260	260	–

The company's cost of capital is 15%.

1. You are required to calculate for each project:
    (a) the net present value
    (b) the payback period
    (c) the accounting rate of return
2. Advise the management of Lewis Ltd. which project should be accepted, giving reasons for your recommendation.

16.10 CSL Ltd. has a cost of capital of 15%. The relevant discount rates are as follows:

Year	Discount factor
1	0.8696
2	0.7561
3	0.6575
4	0.5718
5	0.4972

The company is considering investing in two mutually exclusive projects and has produced the following schedule of profits and cash flows:

	Project 1		Project 2	
Year	Profit £'000s	Cash flow £'000s	Profit £'000s	Cash flow £'000s
0	–	(1,050)	–	(1,050)
1	280	420	210	378
2	210	350	140	308
3	175	315	105	273
4	245	875	175	343
5	–	–	350	728

Required
Determine for both projects:

1. The payback period
2. The accounting rate of return
3. The net present value.

Advise the company which project should be undertaken, giving your reasons.

ANSWERS TO END OF CHAPTER QUESTIONS

NB There are no questions in respect of Chapters 1, 2, 8 and 11.

CHAPTER THREE

3.1 The general ledger entries are:

	Debit	Credit
a. Purchase of raw materials	Purchases account	Bank account
b. Payment of wages	Wages account	Bank account
c. Income from sale of shoes	Bank account	Sales account
d. Purchase of stationery	Stationery account	Bank account
e. Payment of advertising costs	Advertising account	Bank account

3.2 The advice to Franco is as follows:

	Debit	Credit
a. Cash paid into the business by Franco	Bank	Capital
b. Purchase of foodstuffs	Purchases	Bank
c. Cash received from customers	Bank	Sales
d. Cash withdrawn for Franco's personal living expenses	Drawings	Bank
e. Purchase of pizza oven	Fixtures & fittings (or fixed assets)	Bank

Tutorial note:
You may wish to consider the following points.
1. Why was a bank account used and not a cash account?
2. Why was the pizza oven cost not debited to purchases?
  The above answer assumes that all of the above transactions involve sums of money too large to involve the use of notes and coins. Thus, Franco does not hold large amounts of cash on his business premises.

3.3

		Debit	*Credit*
(a)	Fees	Bank account	Fees received account (or sales)
(b)	Rent	Rent account	Bank account
(c)	Electricity	Electricity account	Bank account
(d)	Gas	Gas account	Bank account
(e)	Sheet music	Consumable materials account (or purchases)	Bank account
(f)	Grand piano	Instruments account (or fixed assets)	Bank account

3.4 Eagleburger Hotel nominal ledger (extract)

Bank account

		£			£
20X1			20X1		
February	1 Sales:		February	2 Wine	200
	Accommodation	850		3 Foodstuffs	300
	5 Sales:			4 Wages	1,500
	Functions:	2,500		6 Advertising	500

3.5 Eagleburger Hotel nominal ledger (extract)

Sales: accommodation

	£			£
		20X1		
		Feb 1	Bank	850

Sales: functions

	£			£
		20X1		
		Feb 5	Bank	2,500

Purchases: wine

		£		£
20X1				
Feb 2	Bank	200		

Purchases: foodstuffs

		£		£
20X1				
Feb 4	Bank	300		

Wages account

		£		£
20X1				
Feb 4	Bank	1,500		

Advertising account

	£		£
20X1	500		
Feb 6 Bank			

3.6 Skin Deep general ledger accounts

Bank account

	£		£
		20X1	
		May 31 Property insurance 10,000	

Property insurance account

	£		£
20X1			
May 31 Bank	10,000		

3.7 Akiro general ledger accounts

Bank account

	£		£
		20X3	
		August	
		Repairs	570
		Telephone	450
		Advertising	120

Repairs account

	£		£
20X1			
August Bank	570		

Telephone account

	£		£
20X3			
August Bank	450		

Advertising account

	£		£
20X3			
August Bank	120		

3.8 Advice to Silvana:

Transaction No.

1	Sales	Correct entry.
2	Rent	Incorrect entry. The entry in the bank account should be a credit not a debit.
3	Electricity	Incorrect entry. Silvana should have debited the electricity account and credited the bank account.
4	Sales	Incorrect entry. Silvana should have debited the bank account and credited the sales account.
5	Advertising	Correct entry. NB The electricity entry should be transferred to the correct account.

Bank

		£			£
(1)	Sales	13,000	(2)	Rent	1,000
(4)	Sales	5,000	(3)	Electricity	700
			(5)	Advertising	350

Sales

		£			£
			(1)	Bank	13,000
			(4)	Bank	5,000

Electricity

		£		£
(3)	Bank	700		

Rent

		£		£
(2)	Bank	1,000		

Advertising

		£		£
(5)	Bank	350		

3.9   James Clay general ledger (extract)

Bank account

		£				£
20X3			20X3			
Dec 1	Subscription received	1,500	Dec 3	Wages paid		2,500
Dec 2	Grant from Athletics		Dec 4	Subscription refunded		120
	Council	8,000	Dec 10	Purchase of equipment		4,500
Dec 15	Bar sales	3,850	Dec 12	Purchase of bar supplies	1,700

3.10   Pacioli's statements:

One	Correct
Two	Correct
Three	False
Four	Correct
Five	Correct

3.11   Statements:

(a)	True
(b)	False
(c)	True
(d)	True
(e)	False

3.12   Dragonquest's general ledger accounts

Bank account

		£				£
20x5			20X5			
Oct 30	Balance b/d	37,500	Oct 30	Packaging		8,700
				Software		25,000
				Salaries		97,500
				Rent		10,000
Oct 30	Balance c/d	107,400		Electricity		3,700
		144,900				144,900
			Oct 30	Balance b/d		107,400

Packaging costs account

		£		£
20X5				
Oct 30	Bank	8,700		

Purchases: software account

		£		£
20X5				
Oct 30	Bank	25,000		

Salaries account

		£		£
20X5				
Oct 30	Bank	97,500		

Rent account

		£		£
20X5				
Oct 30	Bank	10,000		

Electricity account

		£		£
20X5				
Oct 30	Bank	3,700		

3.13 Goldenear nominal ledger entries

Bank account

	£			£
		20X9		
		June 30	Aviation fuel	72,000
			Film	110,000
			Equipment repairs	12,500
			Stuntmen fees	65,000
			Catering	95,000
			Aircraft hire	200,000
			Vehicle leasing	30,000
			Legal fees	57,000
			Scriptwriters' fees	1,250

Aviaton fuel account

		£		£
20X9				
June 30	Bank	72,000		

Purchases: film account

		£		£
20X9				
June 30	Bank	110,000		

Equipment repairs account

		£		£
20X9				
June 30	Bank	12,500		

Stuntmen fees account

		£		£
20X9				
June 30	Bank	65,000		

Catering account

		£			£
20X9					
June 30	Bank	95,000			

Aircraft hire account

		£			£
20X9					
June 30	Bank	200,000			

Vehicle leasing account

		£			£
20X9					
June 30	Bank	30,000			

Legal fees account

		£			£
20X9					
June 30	Bank	57,000			

Scriptwriters' account

		£			£
20X9					
June 30	Bank	1,250			

3.14

(1) Debit and credit entries

		Debit entry	Credit entry
Jan			
2	£1,000 into bank account	Bank account	Capital account
	£40 petty cash	Cash account	Bank account
3	£371 goods supplied	Purchases account	Bank account
4	Cheques received	Bank account	Sales account
5	£30 postage paid	Postage account	Cash account
6	£80 stationery	Stationery account	Bank account
7	£8 cheque received	Bank account	Sales account
8	£112 goods supplied	Purchases account	Bank account

(2)

Bank account

		£			£
Jan 2	Capital	1,000	Jan 2	Cash	40
Jan 4	Sales	355	Jan 3	Purchases	371
Jan 7	Sales	8	Jan 6	Stationery	80
			Jan 8	Purchases	112

Cash account

		£			£
Jan 2	Bank	40	Jan 5	Postage	30

Capital account

		£				£
			Jan 2	Bank		1,000

Purchases

		£				£
Jan 3	Bank	371				
Jan 8	Bank	112				

Sales

		£				£
			Jan 4	Bank		355
			Jan 7	Bank		8

Postage

		£			£
Jan 5	Cash	30			

Stationery

		£			£
Jan 6	Bank	80			

3.15   Letter to John

> 25 Reader Street
> Colchester
> CPO RD2
> 31 March 20X1

Dear John

Debit and Credit Entries

With reference to our recent discussion, I have set out below a number of points which should assist you in understanding the terms debit and credit in an accounting system. These points are:

1. Debit means receiving value.
2. Credit means giving value.
3. In your accounting records, your bank account would show receipts on the debit side of the account. The bank account has received value.
4. A bank statement is NOT a record of entries in your accounting system. It is a copy of records in the bank's accounting system. Thus, value received by you on the bank statement is shown as a credit entry, i.e. the bank must give value to you.

Please do not hesitate to contact me if you require any further information.

Yours sincerely

3.16   Reply to Ivan
- The double-entry system is more than a numerical control process. It contains the basic ideas of accounting theory.
- An understanding of accounting ideas is necessary to safeguard against computer error and fraud.
- Accounting processes may be hidden deep within the operating system of a computer. An understanding of these processes is necessary for an understanding of computerized accounting systems. For example, you must know English grammar before you can write a letter in English on a word processor.
- Manual systems are still widely used in practice, particularly in smaller businesses.

CHAPTER FOUR

4.1   Michelle Lee nominal ledger accounts.

Bank account

20X3		£	20X3		£
June 1	Capital	1,500	June 3	Purchases	255
June 10	Sales	126	June 25	Creditors	88
June 30	Debtor	55			

Capital account

20X3		£	20X3		£
June			June 1	Bank	1,500

Purchases account

20X3		£	20X3		£
June 3	Bank	255	June		
June 7	Creditors	348			
June 18	Creditors	294			

Creditors account

20X3		£	20X3		£
June 14	Returns	84	June 7	Purchases	348
June 21	Returns	57	June 18	Purchases	294
June 25	Bank	88			

Sales account

20X3		£	20X3		£
June			June 10	Bank	126
			June 21	Debtors	165

Purchase returns account

20X3		£	20X3		£
June			June 14	Creditors	84
			June 21	Creditors	57

Debtors account

20X3		£	20X3		£
June 21	Sales	165	June 30	Bank	55

4.2 Pandro Goodlad nominal ledger accounts

Bank account

20X5		£	20X5		£
June 1	Capital	5,000	June 3	Motor vehicle	2,500
June 19	Sales	140	June 5	Purchases	275
June 24	Loan	500	June 22	Computers	750
			June 29	Creditors	300

Capital account

20X5		£	20X5		£
July			July 1	Bank	5,000

Purchases account

20X5		£	20X5		£
July 2	Creditor	390	July		
July 5	Bank	275			

Creditors account

20X5		£	20X5		£
July 12	Returns	90	July 2	Purchases	390
July 29	Bank	300			

Motor vehicles account

		£			£
20X5			20X5		
July 3	Bank	2,500	July		

Sales account

		£			£
20X5			20X5		
July			July 10	Debtors	490
			July 19	Bank	140

Debtors account

		£			£
20X5			20X5		
July 10	Sales	490	July		

Purchase returns account

		£			£
20X5			20X5		
July			July 12	Creditors	90

Computers account

		£			£
20X5			20X5		
July 22	Bank	750	July		

Loan account: Arthur Smith

		£			£
20X5			20X5		
July			July 24	Bank	500

4.3   Tara McCarthy's bank account balance

Bank account

		£			£
20X3			20X3		
July 3	Sales	75	July 1	Balance brought	
July 5	Debtors	125		down	1,500
July 6	Loan	1,000	July 4	Purchases	248
July 7	Sales	50	July 7	Creditors	710
July 9	Sales	65	July 23	Creditors	489
July 15	Debtors	1,175	July 31	Creditors	527
July 22	Sales	205			
July 25	Debtors	310			
		3,005			3,474
July 31	Balance carried				
	down	469			
		3,474			3,474
			July 31	Balance brought	
				down	469

The balance on the account at 31 July 20X3 is a credit balance.

4.4   Creditors account: David Smith

Creditors account

		£			£
20X5			20X5		
Aug 1	Purchase returns	100	Aug 5	Purchases	475
Aug 8	Purchase returns	15	Aug 17	Purchases	321
Aug 10	Bank	360	Aug 23	Purchases	407
Aug 31	Bank	321	Aug 25	Purchases	835
			Aug 25	Purchases	915
			Aug 27	Purchases	1,127
		796			4,080
Aug 31	Balance carried				
	down	3,284			
		4,080			4,080
			Aug 31	Balance brought	
				down	3,284

4.5   Pamela Tanzer nominal ledger entries

Tutorial note:

Question 4.5 asks for the nominal ledger entries only. Account balances are shown in order to save space in the suggested answer to question 4.6. (c/d = carried down; b/d = brought down).

Bank account

20X6		£	20X6		£
Sept 1	Capital	50,000	Sept 19	Office	
Sept 2	Loan	2,000		furniture	3,000
Sept 4	Sales	1,000	Sept 21	Purchases	1,100
			Sept 17	Creditors	13,000
			Sept 25	Creditors	5,350
			Sept 30	Balance c/d	30,550
		53,000			53,000
Sept 30	Balance b/d	30,550			

Capital account

20X6		£	20X6		£
Sept			Sept 1	Bank	50,000

Loan account: Brian Hope

20X6		£	20X6		£
Sept			Sept 2		2,000

Purchases account

20X6		£	20X6		£
Sept 3	Creditors	22,200	Sept 30	Balance c/d	25,150
Sept 11	Creditors	1,850			
Sept 21	Bank	1,100			
		25,150			25,150
Sept 30	Balance b/d	25,150			

Purchase returns account

20X6		£	20X6		£
Sept 30	Balance c/d	1,250	Sept 15	Creditors	700
			Sept 20	Creditors	550
		1,250			1,250
			Sept 30	Balance b/d	1,250

Creditors account

20X6		£	20X6		£
Sept 30	Returns	700	Sept 3	Purchases	22,200
Sept 20	Returns	550	Sept 11	Purchases	1,850
Sept 25	Bank	5,350	Sept 17	Motor vehicle	13,000
Sept 27	Bank	13,000			
Sept 30	Balance c/d	17,450			
		37,050			37,050
			Sept 30	Balance b/d	17,450

Debtors account

20X6		£	20X6		£
Sept 5	Sales	2,000	Sept 12	Returns	200
Sept 14	Sales	2,550	Sept 26	Returns	150
			Sept 30	Balance c/d	4,200
		4,550			4,550
Sept 30	Balance b/d	4,200			

Sales account

20X6		£	20X6		£
Sept 30	Balance c/d	5,550	Sept 4	Bank	1,000
			Sept 5	Debtors	2,000
			Sept 14	Debtors	2,550
		5,550			5,550
			Sept 30	Balance b/d	5,550

Sales returns account

20X6		£	20X6		£
Sept 12	Debtors	200	Sept 30	Balance c/d	350
Sept 26	Debtors	150			
		350			350
Sept 30	Balance b/d	350			

Motor vehicles account

20X6		£	20X6	£
Sept 17	Creditors	13,000	Sept	

Office furniture account

20X6		£	20X6	£
Sept 19	Bank	3,000	Sept	

4.6

Pamela Tanzer
Trial balance as at 30 September 20X6

	£ Debit	£ Credit
Bank	30,550	
Capital		50,000
Loan		2,000
Purchases	25,150	
Purchase returns		1,250
Creditors		17,450
Debtors	4,200	
Sales		5,550
Sales returns	350	
Motor vehicle	13,000	
Office furniture	3,000	
	76,250	76,250

4.7   David Jensen: Nominal ledger accounts and trial balance

Bank account

20X4		£	20X4		£
May 1	Capital	20,000	May 21	Machinery	5,500
May 5	Sales	1,800	May 29	Creditors	8,600
May 12	Sales	2,100	May 31	Balance c/d	9,800
		23,900			23,900
May 31	Balance b/d	9,800			

Capital account

20X4		£	20X4		£
May			May 1	Bank	20,000

Purchases account

20X4		£	20X4		£
May 2	Creditors	11,500	May 31	Balance c/d	13,400
May 7	Creditors	1,900			
		13,400			13,400
May 31	Balance b/d	13,400			

Creditors account

20X4		£	20X4		£
May 6	Returns	400	May 2	Purchases	11,500
May 28	Returns	300	May 7	Purchases	1,900
May 29	Bank	8,600	May 31	Computer	2,700
May 31	Balance c/d	6,800			
		16,100			16,100
			May 31	Balance b/d	6,800

Sales account

20X4		£	20X4		£
May 31	Balance c/d	10,000	May 5	Bank	1,800
			May 10	Debtors	3,900
			May 12	Bank	2,100
			May 22	Debtors	2,200
		10,000			10,000
			May 31	Balance b/d	10,000

Purchases returns account

20X4		£	20X4		£
May 31	Balance c/d	700	May 6	Creditors	400
			May 28	Creditors	300
		700			700
			May 31	Balance b/d	700

Debtors account

20X4		£	20X4		£
May 10	Sales	3,900	May 23	Returns	1,400
May 22	Sales	2,200	May 31	Balance c/d	4,700
		6,100			6,100
May 31	Balance b/d	4,700			

Machinery account

20X4		£	20X4		£
May 21	Bank	5,500	May		

Sales returns account

20X4		£	20X4		£
May 23	Debtors	1,400	May		

Computers account

20X4		£	20X4		£
May 31	Creditors	2,700	May		

David Jensen
Trial balance as at 31 May 20X4

	£ Debit	£ Credit
Bank	9,800	
Capital		20,000
Purchases	13,400	
Creditors		6,800
Sales		10,000
Purchase returns		700
Debtors	4,700	
Machinery	5,500	
Sales returns	1,400	
Computers	2,700	
	37,500	37,500

CHAPTER FIVE

5.1   Capital expenditure and revenue expenditure.

Capital Expenditures are those related to the purchase of assets for long-term use in the business. Thus, purchases of land and buildings, motor vehicles, plant and machinery, and office equipment, are examples of capital expenditure.

Revenue expenditures are those which are related directly to the generation of trading income. Examples of revenue expenditure will include purchase of materials for resale, wages, insurance, and electricity.

5.2 (1) Memo to Hillary

> MEMO
>
> To: Hillary Hedgemead   Date:
> From: Author's name
> Subject: The layout of a profit and loss account
>
> The general format of a profit and loss account is as follows:

	£	£
Sales		X
Less cost of sales:		
Opening stock	X	
Plus purchases	X	
	—	
	X	
Less closing stock	(X)	
	—	(X)
		—
Gross profit		X
Less overhead expenses:		
[Category of expense	X	
Category of expense]	X	
	—	(X)
		—
Net profit/(loss) for the period		X
		—

> X = monetary amount
>
> (X) = amount deducted from monetary value directly above

Capital introduced by the owner, capital expenditure, and owner's drawings are excluded from the profit and loss account.

(2) Corrected profit and loss account

Hillary Hedgemead
Profit and loss account
for the year ended 31 December 20X8

	£	£
Sales		24,375
Less cost of sales		
Opening stock	1,300	
Purchases	8,000	
	9,300	
Less closing stock	–	
		9,300
Gross profit		15,075
Less overhead expenses:		
Wages	4,375	
Light and heat	550	
Insurance	300	
Advertising	1,000	
Telephone	850	
		7,075
Profit for the year		8,000

Tutorial Note

Hillary's original profit figure was incorrect. It can be reconciled to the true profit figure as follows:

	£
Hillary's original profit figure	4,875
Add back items which should appear on the balance sheet:	
Drawings	1,625
Motor vehicles	1,500
True profit figure per revised profit and loss account	8,000

5.3   Classification of trial balance items

Advertising	P&L
Bank overdraft	BS
Capital account	BS
Cash	BS
Creditors	BS
Drawings	BS
Debtors	BS
Freehold property	BS
Insurance	P&L
Machinery	BS
Professional fees	P&L
Postage and stationery	P&L
Sales	P&L
Stock at 1 November 20X4 (opening stock)	P&L
Travelling expenses	P&L
Wages	P&L

5.4   Reply to Robert

1. *What is a balance sheet?*
   A balance sheet is a statement of the financial position of a business at a specified date. A balance sheet lists the assets and liabilities of a business.

2. *How should a balance sheet be set out?*
   A simple form of balance sheet is set out as follows:

(Business name)
Balance sheet as at (last day of accounting period)

	£	£	£
Fixed assets			
[Category]			X
[Category]			X
			—
			X
Current assets			
Stock (closing stock at period end)		X	
Debtors		X	
Bank and cash		X	
		—	
		X	
Less current liabilities			
Creditors	X		
Bank overdraft	X		
	—	(X)	

	Net current assets	X
		–
A	Net assets	X
		=
	Capital account	
	Opening balance	X
	Plus net profit (or minus net loss)	X
		–
		X
	Less drawings	(X)
		–
		X
	Long-term liabilities	
	Bank loan	X
		–
B		X
		=

The two values at A and B should be equal.

5.5   Explanation of Terms

1. *Fixed assets*

   Assets are items of value that are owned by the business. A fixed asset is one that is retained in the business for use during more than one accounting period. In addition, a fixed asset is an asset that is not held for resale in the normal course of trading.

2. *Current assets*

   These are assets that are held for conversion into cash in the normal course of trading.

3. *Current liabilities*

   These are short-term liabilities which will fall due for payment within one accounting year.

4. *Capital account*

   This account represents the owner's interest in the business. The capital account is, therefore, the liability of the business to its owner.

5.6

Norma
Profit and loss account for the year ended 31 May 20X9

	£	£
Sales		48,750
Less cost of sales		
Opening stock	2,600	
Purchases	16,000	
	18,600	
Less closing stock	–	18,600
Gross profit		30,150
Less overhead expenses		19,250
Net profit for the year		10,900

Norma
Balance sheet as at 31 May 20X9

	£	£
Fixed assets		
Motor vehicles		20,000
Office equipment		3,000
		23,000
Current assets		
Debtors	5,750	
Bank	250	
Cash	50	
	6,050	
Less current liabilities		
Creditors	2,500	
Net current assets		3,550
Net assets		26,550
Capital account		
Opening balance		18,900
Add profit for year		10,900
		29,800
Less drawings		3,250
		26,550

5.7

John
Profit and loss account for the year ended 30 June 20X4

	£	£
Sales		72,000
Less cost of sales		
Opening stock	3,250	
Purchases	47,000	
	50,250	
Less closing stock	–	
		50,250
Gross profit		21,750
Less overhead expenses		
Rent	15,000	
Wages	19,250	
		34,250
Net profit/(loss) for the year		(12,500)

John
Balance sheet as at 30 June 20X4

	£	£
Fixed assets		
Motor vehicles		9,500
Current assets		
Debtors	6,000	
Bank	500	
	6,500	
Less current liabilities		
Creditors	3,750	
Net current assets		2,750
Net assets		12,250
Capital account		
Opening balance		42,875
Less loss for the year		(12,500)
		30,375
Less drawings		18,125
		12,250

5.8

Tony

Profit and loss account for the year ended 31 August 20X8

	£	£
Sales		121,875
Less cost of sales		
Opening stock	6,500	
Purchases	40,000	
	46,500	
Less closing stock	–	
		46,500
Gross profit		75,375
Less expenses		
Wages	21,875	
Rates and water	4,625	
Light and heat	2,750	
Repairs and renewals	1,875	
Insurance	1,500	
Professional fees	3,125	
Postage and stationery	875	
Advertising	5,000	
Telephone	4,250	
Travelling expenses	2,250	
		48,125
Net profit for the year		27,250

Tony

Balance sheet as at 31 August 20X8

	£	£	£
Fixed assets			
Freehold property			31,250
Motor vehicles			7,500
Machinery			18,750
			57,500
Current assets			
Debtors		15,000	
Cash		125	
		15,125	
Less current liabilities			
Creditors	5,625		
Bank overdraft	625		
		6,250	
Net current assets			8,875
Net assets			66,375

Capital account
Opening balance   47,250
Add net profit for the year   27,250
                                                       _____
                                                       74,500
Less drawings   8,125
                                                       _____
                                                       66,375
                                                       _____

5.9 1. *Drawings and wages*
Drawings are cash and other items of value which are withdrawn from the business by
the owner for his or her own use. Wages are amounts paid to employees and not
owners of the business.
2. *Harold's accounts*

Harold
Profit and loss account for the year ended 31 December 20X7

	£'000s	£'000s
Sales		31,500
Less cost of sales		
Opening stock	800	
Purchases	10,700	
	11,500	
Less closing stock	–	
		11,500
Gross profit		20,000
Less expenses		
Advertising	1,150	
Electricity	650	
Stationery	450	
Wages	19,350	
		21,600
Net profit/(loss) for the year		(1,600)

Harold
Balance sheet as at 31 December 20X7

	£'000s	£'000s
Fixed assets		
Office equipment		5,000
Machinery		10,000
		15,000
Current assets		
Debtors	3,250	
Bank	150	
Cash	50	
	3,450	
Less current liabilities		
Creditors	2,600	
Net current assets		850
Net assets		15,850
Capital account		
Opening balance		25,950
Less loss for the year		1,600
		24,350
Less drawings		8,500
		15,850

5.10

Mary
Profit and loss account for the year ended 31 July 20X5

	£'000s	£'000s
Sales		9,461
Less cost of sales		
Opening stock	1,184	
Purchases	5,937	
	7,121	
Less closing stock	1,473	5,648
Gross profit		3,813
Less expenses		
Wages and salaries	1,931	
Rent	152	
Insurance	39	
Motor expenses	332	
Office expenses	108	
Heat and light	83	
General expenses	514	3,159
Net profit		654

Mary
Balance sheet as at 31 July 20X5

	£'000s	£'000s
Fixed assets		
Freehold property		2,500
Motor vehicles		900
Office equipment		175
		3,575
Current assets		
Stock	1,473	
Debtors	1,948	
Bank	241	
	3,662	
Less current liabilities		
Creditors	865	
Net current assets		2,797
Net assets		6,372
Capital account		
Opening balance		6,318
Profit for the year		654
		6,972
Less drawings		600
		6,372

CHAPTER SIX

6.1   Andrew: comparison of depreciation methods

	Straight line method (SL)	*Reducing balance method (RB)*
	£	£
Cost	24,000	24,000
Depreciation charge 20X1:		
SL: $\dfrac{24{,}000 - 1{,}500}{4}$	5,625	
RB: 24,000 × 50%		12,000
	18,375	12,000
Depreciation charge 20X2:		
SL:	5,625	
RB: 12,000 × 50%		6,000
	12,750	6,000
Depreciation charge 20X3:		
SL:	5,625	
RB: 6,000 × 50%		3,000
	7,125	3,000
Depreciation charge 20X4:		
SL:	5,625	
RB: 3,000 × 50%		1,500
	1,500	1,500

6.2   **(1)** Edward: Depreciation charge for the year ended 30 September 20X8

	£	£
Plant and equipment:		
Cost per trial balance	200,000	
Less accumulated depreciation per trial balance	72,000	
	128,000	
× 20% =		25,600
Motor vehicles:		
Cost per trial balance	75,000	
× 20% =		15,000
		40,600

(2) Balance sheet extract

Fixed assets	Cost	Accumulated depreciation	Net book value
	£	£	£
Plant and equipment	200,000	97,600*	102,400
Motor vehicles	75,000	45,000**	30,000
	275,000	142,600	132,400

* 72,000 + 25,600.
** 30,000 + 15,000.

6.3 (1) Charles: depreciation rate for office equipment
Reducing balance depreciation

$$1 - \sqrt[n]{s/c}$$

where n = number of years of useful life (4 years)
s = residual or scrap value (£10,240)
c = initial cost (£25,000)

$$= 1 - \sqrt[4]{\frac{10,240}{25,000}}$$

$$= 1 - \sqrt[4]{0.4096}$$

$$= 1 - 0.8$$

$$= 0.2 \quad \text{or} \quad 20\%$$

(2) Profit on sale of office equipment

	£
Cost of asset	25,000
Less depreciation 20X1	
25,000 × 20%	5,000
	20,000
Less depreciation 20X2	
20,000 × 20%	4,000
Net book value on disposal	16,000
Sale proceeds	17,500
Profit on sale	1,500

6.4

Tomislav
Profit and loss account for the year ended 31 July 20X9 (ex

		£
Light and heat	(132,000 + 41,500)	173,500
Insurance	(200,500 − 70,000)	130,500
Rates	(80,000 + 30,000)	110,000
Wages		334,000
Advertising	(15,000 − 1,000)	14,000
Telephone		125,000

Tomislav
Balance sheet as at 31 July 20X9 (extract)

		£
Current assets		
Pre-payments	(70,000 + 1,000)	71,000
Current liabilities		
Accruals	(41,500 + 30,000)	71,500

6.5 1. Accounting treatment of bad and doubtful debts

(a) Bad debts are deducted from the balance of outstanding debtors and written off to the profit and loss account as an overhead expense.

(b) Doubtful debts are the subject of an accounting provision. The amount of the provision is deducted from the balance sheet figure of debtors. Increases in the provision are charged to the profit and loss account as an overhead expense. Decreases in the provision are credited to the profit and loss account.

2.

Elizabeth
Balance sheet as at 31 December 20X8 (extract)

		£
Current assets		
Debtors		100,000
Less provision		
100,000 × 10%		10,000
		90,000

Elizabeth
Profit and loss account for the year ended 31 December 20X8 (extract)

		£
Overhead expenses		
Increase in doubtful debts		
provision		
(10,000 − 8,000)		2,000

3.
Elizabeth
Balance sheet as at 31 December 20X9 (extract)

	£
Current assets	
Debtors	70,000
Less provision	
70,000 × 10%	7,000
	63,000

Elizabeth
Profit and loss account for the year ended 31 December 20X9 (extract)

	£
Decrease in doubtful debts provision	
(7,000 − 10,000)	3,000

The decrease in the doubtful debts provision may be added to gross profit or listed as a negative value amongst the overhead expenses.

6.6
Rupert
Profit and loss account for the year ended 31 December 20X2

	£	£
Sales		186,000
Less cost of sales		
Opening stock	18,000	
Purchases	160,000	
	178,000	
Less closing stock	(34,000)	
		144,000
Gross profit		42,000
Less overhead expenses		
Insurance (900 − 100)	800	
Loan interest	3,750	
Miscellaneous expenses	3,850	
Increase in doubtful debts provision (W1)	3,000	
Bad debts	6,500	
Rates (5,000 + 1,000)	6,000	
Depreciation (20,000 × 25%)	5,000	
		28,900
Net profit		13,100

Rupert
Balance sheet as at 31 December 20X2

Fixed assets	£ Cost	£ Accumulated depreciation	£ Net book value
Motor vehicles	20,000	14,500	5,500
Current assets			
Stock		34,000	
Debtors	40,000		
Less provision	(4,000)		
		36,000	
Pre-payments		100	
Bank		17,650	
		87,750	
Less current liabilities			
Creditors	52,500		
Accruals	1,000		
		53,500	
Net current assets			34,250
Net assets			39,750
Capital account			
Opening balance per trial balance			9,650
Add profit for the year			13,100
			22,750
Less drawings			8,000
			14,750
Long-term-loan			25,000
			39,750

Workings:

(W1) Doubtful debts provision

	£
Debtors per trial balance	46,500
Less bad debt	6,500
	40,000
Provision at 10% of debtors	4,000
Previous year's provision per trial balance	1,000
Increase in provision	3,000

6.7

Anne
Profit and loss account for the year ended 30 June 20X6

	£	£
Sales		1,234,200
Less cost of sales		
Opening stock	76,500	
Purchases	975,000	
	1,051,500	
Less closing stock	75,000	
		976,500
Gross profit		257,700
Less overhead expenses		
Advertising	4,500	
Electricity (4,800 + 450)	5,250	
Administration expenses	43,350	
Rates (9,000 − 1,500)	7,500	
Telephone	1,950	
Wages and salaries	116,400	
Depreciation		
Furniture and fittings		
(18,000 × 15%)	2,700	
Vehicles		
(52,500 − 10,500 × 20%)	8,400	
Increase in doubtful debts provision		
(63,000 × 10% = 6,300 − 3,450)	2,850	
		192,900
Net profit		64,800

Anne
Balance sheet as at 30 June 20X6

	£ Cost	£ Accumulated depreciation	£ Net book value
Fixed assets			
Furniture and fittings	18,000	5,400	12,600
Vehicles	52,500	18,900	33,600
	70,500	24,300	46,200
Current assets			
Stock		75,000	
Debtors	63,000		
Less provision	(6,300)		
		56,700	
Pre-payments		1,500	
Bank		600	
		133,800	

	£	£	£
Less current liabilities			
Creditors	19,500		
Accruals	450		
		19,950	
Net current assets			113,850
			160,050
Capital account			
Opening Balance per trial balance			110,250
Add profit for the year			64,800
			175,050
Less drawings			15,000
			160,050

6.8

Margaret

Profit and loss account for the year ended 31 December 20X3

	£	£	£
Sales			492,000
Less cost of sales			
Opening stock		8,400	
Purchases		249,000	
		257,400	
Less closing stock		47,400	
			210,000
Gross profit			282,000
Rent Received			3,900
			285,900
Less overhead expenses			
Office expenses	147,000		
Less drawings	27,000		
	120,000		
Accruals	3,600		
Pre-payments	(1,000)		
		122,600	
Depreciation			
Plant and equipment			
(165,000 × 30%)		49,500	
Motor vehicles			
(192,000—48,000 × 25%)		36,000	
			208,100
Net profit			77,800

Margaret
Balance sheet as at 31 December 20X3

	£ Cost	£ Accumulated depreciation	£ Net book value
Fixed assets			
Land and buildings	50,000	–	50,000
Plant and equipment	165,000	139,500	25,500
Motor vehicles	192,000	84,000	108,000
	407,000	223,500	183,500
Current assets			
Stock		47,400	
Debtors		39,600	
Pre-payments		1,000	
Cash at bank		1,200	
		89,200	
Less current liabilities			
Creditors	28,800		
Accruals	3,600	32,400	
			56,800
			240,300
Capital account			
Opening balance per trial balance			189,500
Add net profit			77,800
			267,300
Less drawings			27,000
			240,300

CHAPTER SEVEN

7.1

Jake and Nog

Profit and loss account for the year ended 31 March 20X6

	£	£
Sales		90,370
Less cost of sales		
Opening stock	24,970	
Purchases	71,630	
	96,600	
Less closing stock	27,340	
		69,260
Gross profit		21,110
Less overhead expenses		
Salaries	8,417	
Office expenses (1,933 + 110)	2,043	
Depreciation		
Motor vehicles (9,200 × 20%)	1,840	
Office equipment (6,500 × 10%)	650	
		12,950
Net profit		8,160
Appropriation account:		
Less interest on capital		
Jake: 27,000 × 10%	2,700	
Nog: 12,000 × 10%	1,200	
		3,900
		4,260
Share of balance of profit		
Jake 60%	2,556	
Nog 40%	1,704	
		4,260
		nil

Jake and Nog
Balance sheet as at 31 March 20X6

	£ Cost	£ Accumulated depreciation	£ Net book value
Fixed assets			
Office equipment	6,500	2,600	3,900
Motor vehicles	9,200	5,520	3,680
	15,700	8,120	7,580
Current assets			
Stock		27,340	
Debtors		20,960	
Cash at bank		755	
		49,055	
Less current liabilities			
Creditors	16,275		
Accruals	110	16,385	
			32,670
			40,250

Capital accounts	Jake	Nog	
per trial balance	27,000	12,000	39,000
Current accounts			
Opening balance			
per trial balance	1,379	1,211	
Add interest on			
capital	2,700	1,200	
Share of balance			
of profits	2,556	1,704	
	6,635	4,115	
Less drawings	5,500	4,000	
	1,135	115	1,250
			40,250

7.2

Carpenter Ltd.

Profit and loss account for the year ended 30 November 20X1

	£'000s	£'000s
Sales		22,320
Less cost of sales		
Opening stock	2,340	
Purchases	12,240	
	14,580	
Less closing stock	2,250	
		12,330
Gross profit		9,990
Dividends received		36
		10,026
Less overhead expenses		
Administrative expenses	1,890	
Distribution costs	5,220	
Depreciation:		
Freehold property (1,800 × 4%)	72	
Vans (6,300 × 25%)	1,575	
		8,757
Net profit before taxation		1,269
Corporation tax		495
Net profit after tax		774
Less dividends:		
Ordinary dividends proposed		
(6,480 × 10p)		648
Retained profit for the year		126
Retained profit brought forward		1,440
Retained profit carried forward		1,566

Tutorial Note:

For the sake of clarity, depreciation charges have been shown on the face of the profit and loss account. However, in practice, these charges would be included in either administrative expenses or distribution costs. It is likely that property depreciation would be included in administrative expenses, and depreciation on vans in distribution costs.

Carpenter Ltd.
Balance sheet as at 30 November 20X1

	£'000s Cost	£'000s Accumulated depreciation	£'000s Net book value
Fixed assets			
Freehold property	1,800	216	1,584
Vans	6,300	4,275	2,025
	8,100	4,491	3,609
Investments			180
Current assets			
Stock		2,250	
Debtors		3,870	
Cash at bank		360	
		6,480	
Less current liabilities			
Creditors	1,080		
Corporation tax	495		
Ordinary dividend	648	2,223	
			4,257
			8,046
Share capital			Authorized and issued
Ordinary shares of £1 each			6,480
Reserves			
Profit and loss account			1,566
			8,046

7.3

Charlene Ltd.
Profit and loss account for the year ended 31 October 20X1

	£	£
Sales		58,300
Less cost of sales		
Opening stock	9,100	
Purchases	45,500	
	54,600	
Less closing stock	10,000	
		44,600
Gross profit		13,700
Less overhead expenses		
Administrative expenses	4,550	
Distribution costs	1,260	
Depreciation:		
Office equipment (14,200 × 10%)	1,420	
		7,230
Net profit before taxation		6,470
Corporation tax		2,500
Net profit after tax		3,970
Less dividends:		
Ordinary dividend		
Paid	–	
Proposed (W1)	1,400	
Preference dividend (W2)	420	
		1,820
Retained profit for the year		2,150
Retained profit brought forward		3,500
Retained profit carried forward		5,650

Charlene Ltd.
Balance sheet as at 31 October 20X1

	£ Cost	£ Accumulated depreciation	£ Net book value
Fixed assets			
Office equipment	14,200	4,940	9,260
Current assets			
Stock		10,000	
Debtors		4,250	
Cash at bank		1,700	
		15,950	
Less current liabilities			
Creditors	3,250		
Corporation tax	2,500		
Ordinary dividend	1,400		
Preference dividend (W2)	210		
		7,360	8,590
			17,850

	Authorized and Issued
Share capital	
Ordinary shares of 50p each	7,000
15% preference shares of £1 each	2,800
	9,800
Reserves	
Profit and loss account	5,650
Share premium account	2,400
	17,850

Workings

		£
(W1)	Ordinary dividends per trial balance ordinary shares of 50p each	7,000
	= 14,000 shares in number	
	Thus, dividend = 14,000 × 10p =	1,400

		£
(W2)	Preference dividend	
	Rate of dividend 15%	
	Shares in issue at nominal value	2,800
	Dividend payable in year	
	2,800 × 15% =	420
	Dividend paid per trial balance	210
	Accrual for balance sheet	210

7.4

Bouncer Ltd.
Profit and loss account for the year ended 31 December 20X2

	£	£
Sales		297,000
Less cost of sales		
Opening stock	45,000	
Purchases	180,000	
	225,000	
Less closing stock	54,000	
		171,000
Gross profit		126,000
Less overhead expenses		
Administrative expenses	53,325	
Distribution costs	20,250	
Depreciation:		
Fixtures and fittings		
$(2,250 \times 10\%)$	225	
Machinery		
$(157,500 - 90,000 \times 50\%)$	33,750	
		107,550
Net profit before taxation		18,450
Corporation tax		11,925
Net profit after tax		6,525
Less dividends:		
Ordinary dividend		
Paid	1,800	
Proposed (W1)	3,600	
Preference dividend (W2)	450	
		5,850
Retained profit for the year		675
Retained profit brought forward		67,500
Retained profit carried forward		68,175

Bouncer Ltd.
Balance sheet as at 31 December 20X2

	£ Cost	£ Accumulated depreciation	£ Net book value
Fixed assets			
Fixtures and fittings	2,250	1,125	1,125
Machinery	157,500	123,750	33,750
	159,750	124,875	34,875
Current assets			
Stock		54,000	
Debtors		78,525	
		132,525	
Less current liabilities			
Creditors	49,500		
Corporation tax	11,925		
Ordinary dividend	3,600		
Preference dividend (W2)	225		
Bank overdraft	2,925		
		68,175	
			64,350
			99,225

Share capital	Authorized and Issued
Ordinary shares of £1 each	18,000
10% preference shares of £1 each	4,500
	22,500
Reserves	
Profit and loss account	68,175
Share premium account	8,550
	99,225

Workings

(W1) Proposed ordinary dividend   £
        Number of shares in issue = 18,000
        Rate of dividend 20p per share
        Dividend = 18,000 × 20p =   3,600

(W2) Preference dividend
        Rate of dividend 10% per annum
        Shares in issue = 4,500
        Total dividend: 4,500 × 10% =   450
        Paid per trial balance   225
        Accrual for balance sheet   225

7.5

Scott Ltd.
Profit and loss account for the year ended 28 February 20X1

	£'000s	£'000s
Sales		11,660
Less cost of sales		
Opening stock	1,820	
Purchases	9,100	
	10,920	
Less closing stock	2,000	
		8,920
Gross profit		2,740
Less overhead expenses		
Administrative expenses	910	
Distribution costs	210	
Depreciation:		
Furniture and equipment		
(2,840 × 10%)	284	
		1,404
Net profit before taxation		1,336
Corporation tax		500
Net profit after tax		836
Less dividends:		
Ordinary dividend–proposed		
(1,400 × 20p)	280	
Preference dividend–paid		
(15% x 560)	84	
		364
Retained profit for the year		472
Retained profit brought forward		700
Retained profit carried forward		1,172

Scott Ltd.

Balance sheet as at 28 February 20X1

	£'000s Cost	£'000s Accumulated depreciation	£'000s Net book value
Fixed assets			
Furniture and equipment	2,840	988	1,852
Current assets			
Stock		2,000	
Debtors		850	
Cash at bank		340	
		3,190	
Less current liabilities			
Creditors	650		
Corporation tax	500		
Ordinary dividend	280		
		1,430	1,760
			3,612

	Authorized and issued
Share capital	
Ordinary shares of £1 each	1,400
15% preference shares of £1 each	560
	1,960
Reserves	
Profit and loss account	1,172
Share premium account	480
	3,612

7.6   Ramsey Ltd.
Profit and loss account for the year ended 31 December 20X2

	£'000s	£'000s
Sales		66,000
Less cost of sales		
Opening stock	10,000	
Purchases	40,000	
	50,000	
Less closing stock	12,000	
		38,000
Gross profit		28,000
Less overhead expenses		
Administrative expenses	11,850	
Distribution costs	4,500	
Depreciation:		
Fixtures and fittings		
(500 × 10%)	50	
Plant and equipment		
(35,000 − 20,000 × 50%)	7,500	
		23,900
Net profit before taxation		4,100
Corporation tax		2,650
Net profit after tax		1,450
Less dividends:		
Ordinary dividend		
Paid	400	
Proposed		
(£4m × 20p)	800	
Preference dividend		
Paid	50	
Accrued (W1)	50	
		1,300
Retained profit for the year		150
Retained profit brought forward		15,000
Retained profit carried forward		15,150

Ramsey Ltd.
Balance sheet as at 31 December 20X2

	£'000s Cost	£'000s Accumulated depreciation	£'000s Net book value
Fixed assets			
Furniture and fittings	500	250	250
Plant and equipment	35,000	27,500	7,500
	35,500	27,750	7,750
Current assets			
Stock		12,000	
Debtors		17,450	
		29,450	
Less current liabilities			
Creditors	11,000		
Corporation tax	2,650		
Ordinary dividend	800		
Preference dividend	50		
Bank overdraft	650		
		15,150	
			14,300
			22,050

Share capital	Authorized	Issued
Ordinary shares of £1 each	4,000	4,000
10% preference shares of £1 each	1,000	1,000
	5,000	5,000

Reserves	
Profit and loss account	15,150
Share premium account	1,900
	22,050

Workings

	£
(W1) Dividend on preference shares	
Rate of dividend–10%	
Shares in issue at nominal value	1,000
Total dividend payable in year	
1,000 × 10%	100
Dividend paid per trial balance	50
Balance of dividend accrued	50

7.7

Madge Ltd.
Profit and loss account for the year ended 30 June 20X3

	£'000s	£'000s
Sales		4,960
Less cost of sales		
Opening stock	520	
Purchases	2,720	
	3,240	
Less closing stock	500	
		2,740
Gross profit		2,220
Dividends received		8
		2,228
Less overhead expenses		
Administrative expenses (420 + 20)	440	
Distribution costs (1,160 − 10)	1,150	
Depreciation:		
Freehold property (400 × 4%)	16	
Motor vehicles (1,400 − 600 × 25%)	200	
		1,806
Net profit before taxation		422
Corporation tax		110
Net profit after tax		312
Less dividends:		
Ordinary dividends proposed		
(1,440 × 10p)		144
Retained profit for the year		168
Retained profit brought forward		320
Retained profit carried forward		488

Madge Ltd.
Balance sheet as at 30 June 20X3

	£'000s Cost	£'000s Accumulated depreciation	£'000s Net book value
Fixed assets			
Freehold property	400	48	352
Motor vehicles	1,400	800	600
	1,800	848	952
Current assets			
Stock		500	
Debtors		900	
Pre-payments		10	
Bank		80	
		1,490	
Less current liabilities			
Creditors	240		
Accruals	20		
Corporation tax	110		
Proposed dividend	144	514	976
			1,928

	Authorized and issued
Share capital	
Ordinary shares of £1 each	1,440
Reserves	
Profit and loss account	488
	1,928

CHAPTER NINE

9.1 Classification of Cash flows

FRS1 requires that cash flows be classified under the following standard headings:

1. *Operating activities*
   These are the cash effects of transactions relating to operating or trading activities.

2. *Returns on investment and servicing of finance*
   These are cash flows resulting from the ownership of an investment and from payments to providers of finance. This heading excludes payments of dividends to ordinary or equity shareholders of the company.

3. *Taxation*
   These are cash flows relating to payment of corporation tax or the receipt of corporation tax rebates or overpayments.

4. *Capital expenditure and financial investment*
   These are cash flows relating to the purchase or sale of fixed assets and investments.

5. *Acquisitions and disposals*
   These cash flows relate to the purchase or sale of subsidiary companies, associated companies or joint ventures.

6. *Equity dividends paid*
   These are dividends paid to ordinary or equity shareholders of the company.

7. *Management of liquid resources*
   These cash flows are those relating to payments into or withdrawals from short-term deposit accounts which do not fall within the definition of 'cash' because they are not repayable on demand without penalty.
   This classification also includes cash flows relating to the purchase or sale of short-term investments which are easily purchased and sold in an active market.

8. *Financing*
   These cash flows are those related to the issue or redemption of shares and debentures.

9.2 Letter to Martin

Your address
Date

Martin's address

Dear Martin

Cash flow statements

Cash flow statements are a report of the significant components of increases or decreases in a business's cash balances. Cash, in this context, means cash in hand, overdrafts, and deposits repayable on demand with no penalty.

The profit and loss account discloses accounting profit for an accounting period. Accounting profit is not the same as cash flow because accountants have to make a number of adjustments to cash flow in order to calculate an accurate figure for profit. These adjustments include:

1. Depreciation of fixed assets.
2. The calculation of debtors and pre-payments.
3. The calculation of creditors and accruals.
4. Inventory valuation.
5. Bad debts and provisions for doubtful debts.

The cash flow statement provides information to assist readers of accounts to assess the liquidity and solvency of the business.

Yours sincerely

Your name

9.3   Net cash flow from operating activities:

	£'000s
Operating profit	12,044
Add: Depreciation Charge	1,798
Increase in creditors	468
Less: Increase in stock	(388)
Increase in debtors	(144)
Net cash inflow from operating activities	13,778

9.4

Torvenas Ltd.
Net cash flow from operating activities

	£
Net profit before tax	135,315
Interest paid	1,800
Interest received	(840)
Operating profit	136,275
Loss on sale of fixed assets	1,485
Depreciation	12,000
Increase in stock	(2,910)
Increase in debtors	(1,080)
Increase in creditors	3,510
Net cash flow from operating activities	149,280

9.5

Nanonics Ltd.
Reconciliation of net cash flow movement to movement in net debt

	£
Increase in cash	31,572
Cash used to redeem debentures	
(16,992 − 15,144)	1,848
Cash used to purchase treasury stock	
(3,000 − 8,400)	5,400
Change in net debt	38,820
Net debt at 1.1.X2	(34,896)
Net funds at 31.12.X2	3,924

Nanonics Ltd.
Analysis of Change in Net Debt

	At 1.1.X2 £	Cash flows £	At 31.12.X2 £
Cash at bank	504	10,164	10,668
Bank overdraft	(21,408)	21,408	–
		31,572	
Debentures	(16,992)	1,848	(15,144)
Treasury stock	3,000	5,400	8,400
	(34,896)	38,820	3,924

9.6

Pico Ltd.
Analysis of change in net debt for the year ended 31 October 20X5

	At 31.10.X4 £	Cash flows £	At 31.10.X5 £
Cash at bank	128,016	(121,968)	6,048
Bank overdraft	(256,896)	156,096	(100,800)
		34,128	
Debt	(203,904)	22,176	(181,728)
Treasury stock	36,000	(36,000)	–
	(296,784)	20,304	(276,480)

9.7   Reconciliation of cash movements to movements in net debt

The original UK Cash flow Standard, FRS1, which was issued in September 1991, merely required businesses to reconcile the increase or decrease in cash and cash equivalents with cash (and cash equivalent) balances on the balance sheet at the start and end of the accounting periods.

The revised standard provides the reader of the cash flow statement with additional information. Net debt is a widely used indication of the financial stability and solvency of a business. It can be defined as borrowings less cash and liquid resources. Borrowings are essentially long-term loans, and the revised standard defines cash as 'cash in hand and deposits repayable on demand'. In addition, the Standard defines liquid resources as 'current asset investments held as readily disposable stores of value'.

9.8

Prime Ltd.
Cash flow statement for the year ended 31 December 20X8

	£'000s	£'000s
Net cash inflow from operating activities		29,856
Returns on investment and servicing of finance		
Interest received	168	
Interest paid	(360)	(192)
Taxation (W2)		(8,766)
Capital expenditure		
Purchase of fixed assets (W4)	(4,701)	
Receipts from sales of fixed assets (W3)	126	(4,575)
Equity dividends paid (W5)		(7,251)
Management of liquid resources		
Purchase of treasury bills	(1,950)	
Sale of treasury bills	600	(1,350)
Financing		
Issue of ordinary shares	633	
Redemption of debentures	(462)	171
Increase in cash		7,893

Notes to Cash flow statement

1. Reconciliation of operating profit to net cash flow from operating activities

	£'000s
Operating profit (W1)	27,255
Depreciation	2,400
Increase in stock	(582)
Increase in debtors	(216)
Increase in creditors	702
Loss on sale of fixed assets	297
Net cash inflow from operating activities	29,856

2. Reconciliation of net cash flow movement to movement in net debt

	£'000s
Increase in cash in the period	7,893
Cash used to redeem debentures	462
Cash used to purchase treasury bills	1,350
Change in net debt	9,705
Net debt at 1.1.X8	(8,724)
Net funds at 31.12.X8	981

3. Analysis of changes in net debt

	At 1 Jan 20X8 £'000s	Cash flows £'000s	At 31 Dec 20X8 £'000s
Cash in hand at bank	126	2,541	2,667
Overdraft	(5,352)	5,352	–
		7,893	
Debt			
Due within 1 year	(462)	462	–
Due after 1 year	(3,786)	–	(3,786)
Treasury bills	750	1,350	2,100
	(8,724)	9,705	981

4. Analysis of changes in financing during the year

	Ordinary shares £'000s	Debentures £'000s
At 1 Jan 20X8	17,554	4,248
Cash flows	633	(462)
At 31 Dec 20X8	18,187	3,786

Workings

(W1) Operating profit

	£'000s
Net profit before tax	27,063
Less interest received	168
Add interest paid	360
Operating profit	27,255

(W2) Taxation cash flow

Taxation account

	£'000s		£'000s
		Creditor at 1.1.X8	8,766
Balance = cash paid	8,766	P&L account	8,327
Creditor at 31.12.X8	8,327		
	17,093		17,093

(W3) Profit on sale of fixed assets

Fixed asset disposal account

	£'000s		£'000s
Cost of disposals	1,058	Accumulated depreciation	635
		P&L loss on sale	297
		Balance = cash rec'd	126
	1,058		1,058

(W4) Purchase of fixed assets

Fixed assets at NBV

	£'000s		£'000s
Per balance sheet 31.12.X7	34,624	Cost of disposal	1,058
Accumulated depreciation on disposal	635	P&L depreciation charge for year	2,400
Balance = cash paid	4,701	Per balance sheet 31.12.X8	36,502
	39,960		39,960

(W5) Equity dividends paid

Dividends account

	£'000s		£'000s
		Creditor 1.1.X8	7,251
Balance = cash paid	7,251	P&L account	7,614
Creditor 31.12.X8	7,614		
	14,865		14,865

9.9   Arvanitis Ltd.
              Cash flow statement for the year ended 31 May 20X5

		£'000s
Net cash inflow from operating activities		522
Returns on investments and servicing of finance		
Interest paid (8% x 175)		(14)
Taxation		(63)
Capital expenditure		
Purchase of fixed assets		(325)
Acquisitions and disposals		
Purchase of subsidiary undertaking		(200)
Equity dividends paid		(123)
Management of liquid resources		
Cash withdrawn from 7 day deposit		2
Financing		
Issue of debentures		175
Decrease in cash		(26)

Notes to cash flow statement

1. Reconciliation of operating profit to net cash inflow from operating activities

	£'000s
Operating profit (W1)	277
Depreciation (W2)	280
Increase in stock	(140)
Decrease in debtors	70
Increase in creditors	35
	522

2. Reconciliation of net cash flow movement to movement in net debt

	£'000s
Decrease in cash in period	(26)
Cash withdrawn from 7 day deposit	(2)
Cash from issue of debentures	(175)
Change in net debt	(203)
Net funds 1.6.X4	35
Net debt 31.5.X5	(168)

Tutorial note
The reconciliation of debt shows increases and decreases in the level of debt. Thus, a cash inflow from the issue of debentures is considered here in terms of its impact on debt *not* as cash inflows and outflows.

3. Analysis of changes in net debt

	At 1 June 20X4 £'000s	Cash flows £'000s	At 31 May 20X5 £'000s
Bank	30	(26)	4
7 day deposit	5	(2)	3
Debt	–	(175)	(175)
	35	(203)	(168)

4. Analysis of changes in financing during they year

	Debentures £'000s
At 31 May 20X4	–
Cash flow	175
At 31 May 20X5	175

Workings

(W1)   Operating profit

	£'000s
Net profit before tax	263
Add debenture interest paid (8% × 175)	14
Operating profit	277

(W2)   Depreciation charge for year

	£'000s
Accumulated depreciation	
31.5.X4	350
31.5.X5	630
Charge in year	280

9.10

NHH Group Plc
Cash flow statement for the year ended 31 December 20X6

	£'000s	£'000s
Cash flow from operating activities		8,011
Returns on investment and servicing of finance		
Interest received	254	
Interest paid	(1,148)	
Preference dividend paid	(225)	
		(1,119)
Taxation		(1,444)
Capital expenditure		
Purchase of tangible fixed assets	(1,756)	
Sale of plant and machinery	1,324	
		(432)
Acquisitions and disposals		
Purchase of subsidiary undertaking	(9,110)	
Sale of business	2,104	
Purchase of interest in joint venture	(1,905)	
		(8,911)
Equity dividends paid		(1,303)
Management of liquid resources		
Cash withdrawn from 7 day deposit	100	
Purchase of government securities	(2,500)	
Sale of government securities	2,150	
Sale of corporate bonds	600	
		350
Financing		
Issue of ordinary shares	300	
Increase in debt	1,173	
		1,473
Decrease in cash in period		(3,375)

Notes to cash flow statement

1. Reconciliation of operating profit to operating cash flows

	£'000s
Operating profit	9,316
Depreciation	1,744
Increase in stock	(6,454)
Increase in debtors	(1,887)
Increase in creditors	5,292
Net cash flow from operating activities	8,011

2.   Reconciliation of net cash flow movement to movement in net debt

	£'000s
Decrease in cash in the period	(3,375)
Cash inflow from increase in debt	(1,173)
Cash inflow from decrease in liquid resources	(350)
Change in net debt	(4,898)
Net debt at 1.1.X6	(6,527)
Net debt at 31.12.X6	(11,425)

3.   Analysis of changes in net debt

	At 1.1.X6	Cash flow	At 31.12.X6
	£'000s	£'000s	£'000s
Cash in hand at bank	118	150	268
Overdraft	(1,264)	(3,525)	(4,789)
		(3,375)	
Debt	(9,781)	(1,173)	(10,954)
7 day deposit	200	(100)	100
Government securities	3,000	350	3,350
Corporate bonds	1,200	(600)	600
	(6,527)	(4,898)	(11,425)

4.   Analysis of changes in financing

	Ordinary shares	Debentures
	£'000s	£'000s
At 1.1.X6	10,000	9,781
Cash inflows	300	1,173
Cash outflows	–	–
At 31.12.X6	10,300	10,954

CHAPTER TEN

10.1 Miklos Ltd.: Ratios for year ended 31 March 20X5

$$\text{ROCE} = \frac{\text{Profit after tax}}{\text{Share capital and reserves}} \times 100$$

$$= \frac{150}{1,550} \times 100$$

$$= 9.7\%$$

Gross profit percentage

$$= \frac{\text{Gross profit}}{\text{Sales}} \times 100$$

$$= \frac{1,500}{3,000} \times 100$$

$$= 50\%$$

Net profit percentage

$$= \frac{\text{Net profit}}{\text{Sales}} \times 100$$

$$= \frac{225}{3,000} \times 100$$

$$= 7.5\%$$

Current ratio

$$= \frac{\text{Current assets}}{\text{Current liabilities}}$$

$$= \frac{688}{600}$$

$$= 1.1 : 1$$

Acid test ratio

$$= \frac{\text{Current assets} - \text{stock}}{\text{Current liabilities}}$$

$$= \frac{688 - 188}{600}$$

$$= 0.8 : 1$$

Fixed asset turnover

$$= \frac{\text{Sales}}{\text{Fixed assets}}$$

$$= \frac{3,000}{1,712}$$

$$= 1.75 \text{ times}$$

Debtor collection period

$$= \frac{\text{Debtors}}{\text{Sales}} \times 365$$

$$= \frac{500}{3,000} \times 365$$

$$= 60.8 \text{ days}$$

Capital gearing ratio

$$= \frac{\text{Debt capital}}{\text{Debt capital} + \text{equity capital}} \times 100$$

$$= \frac{250}{250 + 1,550} \times 100$$

$$= 13.9\%$$

10.2   Harvest Plc: investment ratios for year ended 31 August 20X8

Earnings per share

$$= \frac{\text{Profit after tax}}{\text{No. of ordinary shares in issue}}$$

$$= \frac{500,000}{1,000,000}$$

$$= 50\text{p} \ (\pounds 0.5)$$

Price earnings ratio

$$= \frac{\text{Market price per share}}{\text{Earnings per share}}$$

$$= \frac{175\text{p}}{50\text{p}}$$

$$= 3.5 \text{ years}$$

Dividend yield

$$= \frac{\text{Ordinary dividend per share}}{\text{Market price per share}} \times 100$$

$$= \frac{35p}{175p} \times 100$$

$$= 20\%$$

Dividend cover

$$= \frac{\text{Net profit after tax}}{\text{Ordinary dividends}}$$

$$= \frac{500,000}{350,000}$$

$$= 1.4 \text{ times}$$

10.3   Janeway Ltd.: return on capital employed

$$\text{ROCE} = \frac{\text{Profit before interest and tax}}{\text{Share capital, reserves and loan capital}} \times 100$$

$$= \frac{385 + 70}{2730} \times 100$$

$$= \qquad 16.7\%$$

The interest figure has been calculated as follows:

Balance sheet figure for debentures $\times$ rate of debenture interest.

Capital gearing ratio

$$= \frac{\text{Debt capital}}{\text{Debt capital} + \text{equity capital}} \times 100$$

$$= \frac{700 + 70}{2,730} \times 100$$

$$= \qquad 28.2\%$$

10.4   Johnstone Ltd.

1.   *Ratios of significance to user groups*

Shareholders	**Trade creditors**	**Management**
Earnings per share	Current ratio	ROCE
Dividend cover	Acid test ratio	Debtors collection period

2. *Ratio calculations*

	20X6	20X7

Earnings per share

$$= \frac{\text{Profit after tax}}{\text{No. of ordinary shares in issue}}$$

$$= \frac{14{,}280}{(14{,}880 \times 100/25)}$$

$$= \frac{14{,}280}{59{,}520} \qquad\qquad = \qquad 24\text{p}$$

$$= \frac{17{,}490}{59{,}520} \qquad\qquad = \qquad\qquad 29\text{p}$$

Dividend cover

$$= \frac{\text{Net profit after tax}}{\text{Ordinary dividends}}$$

$$= \frac{14{,}280}{3{,}360} \qquad\qquad = \qquad 4.25 \times$$

$$= \frac{17{,}490}{3{,}600} \qquad\qquad = \qquad\qquad 4.9 \times$$

Current ratio

$$= \frac{\text{Current assets}}{\text{Current liabilities}}$$

$$= \frac{138{,}670}{55{,}293} \qquad\qquad = \qquad 2.5{:}1$$

$$= \frac{149{,}422}{63{,}712} \qquad\qquad = \qquad\qquad 2.3{:}1$$

Acid test ratio

$$= \frac{\text{Current assets—stock}}{\text{Current liabilities}}$$

$$= \frac{138{,}670 - 60{,}217}{55{,}293} \qquad\qquad = \qquad 1.4{:}1$$

$$= \frac{149{,}422 - 75{,}682}{63{,}712} \qquad\qquad = \qquad\qquad 1.2{:}1$$

Return on capital employed

	20X6	20X7

$$\text{ROCE} = \frac{\text{Profit before interest and tax}}{\substack{\text{Share capital, reserves} \\ \text{and loan capital}}} \times 100$$

$$= \frac{25{,}857}{90{,}870} \times 100 \qquad\qquad = \quad 28.4\%$$

$$= \frac{31{,}005}{104{,}760} \times 100 \qquad\qquad = \qquad\qquad 29.6\%$$

Debtors collection period

$$= \frac{\text{Debtors}}{\text{Sales}} \times 365$$

$$= \frac{60{,}315}{729{,}450} \times 365 \qquad\qquad = \quad 30.2 \text{ days}$$

$$= \frac{65{,}055}{875{,}850} \times 365 \qquad\qquad = \qquad\qquad 27.1 \text{ days}$$

3. *Comment on changes between 20X6 and 20X7*

Sales and operating profit have increased by 20% in the period. Shareholders have seen a comensurate increase in eanings per share. Dividend cover has increased from 4.25 times to 4.9 times, while interest paid has remained constant. The shareholders are unlikely to be disapointed by the 20X7 results.

The amount of cash has been reduced, but this appears to have been the result of asset purchases rather than a reduction in liquidity levels. The current ratio and the acid test ratio have improved slightly, and it is encouraging to see that the debtors collection period has been reduced to only 27.1 days.

The return on capital employed has been calculated in terms of a gross return to providers of capital and this appears to be a healthy rate of return. However, further information is required about the operating environment of the company and its future prospects before a more detailed analysis of its results can be made.

10.5 Report to Hector Gladstone

Report on the potential acquisition of Solo Ltd. and Mio Ltd. for Hector Gladstone
By (author name)
Date

Introduction

In accordance with your instructions, I have investigated the latest financial statements of the two companies in terms of their potential as aquisitions. Ratios which form the basis of this report are given in appendix one.

Analysis

The financial statements of the companies indicate their current profitability and not their future prospects. Return on capital employed is 27.2% for Solo Ltd. and 15.6% for Mio Ltd. The gross profit percentages of both companies are identical, but Solo Ltd. has a higher net profit percentage. This suggests that Solo Ltd. has better control over its overhead expenses and this is reflected in its higher level of profitability.

Both companies appear to operate at low levels of liquidity. This is a cause for concern for companies in the engineering industry as they are unlikely to receive cash on a day-to-day basis. The liquidity indicators appear to be more appropriate to companies involved in retailing. Mio Ltd. takes more than four times as long to collect its debtors than Solo Ltd. This may mean that Mio Ltd. could suffer a high incidence of bad debts in 20X8.

Both companies have similar levels of fixed asset utilization, but Solo Ltd. appears to enjoy a net asset turnover of 1.27 times compared to 0.99 times for Mio Ltd.

Mio Ltd. has a capital gearing ratio of 12.4% compared with 28.4% for Solo Ltd.

Advice and recommendations

An analysis of one year's accounting statements cannot provide the basis for a detailed analysis of the results of the two companies. More information is required in respect of the historical results and the future prospects of the companies. In addition, the results of the ratio analysis might be distorted by differences in accounting policies between the two companies.

Conclusion

An initial analysis of the results for the year ended 30 April 20X7 seems to suggest that Solo Ltd. is a better candidate for acquisition than Mio Ltd.

Appendix one: Ratio calculations

	Solo Ltd.	Mio Ltd.

Profitability

ROCE

$$= \frac{\text{Profit before interest and tax}}{\text{Share capital, reserves and loan capital}} \times 100$$

$$= \frac{1{,}408 + 280}{6{,}200} \times 100 \qquad\qquad 27.2\%$$

$$= \frac{624 + 80}{4{,}520} \times 100 \qquad\qquad\qquad\qquad 15.6\%$$

	Solo Ltd.	Mio Ltd.

Gross profit percentage

$$= \frac{\text{Gross profit}}{\text{Sales}} \times 100$$

$$= \frac{5,880}{7,880} \times 100 \qquad\qquad 74.6\%$$

$$= \frac{3,352}{4,480} \times 100 \qquad\qquad\qquad\qquad 74.8\%$$

Net profit percentage

$$= \frac{\text{Net profit}}{\text{Sales}} \times 100$$

$$= \frac{1,408}{7,880} \times 100 \qquad\qquad 17.9\%$$

$$= \frac{624}{4,480} \times 100 \qquad\qquad\qquad\qquad 13.9\%$$

Liquidity

Current ratio

$$= \frac{\text{Current assets}}{\text{Current liabilities}}$$

$$= \frac{3,000}{2,920} \qquad\qquad 1:1$$

$$= \frac{4,640}{3,400} \qquad\qquad\qquad\qquad 1.4:1$$

Acid test ratio

$$= \frac{\text{Current assets} - \text{stock}}{\text{Current liabilities}}$$

$$= \frac{3,000 - 1,240}{2,920} \qquad\qquad 0.6:1$$

$$= \frac{4,640 - 1,120}{3,400} \qquad\qquad\qquad\qquad 1:1$$

	Solo Ltd.	Mio Ltd.

Efficiency

Net asset turnover

$$= \frac{\text{Sales}}{\text{Net assets}}$$

$$= \frac{7,880}{6,200} \qquad 1.27 \times$$

$$= \frac{4,480}{4,520} \qquad\qquad\qquad 0.99 \times$$

Fixed asset turnover

$$= \frac{\text{Sales}}{\text{Fixed assets}}$$

$$= \frac{7,880}{6,120} \qquad 1.3 \times$$

$$= \frac{4,480}{3,280} \qquad\qquad\qquad 1.4 \times$$

Debtor collection period

$$= \frac{\text{Debtors}}{\text{Sales}} \times 365$$

$$= \frac{1,360}{7,880} \times 365 \qquad 63 \text{ days}$$

$$= \frac{3,160}{4,480} \times 365 \qquad\qquad\qquad 257 \text{ days}$$

Investment

Capital gearing ratio

$$\frac{\text{Debt capital}}{\text{Debt capital} + \text{equity capital}} \times 100$$

$$= \frac{1,760}{6,200} \times 100 \qquad 28.4\%$$

$$= \frac{560}{4,520} \times 100 \qquad\qquad\qquad 12.4\%$$

10.6

Zork plc
Report on the performance of Bryzzen plc and Calleva plc
Prepared by (name)
Date

Introduction
This report has been prepared following the decision of the board of Zork plc to review the performance of Bryzzen plc and Calleva plc (hereafter Bryzzen and Calleva). The sources of information for this report are the financial statements of Bryzzen and Calleva for the year ended 31 March 20X5 and the Manufacturers of Office Furniture Trade Association (MOFTA) report of April 20X5. Appendix one contains ratios derived from the 20X5 accounts.

Analysis
A summary of the ratio analysis is as follows:

	Bryzzen	Calleva	Industry average
ROCE	19%	31%	19%
Net profit %	21%	23%	21%
Fixed asset turnover	1.3 ×	1.5 ×	–
Net asset turnover	0.9 ×	1.3 ×	0.9 ×
Current ratio	1.6 :1	1.4 :1	1.7 :1
Capital gearing ratio	13%	43%	28%
Interest cover	12 ×	5 ×	–
Value added Per employee	£21,962	£28,731	£23,500

Bryzzen achieves a return on capital employed and net profit percentage equal to the industry average. Calleva has achieved a higher net profit percentage and a substantially higher ROCE than Bryzzen or the industry. It is not clear whether or not the MOFTA figure of asset turnover relates to fixed or net asset turnover but it is clear that Calleva's superior performance is related to a more efficient use of assets. This is further emphasised by the valued added per employee calculation.

The current ratio reveals that both companies are below the industry average. Calleva has the lowest current ratio but this may reflect the fact that it can operate at lower levels of liquidity due to superior working capital management. This point should be investigated further.

The capital gearing ratios reveal that Bryzzen is below the industry average and could benefit from obtaining further debt capital to finance its future operations. In fact both companies display healthy levels of interest cover suggesting that Calleva could also obtain more debt capital if it chose to do so.

Advice and recommendations
Calleva has produced a better set of financial results than Bryzzen. It is a larger company than Bryzzen; it employs 25% more staff, net assets are 22% higher and sales are 75% higher. Calleva may be benefiting from economies of scale which are not available to Bryzzen. However, it is suggested that Bryzzen should consider methods of reducing its

manufacturing costs which are 79% of sales (if the interest charge is excluded) compared to a value of 77% for Calleva.

Conclusion

The above analysis suggests that Calleva has produced a better set of financial results than Bryzzen and the industry average. It is likely that both companies will have comparable accounting policies because they are members of the same group, however comparisons with the industry average may be distorted because of accounting policy differences and distortions caused to the average by the volatility of trading results within the industry. This is likely given that two companies within the same group can display such different results for the same accounting period. There are a number of other limitations to ratio analysis as an interpretive technique in terms of the variety of methods which can be used to calculate the statistics.

   The analysis of the results of the two companies has been based on the accounting results of one period only. No information has been given about the trend of historical results or about non accounting factors such as staff morale and brand loyalty which might have affected the financial results.

Appendix One   Ratio calculations

	Bryzzen	Calleva

ROCE

$$= \frac{\text{Profit before interest and tax}}{\text{Share capital, reserves and loan capital}} \times 100$$

$$= \frac{1,332 + 120}{7,624} \times 100 \qquad 19\%$$

$$= \frac{2,320 + 560}{9,274} \times 100 \qquad\qquad\qquad 31\%$$

Net profit percentage

$$= \frac{\text{Net profit}}{\text{Sales}} \times 100$$

$$= \frac{1,332 + 120}{7,010} \times 100 \qquad 21\%$$

$$= \frac{2,320 + 560}{12,294} \times 100 \qquad\qquad\qquad 23\%$$

NB. The net profit used above is profit before interest and tax.

Fixed asset turnover

$$= \quad \frac{\text{Sales}}{\text{Fixed assets}}$$

$$= \quad \frac{7,010}{5,270} \qquad\qquad 1.3 \text{ times}$$

$$= \quad \frac{12,294}{7,938} \qquad\qquad 1.5 \text{ times}$$

Net asset turnover

$$= \quad \frac{\text{Sales}}{\text{Net assets}}$$

$$= \quad \frac{7,010}{7,624} \qquad\qquad 0.9 \text{ times}$$

$$= \quad \frac{12,294}{9,274} \qquad\qquad 1.3 \text{ times}$$

Current ratio

$$= \quad \frac{\text{Current assets}}{\text{Current liabilities}}$$

$$= \quad \frac{6,390}{4,036} \qquad\qquad 1.6 :1$$

$$\frac{4,700}{3,364} \qquad\qquad 1.4 :1$$

Capital gearing ratio

$$= \quad \frac{\text{Debt capital}}{\text{Debt capital + equity capital}} \times 100$$

$$= \quad \frac{1,000}{7,624} \times 100 \qquad\qquad 13\%$$

$$= \quad \frac{4,000}{9,274} \times 100 \qquad\qquad 43\%$$

Interest cover

$$= \quad \frac{\text{Profit before interest and tax}}{\text{Interest charge}} \times 100$$

$$= \quad \frac{1,332 + 120}{120} \qquad\qquad 12 \text{ times}$$

$$= \quad \frac{2,320 + 560}{560} \qquad\qquad 5 \text{ times}$$

Value added per employee

$$\frac{\text{Sales—materials and plant hire}}{\text{No. of employees}}$$

$$=\qquad \frac{4,166}{190}\qquad\qquad\qquad\qquad £21,962$$

$$=\qquad \frac{6,838}{238}\qquad\qquad\qquad\qquad £28,731$$

CHAPTER TWELVE

12.1   Apportionment of overhead expenses

Cost	Basis	Total	Department 1	2	3
			£	£	£
Rent	Floor space	20,529	9,238	7,185	4,106
Depreciation of machinery	Machine value	900	400	200	300
Rates	Floor space	5,176	2,329	1,812	1,035
Canteen expenses	No. of employees	384	150	180	54
Machinery Power	Horse power	4,335	2,853	110	1,372
		31,324	14,970	9,487	6,867

12.2   Memo

To: Finance director
From: (author's name)
Date:
Subject: Overhead allocation and apportionment

My advice is as follows:

Cost classification	Basis of allocation/apportionment.
Telephone	Apportionment on the basis of number of handsets or telephone points. If this information is not easily available, a crude measure of apportionment could be floor area.
Depreciation of machinery	Apportionment on the basis of machine value.
Rent and rates	Apportionment on the basis of floor area.
Factory power	Apportionment on the basis of machine hours.
Light and heat	Apportionment on the basis of floor area.

Indirect wages Allocation on the basis of specific employees or apportionment on the basis of employee numbers.

Canteen expenses Apportionment on the basis of number of employees.

12.3 Shadowlands Ltd.

Cost classification

Cost	Classification
Telephone charges	Indirect expenses
Wages of machinists	Direct labour
Lubricant for sewing machines	Indirect materials
Cost of fabric	Direct materials
Royalty	Direct expense

12.4 1.

Perelandra Ltd.
Overhead analysis sheet
for the year ended 31 December 20X2

Cost	Basis code	Total £	Machining £	Department assembly £	Finishing £
Indirect wages and salaries	(a)	1,347,072	361,062	716,910	269,100
Rent	(b)	38,056,500	17,125,425	13,319,775	7,611,300
Rates	(b)	10,352,700	4,658,715	3,623,445	2,070,540
Light and heat	(b)	2,956,050	1,330,222	1,034,618	591,210
Machinery power	(c)	8,671,800	5,636,670	216,795	2,818,335
Depreciation	(d)	1,800,000	1,125,000	135,000	540,000
Canteen expenses	(e)	768,000	299,520	360,960	107,520
		63,952,122	30,536,614	19,407,503	14,008,005

Key to basis code:
(a) Allocated
(b) Floor space occupied
(c) HP of machinery
(d) Value of machinery
(e) Number of employees

2. Overhead absorption rates

	Machining	Assembly	Finishing
Allocated and apportioned overheads per analysis sheet	30,536,614	19,407,503	14,008,005
No. of machine hours	400,000		180,000
No. of labour hours		280,000	
Overhead absorption rates	£76.34	£69.31	£77.82

Workings

1. Apportionment bases

	Total	Machining	Assembly	Finishing
No. of machine hours	326,000	200,000	36,000	90,000
%	100%	61%	11%	28%
No. of labour hours	275,000	100,000	140,000	35,000
%	100%	36%	51%	13%
Value of machinery (£'000s)	1,200	750	90	360
%	100%	62.5%	7.5%	30%
Floor space occupied	4,000	1,800	1,400	800
%	100%	45%	35%	20%
No. of employees	128	50	60	18
%	100%	39%	47%	14%

2. Overhead absorption rate bases

Machining	Assembly	Finishing
machine hours	labour hours	machine hours

It has been assumed that the number of hours spent in each department is an indication of relative activity. Thus, where machine hours are higher than labour hours, machine hours are an appropriate absorption base.

12.5

Roundup Ltd.
Unit cost of product 507 Alpha

			£	£
Direct materials				800

Direct labour costs:

Dept	Hours	Wage rate		
A	40	£7	280	
B	60	£5	300	
C	15	£8	120	
				700
				1,500

Overhead costs:

Dept	Hours	Overhead rate		
A	40	£75	3,000	
B	60	£70	4,200	
C	15	£80	1,200	
				8,400
Unit cost				9,900

12.6

Lewis Ltd.
Unit cost of contract WPO 2751

			£	£
Direct materials				1,600.00

Direct labour costs:

Dept	Hours	Rate		
X	30	£7.72	231.60	
Y	10	£7.00	70.00	
Z	5	£5.00	25.00	
				326.60
				1,926.60

Overhead costs:

Dept	Hours	Rate		
X	30	£3.70	111.00	
Y	10	£3.31	33.10	
Z	5	£3.00	15.00	
				159.10
Unit cost				2,085.70

Workings

1. Hourly wage rates per department:

	Department		
	X	Y	Z
Direct wage cost (£)	772,000	420,000	200,000
Direct labour hours	100,000	60,000	40,000
Wage rates per hour (£)	7.72	7	5

2. Overhead analysis sheet and absorption rates:

Cost	Basis code	Total	Department		
			X	Y	Z
Repairs & maintenance	(a)	124,000	84,000	20,000	20,000
Depreciation	(b)	80,000	34,000	28,000	18,000
Consumable supplies	(c)	18,000	9,000	5,400	3,600
Wage-related costs	(d)	174,000	96,500	52,500	25,000
Indirect labour	(c)	180,000	90,000	54,000	36,000
Canteen expenses	(e)	60,000	30,000	18,000	12,000
Rates and insurance	(f)	52,000	26,000	20,800	5,200
		688,000	369,500	198,700	119,800
Direct labour hours			100,000	60,000	40,000
Overhead absorption rates			£3.70	£3.31	£3.00

Basis code:
(a) Allocation
(b) Plant cost
(c) Direct labour hours
(d) 12.5% direct wage costs
(e) No. of direct workers
(f) Floor area

12.7   Bascombe Ltd.
              Re-apportionment of service centre costs

	Department				
	1	2	3	4	5
per question (£'000s)	90	70	320	120	68
Re-apportionment Dept 4	30	24	54	(120)	12
	120	94	374	–	80
Dept 5	24	32	24	–	(80)
	144	126	398	–	–

12.8

1. Overhead analysis sheet and absorption rates

				Department			
Cost	Basis code	Total	A	B	C	X	Y
Overheads	(a)	3,550	1,400	850	600	400	300
Rent and rates	(b)	6,400	3,000	1,800	600	600	400
Machine insurance	(c)	3,000	1,500	625	500	250	125
Telephone	(b)	1,600	750	450	150	150	100
Depreciation	(c)	9,000	4,500	1,875	1,500	750	375
Supervisor's salary	(d)	12,000	6,400	3,600	2,000	–	–
Heat and light	(b)	3,200	1,500	900	300	300	200
		38,750	19,050	10,100	5,650	2,450	1,500
Re-apportionment of service dept overheads			1,225	612	613	(2,450)	
			300	450	750		(1,500)
			20,575	11,162	7,013	–	–
Direct labour Hours			1,600	900	500		
Overhead Absorption Rates			£12.86	£12.40	£14.03		

Basis code:
(a) Allocation
(b) Floor area
(c) Value of machinery
(d) Direct labour hours

2. Product costs

			Machine	
			123 £	124 £
Direct material			77.00	54.00
Direct labour:				
Dept	Hours	Rate		
A	20	£3.80	76.00	
B	12	£3.50	42.00	
C	10	£3.40	34.00	
A	16	£3.80		60.80
B	10	£3.50		35.00
C	14	£3.40		47.60
			229.00	197.40

Overhead costs:

Dept	Hours	Rate	£	£
A	20	£12.86	257.20	
B	12	£12.40	148.80	
C	10	£14.03	140.30	
A	16	£12.86		205.76
B	10	£12.40		124.00
C	14	£14.03		196.42
Total costs			775.30	723.58

3. Selling prices

	Machine	
	123	*124*
	£	£
Cost	775.30	723.58
Selling price = cost × 100/75	1,033.73	964.77

12.9 1.

XLS Ltd.
Overhead Analysis sheet
for the year ended 31 December 20X9

Cost	Basis code	Total £'000s	Department A £'000s	B £'000s	C £'000s	D £'000s
Indirect wages	(a)	48	20	12	16	–
Indirect materials	(a)	94	30	8	16	40
Power	(b)	204	160	20	24	–
Light and heat	(c)	20	10	4	3	3
Depreciation	(d)	14	8	3.2	1.2	1.6
Rent and Rates	(c)	50	25	10	7.5	7.5
Personnel	(e)	126	36	24	48	18
		556	289	81.2	115.7	70.1
Re-apportionment of service dept costs			42.06	14.02	14.02	(70.1)
			331.06	95.22	129.72	–

Basis code:
(a) Allocation
(b) Machine hours
(c) Floor area
(d) Value of assets
(e) No. of employees

2.   Overhead absorption rates

	Department		
	A	*B*	*C*
Per overhead analysis sheet (£'000s)	331.06	95.22	129.72
Machine hours ('000s hours)	80		
Direct labour hours ('000s hours)		16	32
Absorption rates per:			
Machine hour	£4.15		
Direct labour hour		£5.95	£4.05

3.   Cost estimate

	£	£
Direct materials (5,000 + 800 + 400)		6,200

Direct labour cost:

Dept	Hours	Rate*		
A	1,600	£5	8,000	
B	700	£4	2,800	
C	280	£4.50	1,260	
				12,060
				18,260

Overhead costs:

Dept	Hours	Rate		
A	1,600	£4.15	6,640	
B	700	£5.95	4,165	
C	280	£4.05	1,134	
				11,939
				30,199

* Direct labour rate = cost/number of hours.

   Dept A: £120,000/24,000 hours = £5.
   Dept B: £64,000/16,000 hours = £4.
   Dept C: £144,000/32,000 hours = £4.50.

CHAPTER THIRTEEN

13.1

Wood Ltd.
Variable costing statement

	Output 15,000 units £'000s	Output 30,000 units £'000s
Sales revenue	300	600
Variable costs		
Direct wages	60	120
Direct materials	135	270
Manufacturing overheads	15	30
Contribution	90	180
Fixed costs	25	25
Profit	65	155

13.2 Drury Ltd.

1. Number of units to break-even

	£
Sales revenue per unit	200
Contribution per unit: 200 × 20%	40
Fixed costs	600,000

Number of units to break-even =

$$\frac{\text{Fixed costs}}{\text{Contribution per unit}} = \frac{600,000}{40} = 15,000 \text{ units}$$

2. Number of units to make a profit of £400,000

$$\frac{\text{Fixed costs + Desired profit}}{\text{Contribution per unit}} = \frac{600,000 + 400,000}{40} = 25,000 \text{ units}$$

13.3   Pendrill Plc

1.   Break-even point in terms of sales revenue

(a)   Variable costing statement
                    for the year ended 31 December 20X3

	per unit £	4m units £'000s
Sales revenue	0.25	1,000
Variable costs (Sales − Contribution)	0.15	600
Contribution (Sales × 40%)	0.10	400
Fixed costs (Contribution − Net profit)	0.05	200
Net profit	0.05	200

(b)   Break-even sales revenue

$$\frac{\text{Fixed costs}}{\text{PV Ratio}} = \frac{200,000}{40\%} = £500,000$$

2.   Break even point in 20X4 if fixed costs increase by 50%

	£
20X3 fixed costs	200,000
50% increase	100,000
20X4 fixed costs	300,000

Break-even units:

$$\frac{\text{Fixed costs}}{\text{Contribution per unit}} = \frac{300,000}{0.10} = \text{3m units}$$

13.4   Advice to directors of Weetman Ltd.

The options may be summarized as follows:

	Current Position per unit £	Option 1 per unit £	Option 2 per unit £	Option 3 per unit £
Sales revenue	10	9	10	10
Variable costs	7	7	8.5	7
Contribution	3	2	1.5	3
Fixed costs (£'000s)	120	120	120	160
Number of units to break even ('000s)	40	60	80	53

It would seem that, with the available information, option 3 would be the one to adopt as this requires the smaller increase in sales volume in order for the company to break even. In fact, if sales were increased by 30%, as a result of choosing option 3, the company would earn a profit of £35,000 (65,000 units × £3 contribution less fixed costs of £160,000).

13.5   Acre Ltd.

The effect of ceasing to produce product B would be as follows:

	£'000s
Loss of contribution	30
Savings in fixed costs	10
Net loss	20

Profits for the company would now be:

Product	A	C	Total
Contribution	40	50	90
Fixed costs (110 − 10)			100
Profit/(loss)			(10)

13.6 Brittan Plc

Contribution per unit of product and per labour hour:

	Product		
	X	Y	Z
	£	£	£
Sales revenue	100	110	70
Less variable costs:			
Direct materials	16	31	12
Direct labour	24	36	12
Variable overheads	10	10	10
Contribution per unit	50	33	36
Number of labour hours per unit	2	3	1
Contribution per labour hour	25	11	36

Product Z has the highest contribution per labour hour. The company should, therefore, produce as much of this product as possible. Product X has the next highest contribution per labour hour. This should be produced in preference to product Y.

Brittan Plc
Production budget
June 20X1

	No. of units of production	*No. of hours requ'd*	*No. of hours remaining*	*£'000s Contribution*
Available hours			47,000	
Product Z:				
15,000 units	15,000	15,000	32,000	540(a)
Product X:				
10,000 units	10,000	20,000	12,000	500
Product Y:				
4,000 units	4,000(b)	12,000	–	132
Total contribution				1,172
Fixed costs				900
Profit				272

(a) 15,000 hours × £36 per hour
(b) 12,000 hours will only allow the production of 4,000 units

13.7
Berry Plc
Schedule of contribution earned per display case per week

	Contribution earned		
	One	Two	Incremental
Range	case	cases	contribution
	£	£	£
Classic	675(a)	1,250(b)	575
Elegance	700	1,260	560
Sport	600	1,150	550
Continental	800	1,300	500
Hi Tech	500	1,020	520

(a) £3,375 × 20%
(b) (£3,125 × 2) x 20%

Optimum allocation of shop space
(The suggested answer to this question is presented in the form of a tutorial note.)
If we assume that Berry Plc is a profit maximizer, the optimum allocation of shop space may be found by choosing a combination of display cases with the highest contribution.
In respect of each range, consider the contribution earned from one display case and the incremental contribution earned from the second display case. If we choose the highest value of contribution and then the next highest, and so on, we will end up with the following contribution from display cases:

Range	Contribution
	£
Contribution from one display case	
Continental	800
Elegance	700
Classic	675
Sport	600
Incremental contribution	
Classic	575
Elegance	560
Sport	550
Total contribution	4,460

Thus, Berry Plc should be advised that contribution will be maximized if space is allocated to two cases of the Classic, Elegance, and Sport ranges, and one case of the Continental range.
A further assumption that we need to make is that the company will not be disadvantaged in marketing or production terms by discontinuing the sale of the Hi Tech range.
Answers may also contain points relating to the underlying assumptions of cost volume profit analysis.

13.8   Advice to Glautier Ltd. in respect of Theta campaign

	Without promotion £	*With promotion* £
Sales revenue per unit	5.60	4.48
Variable costs (5.60 − 2.52)	3.08	3.08
Contribution per unit	2.52	1.40
Units sold per week	4,800	12,000
	£	£
Total weekly contribution	12,096	16,800
Additional fixed costs	–	2,700
	12,096	14,100

Weekly sales volume for promotion to break-even

$$= \frac{\text{Current level of weekly contribution} + \text{Additional fixed costs}}{\text{Revised contribution per unit}}$$

$$= \frac{12,096 + 2,700}{1.40}$$

$$= \quad 10,569 \text{ units}$$

If the promotion is considered in purely financial terms, the company should be advised to undertake the promotion, as it results in an incremental increase in profit of £14,100 − £12,096 = £2,004 per week. In addition, the predicted sales level is above the break-even point for the promotion. The company may wish to reduce the selling price further in order to boost sales.

Other factors to be considered would include:

- the accuracy of the financial predictions
- the limitations of cost volume profit analysis
- the longer term effect of the promotion
- the impact of the promotion on sales of other products
- the impact of the promotion on staff and suppliers.

CHAPTER FOURTEEN

14.1   1. *Master budget*

When budgets for organizational sub-units have been co-ordinated and reviewed, a master budget is produced. This can be seen as a summary of the sub-unit budgets in their final form. The master budget is often presented as a budgeted profit and loss account, balance sheet and cash flow schedule.

2. *Stages in the budget preparation process:*

(a) Identification of the principal budget factor:

This is the factor which limits the activities of the business. Examples of principal budget factors are sales demand and the availability of materials. Once the principal budget factor has been identified, all the elements of the master budget must reflect this constraint.

(b) Preparation of business sub-unit budgets:
The starting point is the preparation of the budget for the business sub-unit most closely associated with the principal budget factor. If sales demand is the principal budget factor, the sales budget is produced first. Other sub-unit budgets are produced in a logical sequence, i.e. the production budget must normally be prepared before the materials purchase budget is prepared.

(c) Co-ordination and revision of budgets:
Once sub-unit budgets are prepared, they are reviewed and amended to remove errors and inconsistencies.

(d) Preparation of the master budget.

Once the budget has been prepared for the business, it is used to compare actual results with budgeted results. In addition, the budgetary targets should be reviewed in the light of changing operating conditions.

14.2   The advantages to an organization of preparing a budget

1. Managers are encouraged to consider organizational objectives. In practice, organizations will have a number of objectives. The process of preparing a budget allows managers to focus upon these objectives.

2. Managers are encouraged to plan output targets and resource allocations so as to achieve organizational objectives.

3. The preparation of budgetary targets provides an effective resource for the communication of the results of business activity across disciplinary boundaries.

4. The co-ordination of business sub-unit activity is assisted by the preparation and dissemination of budgetary targets.

5. Control of operational activity can be maintained by comparing budgetary targets to actual results.

6. Employees may be motivated to improve their performance as budgets will provide target levels of attainment for collective and individual effort.

14.3   1. *Zero based budgeting (ZBB)*
This method of budgeting requires budgeted expenditures to be determined from a zero base, as it is assumed that there is no initial commitment to incur expenditure in respect of any activity.

2. *The preparation of budgets using ZBB*
(a) Decision packages are defined and quantified. These identify and describe specific activities from a number of perspectives. The status quo is questioned. Alternative methods of getting the same job done are analysed and compared.
(b) Decision packages are evaluated and ranked. A consensus about the optimal combination of decision packages is reached.
(c) Resources are allocated based on the chosen combinations of decision packages.

3. Advantages and disadvantages of ZBB

Advantages	Disadvantages
Efficient resource allocation	Time and effort required to define and quantify decision packages
Encourages managers to consider alternative methods of completing tasks	Assumption that current methods are inefficient
	Individuals and organizations are often highly resistant to change

14.4 Flexible budget

A flexible budget is one which has been adjusted to account for changes in output volume. It can be compared with a fixed budget which is based on an estimated volume of output and is not adjusted when actual activity differs from budgeted activity.

In order to produce a flexible budget, fixed and variable costs must be identified. The variable elements of budgeted income and expenditures are then adjusted to reflect actual output levels.

14.5 1. *Responsibility accounting*

Responsibility accounting is a management accounting system based upon the idea that named individuals are made responsible for items of expenditure or income in respect of defined sub-units of an organization. These organizational sub-units are known as responsibility centres.

2. *Types of responsibility centre*

(a) Responsibility cost centre:

In a responsibility cost centre, individuals are responsible for costs incurred.

(b) Profit centre:

In this type of responsibility centre, individuals are responsible for costs and revenues.

(c) Investment centre:

Individuals given responsibility for an investment centre are responsible for costs, revenues, and capital expenditure.

14.6

MacHeath Ltd.

Sales budget for the year ended 31 December 20X9

Product	Demand	Unit selling price	Sales value
	Units	£	£'000s
A	18,000	128	2,304
B	16,000	176	2,816
C	24,000	264	6,336
			11,456

14.7

Peachum Ltd.
Raw materials usage budget
for the year ended 30 December 20X7

	Units
Sales demand	1,125
Less opening stock of finished goods	(225)
Add closing stock of finished goods	100
Number of units to be produced	1,000

Material requirements:	kg
Material J167: 1,000 × 3 kg	3,000
Material L345: 1,000 × 4 kg	4,000
	7,000

Note

In order to calculate the raw materials purchases budget, we will need to obtain information in respect of stocks of raw materials at the start and end of the budget period.

14.8

Lockit Ltd.
Cash budget for the six months ended 31 December 20X6

	Jul £'000s	*Aug* £'000s	*Sept* £'000s	*Oct* £'000s	*Nov* £'000s	*Dec* £'000s	*Total* £'000s
Receipts	120	600	800	400	700	900	3,520
Payments:							
Materials	50	200	300	200	500	100	1,350
Wages	220	240	250	250	275	290	1,525
Overhead expenses	30	25	25	30	35	40	185
	300	465	575	480	810	430	3,060
Net receipts	(180)	135	225	(80)	(110)	470	460
Opening balance	50	(130)	5	230	150	40	50
Closing balance	(130)	5	230	150	40	510	510

14.9

Polly Ltd.
Purchases budget
for the year ended 31 March 20X5

	Material A kg	*Material B* kg
Materials requirement from production budget	68,000	224,000
Less opening stock of raw materials	(4,400)	(24,000)
Add closing stock of raw materials	2,400	4,000
Number of units to purchase	66,000	204,000
	£	£
Cost per unit	6	4
Cost of materials	396,000	816,000
Total cost of materials	£1,212,000	

14.10

Lucy Ltd.
Budgeted profit for the year ended 31 August 20X4

		£	£
Sales	(W5)		11,253,456
Less variable costs:			
Direct materials	(W1)	2,615,200	
Direct wages	(W2)	4,576,600	
Product overheads	(W3)	1,515,320	
Non-production overheads	(W4)	430,760	
			9,137,880
Contribution			2,115,576
Less fixed costs	(W4)		240,000
Profit			1,875,576

Workings

(W1)   Direct materials

	£
Capacity level of 55%	1,692,400
Increase	307,600
Capacity level of 65%	2,000,000

A 10% increase in capacity results in a cost increase of £307,600. The direct material cost at 85% capacity is therefore:

	£
Direct material cost at 75% capacity	2,307,600
Increase	307,600
Direct material cost at 85% capacity	2,615,200

(W2)   Direct wages

Costs increase by £538,300 for a 10% increase in capacity. At 85% capacity, the costs will be:

	£
£4,038,300 + £538,300 =	4,576,600

(W3)   Production overheads

Costs increase by £107,660 for a 10% increase in capacity. At 85% capacity, the costs will be:

	£
£1,407,660 + £107,660 =	1,515,320

(W4)   Non-production overheads and fixed costs

Non-production overheads are a semi-variable cost. The variable element of the costs increases by £15,380 for a 10% increase in capacity. At 85% capacity the costs will be:

	£
Total non-production overheads at 75% capacity	655,380
Add increase in variable element	15,380
Total non-production overheads at 85% capacity	670,760
Less fixed costs	240,000
Variable costs at 85% capacity	430,760

(W5)   Sales

			£
Total costs	5/6	9,137,880 + 240,000	9,377,880
Plus profit	1/6		1,875,576
Sales Value	6/6		11,253,456

CHAPTER FIFTEEN

15.1   Wyngarde Ltd.: production cost variances

		Standard cost £	Actual cost £	Variance: favourable/(adverse) £
Materials	(W2)	27,000	26,600	400
Labour	(W4)	15,000	16,800	(1,800)
Machining	(W6)	18,800	18,900	(100)
Overheads	(W7)	9,200	8,800	400
		70,000	71,100	(1,100)

Workings

(W1)   Materials used

	Budget kg	Actual kg
Product A (8 kg × 1200 units)	9,600	
(8 kg × 1000 units)		8,000
Product B (10 kg × 800 units)	8,000	
(10 kg × 1000 units)		10,000
	17,600	18,000

(W2)   Standard cost of materials

Budgeted cost	£26,400
Budgeted usage (W1)	17,600 kg

Standard cost per kg

$$= \frac{£26,400}{17,600 \text{ kg}} \qquad £1.50 \text{ per kg}$$

Standard cost of output

$$= 18,000 \text{ kg} \times £1.50 \qquad £27,000$$

(W3)   Labour hours used in production

	Budget hrs	Actual hrs
Product A (2 hrs × 1200 units)	2,400	
(2 hrs × 1000 units)		2,000
Product B (4hrs × 800 units)	3,200	
(4 hrs × 1000 units)		4,000
	5,600	6,000

(W4)   Standard cost of labour

Budgeted cost	£14,000
Budgeted usage (W3)	5,600 hrs

Standard cost per hour

$$= \frac{£14,000}{5,600 \text{ hrs}} \qquad £2.50 \text{ per hour}$$

Standard cost of output
= 6,000 hrs × £2.50   £15,000

(W5)   Machining hours used in production

	Budget hrs	Actual hrs
Product A (1 hr × 1,200 units)	1,200	
(1 hr × 1,000 units)		1,000
Product B (0.5 hrs × 800 units)	400	
(0.5 hrs × 1,000 units)		500
	1,600	1,500

(W6)   Standard cost of machining hours

		£
Budgeted cost		19,200
Budgeted usage (W5)	1,600 hrs	
Variable element of machining cost		
= 1,600 hrs × £4 per hr		6,400
Fixed element of machining cost		12,800

	£
Standard cost of output	
Fixed element of machining cost	12,800
Variable element of machining cost	
= 1,500 (W5) hrs × £4 per hr	6,000
	18,800

(W7)   Standard cost of overheads

		£
Budgeted cost		8,800
Budgeted labour hours (W3)	5,600	
Variable element of overhead cost		
= 5,600 hrs × £1 per hr		5,600
Fixed element of overhead cost		3,200

	£
Standard cost of output	
Fixed element of overhead cost	3,200
Variable element of overhead cost	
= 6,000 (W3) hrs × £1 per hr	6,000
	9,200

15.2   Cain Ltd.: production cost variances

Materials
Total variance
= Standard cost of output − Actual cost of output

	£
Standard cost of output	
16,400 packs × 2 kg × £2	65,600
Actual cost of output	
42,000 kg × £1.96	82,320
Total adverse variance	(16,720)

Price variance   £
= Standard price − Actual price
  × Actual quantity
= (£2 − £1.96) × 42,000   1,680

Usage variance
= Standard quantity − Actual quantity
  × Standard price
= (16,400 packs × 2 kg − 42,000 kg)
  × £2
= (32,800 − 42,000) × £2   (18,400)
Total adverse variance   (16,720)

Labour
Total variance
= Standard cost of output − Actual cost of output

	£
Standard cost of output	
16,400 packs × 2 hrs × £4.40	144,320
Actual cost of output	126,400
Total favourable variance	17,920

Rate variance   £
= Standard rate − Actual rate
  × Actual hours
= (£4.40 − £4) × 31,600   12,640

Usage variance
= Standard hours − Actual hours
  × Standard rate
= (16,400 packs × 2 hrs − 31,600)
  × £4.40
= (32,800 − 31,600) × £4.40   5,280
Total favourable variance   17,920

Variable overheads
Total variance
= Standard cost of output − Actual cost of output

	£
Standard cost of output	
16,400 packs × 2 hrs × £2	65,600
Actual cost of output	28,500
Total favourable variance	37,100

Expenditure variance   £
= (Standard rate × Actual hours)
     − Actual cost

= (£2 × 31,600) − 28,500	34,700

Efficiency variance
= Standard hours − Actual hours
     × Standard rate
= (16,400 packs × 2 hrs − 31,600)
     × £2

= (32,800 − 31,600) × £2	2,400
Total favourable variance	37,100

15.3   Fabbianni Ltd.: sales variances

Total variance
= Actual contribution − budgeted contribution

	£
Actual contribution	
£16 × 240 units	3,840
Budgeted contribution	
£20 × 200 units	4,000
Total adverse variance	(160)

Sales margin price variance   £
= Actual contribution − (Standard
     unit contribution × Actual sales volume)

= £3,840 − (£20 × 240 units)	
= £3,840 − £4,800	(960)

Sales margin volume variance
= (Standard unit contribution × Actual
     sales volume) − Budgeted contribution

= (£20 × 240 units) − £4,000	
= £4,800 − £4,000	800
Total adverse variance	(160)

NB In this question actual contribution equals actual sales revenue minus standard variable costs.

15.4   Jason Ltd.: sales and production cost variances

Sales variances

Sales margin price variance   £
= Actual contribution − (Standard
  unit contribution × Actual sales volume)

= £176,000 (W4) − [£50 (W3) × 4,400 units)

= £176,000 − £220,000   (44,000)

Sales margin volume variance
= (Standard unit contribution × Actual
  sales volume) − Budgeted contribution

= £220,000 − £200,000 (W3)   20,000

Total adverse variance   (24,000)

Production cost variances

Materials
Price variance   £
= Standard price − Actual price
  × Actual quantity

= (£10 − £9) × (16 kg × 4,400 units)

= £1 × 70,400 kg   70,400

Usage variance
= Standard quantity − Actual quantity
  × Standard price

= (4,400 units × 14 kg − 70,400 kg)
  × £10

= (61,600 − 70,400) × £10   (88,000)

Total adverse variance   (17,600)

Labour

Rate variance   £
= Standard rate − Actual rate
  × Actual hours

= (£5 − £6) × (8 hrs × 4,400 units)

= £1 × 35,200   (35,200)

Usage variance
= Standard hours − Actual hours
  × Standard rate

= (4,400 units × 10 hrs − 35,200)
  × £5

= (44,000 − 35,200) × £5   44,000

Total favourable variance   8,800

Variable overheads

	£
Expenditure variance = (Standard rate × Actual hours) − Actual cost	
= (£6 × 35,200) − £130,000	
= £211,200 − £130,000	81,200
Efficiency variance = Standard hours − Actual hours × Standard rate	
= (4,400 units × 10 hrs − 35,200) × £6	
= (44,000 − 35,200) × £6	52,800
Total favourable variance	134,000

Workings

		Budget £	Actual £
(W1)	*Sales revenue*		
	£300 × 4,000 units	1,200,000	
	£290 × 4,400 units		1,276,000
(W2)	*Variable cost*	Budget £	Actual £
	Direct materials		
	£140 × 4,000 units	560,000	
	£144 × 4,400 units		633,600
	Direct wages		
	£50 × 4,000 units	200,000	
	£48 × 4,400 units		211,200
	Overheads		
	£60 × 4,000 units	240,000	
	per question		130,000
		1,000,000	974,800
	Variable costs per unit	£250	£221.54
(W3)	*Budgeted contribution*	£	
	Sales revenue (W1)	1,200,000	
	Variable cost (W2)	1,000,000	
		200,000	
	per unit £200,000/4,000	£50	

(W4)   *Actual contribution*

The actual contribution for the purposes of calculating the sales margin price variance is sales revenue minus *standard variable costs*. This is because the sales department is responsible for sales price and sales volume, and not production cost. The 'actual' contribution is therefore:

	£
Sales revenue (W1)	1,276,000
Standard variable cost	
= 4,400 units × £250 (W2)	
=	1,100,000
	176,000

CHAPTER SIXTEEN

16.1

Malacandra Ltd.
Net present value calculation

Year	Cash flow £'000s	Discount factor	Present value £'000s
0	(5,000)	1	(5,000)
1	1,600	0.8696	1,391
2	1,700	0.7591	1,290
3	1,660	0.6575	1,091
4	2,400	0.5718	1,372
5	1,400	0.4972	696
Net present value			840

16.2 Meldilorn Ltd.

Project A:

Year	Cash flow £'000s	Discount factor	Present value £'000s
0	400	1	(400)
1	160	0.8475	136
2	140	0.7182	101
3	130	0.6086	79
4	120	0.5158	62
5	130 (110 + 20)	0.4371	57
Net present value			35

Project B:

Year	Cash flow £'000s	Discount factor	Present value £'000s
0	460	1	(460)
1	200	0.8475	169
2	140	0.7182	101
3	100	0.6086	61
4	100	0.5158	52
5	130 (100 + 30)	0.4371	57
Net present value			(20)

The company should be advised to accept project A as this has a positive net present value. The company may wish to consider alternative projects with a higher positive net present value than project A.

16.3 Internal rate of return

Year	Cash flow £'000s	Discount factors 5%	Discount factors 10%	Present values 5% £'000s	Present values 10% £'000s
0	(2,900)	1	1	(2,900)	(2,900)
1	460	0.9524	0.9091	438	418
2	740	0.9070	0.8264	671	612
3	1,200	0.8638	0.7513	1,037	902
4	840	0.8227	0.6830	691	574
5	220	0.7835	0.6209	172	137
Net present values				109	(257)

$$\text{IRR} = 0.05 + \left[\frac{109}{109 + 257} \times (0.10 - 0.05) \right]$$

$$= 0.05 + [0.2978 \times 0.05]$$

$$= 0.06489 \quad \text{or} \quad 6.5\%$$

16.4

Dr Ransome
Internal rate of return calculation

Year	Cash flow £'000s	Discount factors 15%	Discount factors 20%	Present values 15% £'000s	Present values 20% £'000s
0	(950)	1	1	(950)	(950)
1	100	0.8696	0.8333	87	83
2	400	0.7561	0.6944	302	278
3	450	0.6575	0.5787	296	260
4	450	0.5718	0.4823	257	217
5	150	0.4972	0.4019	75	60
Net present values				67	(52)

$$\text{IRR} = 0.15 + \left[\frac{67}{67 + 52} \times (0.20 - 0.15)\right]$$

$$= 0.15 + [0.5630 \times 0.05]$$
$$= 0.15 + 0.02815$$
$$= 0.17815 \quad \text{or} \quad 18\%$$

16.5   Payback Period

Year	Cash flow £'000s	Cumulative cash flow £'000s
0	(360)	(360)
1	110	(250)
2	130	(120)
3	190	70
4	216	

Year $n = 3$

$$\text{Payback period} = \text{year } n - 1 + \frac{\text{Cumulative cash flow year } n - 1}{\text{Actual cash flow year } n}$$

$$= 2 + \frac{120}{190}$$

$$= 2.63 \text{ years}$$

16.6   1.

Perelandra Ltd.
Payback periods

Year	Project A Cash flow £	cumulative cash flow £	Project B cash flow £	Cumulative cash flow £
0	(2,000)	(2,000)	(20,000)	(20,000)
1	720	(1,280)	4,600	(15,400)
2	576	(704)	5,280	(10,120)
3	692	(12)	6,080	(4,040)
4	828	816	7,000	2,960
5	996		8,040	
n	$=$	4		4
$n - 1$	$=$	3		3
Payback	$=$	$3 + \dfrac{12}{828}$		$3 + \dfrac{4,040}{7,000}$
	$=$	3.01 years		3.58 years

2. *Choice of projects using the payback method*
   The strict application of the payback period suggests that project A is preferred as it has the shortest payback period.

3. *Disadvantages of payback method*
   (a) Cash flows after the payback period are ignored.
   (b) The payback period decision rule ignores the absolute size of cash flows. Note that project B is rejected even though it results in considerably larger cash inflows than project A.
   (c) It ignores the time value of money. This can result in the acceptance of projects with a negative net present value.

16.7   Accounting rate of return (ARR)

$$\text{ARR} = \frac{\text{Average Annual profit}}{\text{Average investment}} \times 100$$

$$= \frac{(200 + 500 + 500 + 400) \times 1/4}{1,000/2} \times 100$$

$$= \frac{400}{500} \times 100$$

$$= 80\%$$

16.8   Treatment of depreciation

1. *Accounting rate of return*
   Depreciation should be reflected in the computation of average annual profit and in the calculation of the average investment.

2. *Payback and net present value*
   These capital investment appraisal methods focus upon cash flows rather than accounting profit. Depreciation should, therefore, be excluded from payback and net present value calculations.

16.9   Lewis Ltd.

1. *Calculations*

		Project Alpha £'000s	Project Beta £'000s	Project Gamma £'000s
(W1)	Net present value	127	15	165
		years	years	years
(W2)	Payback period	2.77	3.2	2.63
		%	%	%
(W3)	Accounting rate of return	28	18.3	39.7

2. *Advice to management*

The decision rules of the capital investment appraisal methods suggest that the projects should be ranked in order of preference as follows:

Preferred project:

Net present value	Gamma—as it has the highest positive net present value
Payback period	Gamma—as it has the lowest payback period
Accounting rate of return	Gamma—as it has the highest ARR

Project Gamma should therefore be chosen.

Workings

(W1)   Net present value calculations

Project Alpha:

Year	Cash flow	Discount factor	Present Value
	£'000s		£'000s
0	(800)	1	(800)
1	320	0.8696	278
2	280	0.7561	212
3	260	0.6575	171
4	240	0.5718	137
5	260	0.4972	129
	Net present value		127

Project Beta:

Year	Cash flow	Discount factor	Present value
	£'000s		£'000s
0	(920)	1	(920)
1	400	0.8696	348
2	280	0.7561	212
3	200	0.6575	132
4	200	0.5718	114
5	260	0.4972	129
	Net present value		15

Project Gamma:

Year	Cash flow	Discount factor	Present value
	£'000s		£'000s
0	(720)	1	(720)
1	220	0.8696	191
2	260	0.7561	197
3	380	0.6575	250
4	432	0.5718	247
Net present value			165

(W2)   Payback periods

	Project Alpha		Project Beta		Project Gamma	
Year	Cash flow	Cumulative cash flow	Cash flow	Cumulative cash flow	Cash flow	Cumulative cash flow
	£	£	£	£	£	£
0	(800)	(800)	(920)	(920)	(720)	(720)
1	320	(480)	400	(520)	220	(500)
2	280	(200)	280	(240)	260	(240)
3	260	60	200	(40)	380	140
4	240		200	160	432	
5	260		260			
n =	3		4		3	
$n-1$ =	2		3		2	
Payback =	$2 + \dfrac{200}{260}$		$3 + \dfrac{40}{200}$		$2 + \dfrac{240}{380}$	
=	2.77 years		3.2 years		2.63 years	

(W3)   Accounting rate of return calculation

1.   Calculation of averaging accounting profit

$$\frac{\text{Accounting}}{\text{profit}} = \frac{\text{Annual}}{\text{cash flow}} - \frac{\text{Annual depreciation}}{\text{charge}}$$

Project Alpha:

Year	Cash flow £'000s	−	Depreciation charge £'000s	=	Account profit £'000s
1	320		160 (800/5)		160
2	280		160		120
3	260		160		100
4	240		160		80
5	260		160		100
					560

Average profit = 560/5 =   112

Project Beta:

Year	Cash flow £'000s	−	Depreciation charge £'000s	=	Account profit £'000s
1	400		184 (920/5)		216
2	280		184		96
3	200		184		16
4	200		184		16
5	260		184		76
					420

Average profit = 420/5 =   84

Project Gamma:

Year	Cash flow £'000s	−	Depreciation charge £'000s	=	Account profit £'000s
1	220		180 (720/4)		40
2	260		180		80
3	380		180		200
4	432		180		252
					572

Average profit = 572/4 =   143

2. Calculation of average investment

Average investment = (Initial − Residual) × 1/2
                          cost   value

There are no residual values for the assets used in projects Alpha, Beta, and Gamma.

Project	Alpha £'000s	Beta £'000s	Gamma £'000s
Average investment	$\frac{800}{2}$	$\frac{920}{2}$	$\frac{720}{2}$
=	400	460	360

3. Calculation of accounting rate of return

$$ARR = \frac{\text{Average annual profit}}{\text{Average investment}} \times 100$$

Project	Alpha	Beta	Gamma
Average annual profits (£000's)	112	84	143
Average investment (£000's)	400	460	360
ARR	28%	18.3%	39.7%

16.10

CSL Ltd.

Payback period

Year	Project 1 Cash flow £'000s	Project 1 Cumulative cash flow £'000s	Project 2 Cash flow £'000s	Project 2 Cumulative cash flow £'000s
0	(1,050)	(1,050)	(1,050)	(1,050)
1	420	(630)	378	(672)
2	350	(280)	308	(364)
3	315	35	273	(91)
4	875		343	252
5	–		728	

year n	=		3	4
year $n-1$	=		2	3

$$\text{Payback} = \text{year } n-1 + \frac{\text{Cumulative cash flow year } n-1}{\text{Actual cash flow year } n}$$

$$\text{Payback} = 2 + \frac{280}{315} \qquad\qquad 3 + \frac{91}{343}$$

$$= 2.89 \text{ years} \qquad\qquad 3.27 \text{ years}$$

Accounting rate of return

		Project 1 £'000s	Project 2 £'000s
Average Profits	=	$\dfrac{280 + 210 + 175 + 245}{4}$	$\dfrac{210 + 140 + 105 + 175 + 350}{5}$
	=	227.5	196
Average investment	=	$\dfrac{1,050}{2}$	$\dfrac{1,050}{2}$
	=	525	525
ARR	=	43.3%	37.3%

Tutorial Note
In this question, the actual accounting profits in respect of the project are given. We do not have to estimate accounting profit by deducting depreciation from cash flows. In fact, the difference between the cash flows and accounting profits in this question is the depreciation charge on the asset used, but CSL Ltd. does not charge depreciation on a consistent basis over the life of the asset. In the final year of ownership, all the outstanding depreciation on the asset is charged against profit.

Net present value

Year	Cash flows		Discount factor	Present values	
	Project 1	Project 2		Project 1	Project 2
	£'000s	£'000s		£'000s	£'000s
0	(1,050)	(1,050)	1	(1,050)	(1,050)
1	420	378	0.8696	365	329
2	350	308	0.7561	265	233
3	315	273	0.6575	207	179
4	875	343	0.5718	500	196
5	–	728	0.4972	–	362
Net present values				287	249

Summary

	Project 1	Project 2
Payback period	2.89 years	3.27 years
Accounting rate of return	43.3%	37.3%
Net present value (£'000s)	287	249

Advice to CSL Ltd.

Project 1 should be chosen. It has a higher net present value and accounting rate of return than project 2. In addition, it has a shorter payback period.

TABLE OF DISCOUNT FACTORS

This table gives the present value of £1 received after n years discounted at r%.

r% n	1	2	3	4	5
1	0.9901	0.9804	0.9709	0.9615	0.9524
2	0.9803	0.9612	0.9426	0.9246	0.9070
3	0.9706	0.9423	0.9151	0.8890	0.8638
4	0.9610	0.9238	0.8885	0.8548	0.8227
5	0.9515	0.9057	0.8626	0.8219	0.7835

r% n	6	7	8	9	10
1	0.9434	0.9346	0.9259	0.9174	0.9091
2	0.8900	0.8734	0.8573	0.8417	0.8264
3	0.8396	0.8163	0.7938	0.7722	0.7513
4	0.7921	0.7629	0.7350	0.7084	0.6830
5	0.7473	0.7130	0.6806	0.6499	0.6209

r% n	11	12	13	14	15
1	0.9009	0.8929	0.8850	0.8772	0.8696
2	0.8116	0.7972	0.7831	0.7695	0.7561
3	0.7312	0.7118	0.6931	0.6750	0.6575
4	0.6587	0.6355	0.6133	0.5921	0.5718
5	0.5935	0.5674	0.5428	0.5194	0.4972

r% n	16	17	18	19	20
1	0.8621	0.8547	0.8475	0.8403	0.8333
2	0.7432	0.7305	0.7182	0.7062	0.6944
3	0.6407	0.6244	0.6086	0.5934	0.5787
4	0.5523	0.5337	0.5158	0.4987	0.4823
5	0.4761	0.4561	0.4371	0.4190	0.4019

GLOSSARY OF ACCOUNTING TERMS

ABSORPTION COSTING

A method of ascertaining the cost of products or services which includes both fixed and variable costs. This may be contrasted with variable or marginal costing where costs of products or services are calculated using variable costs only.

ACCOUNTING

The process of recording and communicating the economic activities of business units.

ACCOUNTING STANDARDS

A set of rules which provide guidance for measuring and disclosing accounting transactions. In the UK these take the form of Statements of Standard Accounting Practice (SSAPs) and Financial Reporting Standards (FRSs). It is envisaged that SSAPs will be gradually replaced by FRSs.

ACCOUNTING RATE OF RETURN

A calculation used to evaluate capital expenditure projects by comparing the average annual accounting profits with either the initial capital investment or the average capital investment.

ACCRUALS

An accrual is an item of expenditure which has not been paid at the end of the accounting period, but which must be included in the expenditures of the current accounting period. It is often the case that an accrual is not supported by a specific invoice and must, therefore, be estimated.

ACID TEST RATIO

A measure of liquidity. An accounting ratio which compares current assets minus stock with current liabilities.

ALLOCATION OF COSTS

Where overheads are analysed to support an overhead absorption rate calculation. Some indirect costs may be directly identified with cost centres. These costs are said to be allocated to such cost centres.

ANNUAL REPORT

A published set of narrative and numerical reports which describes an organization's economic activity for a defined accounting period.

APPORTIONMENT OF COSTS

Where overheads are analysed to support an overhead absorption rate calculation, some indirect costs cannot be directly identified with cost centres. These costs must be identified with cost centres on the basis of subjective judgement. Thus the cost of electricity used for lighting and heating may be apportioned on the basis of the floor area or physical volume occupied by cost centres.

ASSET

An item owned by a business. Fixed assets are those assets which are intended to be retained for a number of accounting periods. Current assets are those assets which are intended to be constantly replaced in the normal course of trading activities.

ASSET TURNOVER

A measure of the productivity of the assets of a business achieved by comparing asset values with sales revenue.

BAD DEBTS

Specific debts which will not be paid by the debtor.

BALANCE SHEET

A primary financial accounting statement that lists the assets and liabilities of a business at the end of its accounting period.

BREAK EVEN POINT

The point, indicated by a comparison between costs and revenues, where neither profit nor loss is made because sales revenue equals total cost.

BUDGET

A plan of future economic activity expressed mainly in monetary terms.

CAPITAL ACCOUNT

An account used to record the owners interest in the business. In partnership accounts, capital accounts are supplemented by current accounts.

CAPITAL EMPLOYED

A measure of the resources used by a business.

CAPITAL EXPENDITURE

Expenditure for the purchase of assets for long term use in the business.

CASH

(1) Monetary transfer

(2) Cash in hand plus deposits and overdrafts repayable on demand.

CASH BUDGET

A forecast of future cash flows.

CASH FLOW STATEMENT

(1) A financial accounting statement which analyses the historical cash flows of an entity's accounting period into defined categories.

(2) A management accounting statement which may also be termed a cash budget.

CASH TRANSACTION

An accounting transaction settled by an immediate monetary transfer. This may be compared to a credit transaction where there is a delay before a monetary transfer is effected.

CONTRIBUTION

Sales revenue minus variable costs.

COST CENTRE

(1) A department or other organizational sub-unit where costs may be accumulated.

(2) A type of responsibility centre where a named individual is made responsible for designated costs.

COST OF SALES

Costs which vary with sales. In this text this is interpreted as: Opening Stock plus Purchases minus Closing Stock.

COST VOLUME PROFIT (CVP) ANALYSIS

A study of the effect on short-term costs and revenues of changes in output.

COST UNIT

A unit of product or service where costs may be accumulated.

CREATIVE ACCOUNTING

The manipulation of the presentation of accounting information with the intention to mislead users of the accounts.

CREDIT

A double entry posting indicating value given.

CREDITORS

Amounts owed by a business to other entities or individuals.

CREDIT TRANSACTION

An accounting transaction where there is a delay between transfer of goods (or services) and transfer of monetary value.

CURRENT ASSETS

Short-term assets which are intended to be constantly replaced in the normal course of trading activity. Current assets typically comprise: Stock, Debtors, Prepayments, Positive bank balances and Cash.

CURRENT RATIO

A measure of liquidity. An accounting ratio which compares current assets with current liabilities.

CURRENT LIABILITIES

Short-term liabilities which are intended to be constantly replaced in the normal course of trading activity. Current liabilities typically comprise: Creditors, Accruals and Bank Overdrafts.

DEBENTURE

A formal agreement used to secure a long-term loan. In this text the words 'debenture' and 'long-term loan' are used synonymously.

DEBIT

A double entry posting indicating value received.

DEBTORS

Amounts owed to a business by other entities or individuals.

DEPRECIATION

A measure of the wearing out or other loss in value of fixed assets. In this text depreciation calculations are described using the straight line method and the reducing balance method. The straight line method charges an equal amount of depreciation to the Profit and Loss Account over the useful life of the asset. The reducing balance method charges proportionately more depreciation to the Profit and Loss Account early in the asset's useful life and lower amounts of depreciation later in the asset's useful life.

DIRECT COSTS

Costs which may be directly identified with a unit of product or service. Direct costs typically comprise: Direct Labour, Direct Materials and Direct Expenses.

DIRECT METHOD

A method of presenting operating cash flows in a Cash Flow Statement. The direct method is based upon an analysis of operating cash flows and the results of this analysis is presented in the following categories: cash received from customers, cash payments to suppliers, cash paid to or on behalf of employees and other cash payments. This method is not widely used in UK financial reporting.

DISCOUNT FACTORS

Factors which express the time value of money for defined periods and opportunity costs of capital.

DISCOUNTED CASH FLOW METHODS

Methods of capital investment appraisal which employ the concept of the time value of money. This book considers two main discounted cash flow methods: the Net Present Value (NPV) method and the Internal Rate of Return (IRR) method.

DIVIDENDS

Appropriations of profit paid to shareholders. Interim dividends may be paid during an accounting period and final or proposed dividends are payable at the end of the accounting period and are normally treated as creditors.

DIVIDEND COVER

A measure of an entity's ability to pay dividends. It is calculated by comparing dividends with net profit after tax.

DIVIDEND YIELD

A measure of the return on the market value of shares. It is calculated by comparing dividend payments with the market value of shares.

DOUBLE ENTRY SYSTEM

A method of recording and processing accounting transactions based upon the concept that each transaction has a dual aspect; a debit entry and a credit entry.

DOUBTFUL DEBTS

These are non-specific debtors who may not pay their debts when due.

DOUBTFUL DEBTS PROVISION

An accounting provision for doubtful debts normally calculated as a percentage of outstanding debtors at the end of an accounting period. The doubtful debts provision is shown as a deduction from debtors on the Balance Sheet. Increases or decreases in the provision (which are identified by comparing the current period end provision with the previous period end provision) are charged or credited to the Profit and Loss Account.

EARNINGS PER SHARE (EPS)

A measure of profit from the (ordinary) shareholder's viewpoint. It is calculated by dividing profit after tax (and preference dividend) by the number of issued ordinary shares.

EQUITY CAPITAL

Ordinary share capital. This normally comprises Ordinary Shares and Reserves.

FINANCIAL ACCOUNTING

The recording and presentation of accounting transactions with a view to determining the results of economic activity for the whole entity for a defined accounting period which is normally of one year's duration.

FIXED ASSETS

Assets which are intended to be retained for a number of accounting periods, are not acquired, primarily, for resale and involve large enough expenditures for such assets to be economically identified as fixed assets. Thus the acquisition of a paper clip would not satisfy all of the above criteria, whereas the acquisition of a vehicle could.

FIXED COSTS

Cost which do not, in the short-term, vary with levels of output or sales.

FLEXIBLE BUDGET

A budget which allows variable costs to be adjusted for changes in output or sales levels.

GEARING RATIO

The expression of debt capital as a proportion of total capital. The US term for gearing is 'leverage'.

GROSS PROFIT

Sales minus Cost of Sales.

HISTORICAL COST

The original value of items of revenue and expenditure unadjusted for changes in price levels.

HORIZONTAL ANALYSIS

A method of interpreting financial statements whereby changes in revenues, expenditures, assets and liabilities are compared over more than one time period.

INDIRECT COSTS

Costs which cannot be directly identified with a unit of product or service.

INDIRECT METHOD

A method of calculating the operating cash flows in a Cash Flow Statement based upon adjustments to accounting profit. A summary of these calculations is presented as a note to the Cash Flow Statement and is described as a reconciliation between operating cash flows and operating profits.

INTERNAL RATE OF RETURN (IRR)

A method of appraising capital expenditure projects. The Internal Rate of Return is the discount rate that, when applied to project cash flows, gives a net present value of zero.

INVENTORIES

The US term for stocks of raw materials, work in progress or finished goods.

INVESTMENT CENTRE

A type of Responsibility Centre where a named individual is made responsible for costs, revenues and capital expenditures.

LIABILITY

An amount owed by a business to other entities or individuals. Long-term liabilities are those liabilities (normally loans) which are repayable after more than one year. Current liabilities are short-term liabilities which are intended to be replaced in the normal course of trading activities.

LIMITING FACTOR

A constraint which limits business activities, for example, labour or materials which are in short supply.

LIQUIDITY RATIOS

Statistics such as the Current Ratio and the Acid Test Ratio which measure the relationship between current assets and current liabilities.

LIQUID RESOURCES

In the context of a financial accounting Cash Flow Statement, liquid resources have been defined by FRS1 (revised 1996) as "current asset investments held as readily disposable stores of value".

MANAGEMENT ACCOUNTING

The recording and presentation of accounting and other quantitative data to enable business managers to make informed judgements about the direction and control of the entity's economic activities.

MASTER BUDGET

A summary of an organization's sub-unit budgets. In this text the Master Budget is presented in the form of a budgeted Profit and Loss Account, Balance Sheet and a (management accounting) Cash Flow Schedule.

NET ASSETS
Fixed Assets plus Current Assets minus Current Liabilities.
NET CURRENT ASSETS
Current Assets minus Current Liabilities.
NET CURRENT LIABILITIES
Current Assets minus Current Liabilities where there is an excess of Current Liabilities.
NET PRESENT VALUE (NPV)
A method of appraising capital expenditure projects. The Net Present Value of a capital expenditure project is the sum of the present values of the projected cash flows. The present value is found by applying discount factors to project cash flows.
NET PROFIT
Gross Profit minus Overhead Expenses.
NOMINAL LEDGER
An accounting record which contains a number of designated accounts which classify the Revenues, Expenditures, Assets and Liabilities of a business.
OPERATING PROFIT
The profit earned from trading activities.
ORDINARY SHARES
Documents used to indicate an interest in a limited company. Ordinary Shares may be equated to the capital account of the sole trader. The holders of Ordinary Shares vote to exercise overall control of a company in general meetings and, in addition, have the right to receive a share, in part or all, of the company's profits.
OVERHEAD ABSORPTION RATES
A method of allowing cost centre indirect expenses to be identified with cost units. An overhead analysis sheet is used to allocate and apportion indirect costs to cost centres. The sum of cost centre indirect costs for each cost centre is then divided by a suitable absorption base (such as labour hours or machine hours) in order to calculate overhead absorption rates. Indirect expenses are identified with cost units by multiplying units of the absorption base, utilised by the cost unit in each cost centre, by the corresponding overhead absorption rates for each cost centre.
OVERHEAD EXPENSES
Indirect Costs. In financial accounting these are listed after gross profit in the Profit and Loss Account.
PAYBACK
A method of capital investment appraisal. The initial outlay of a project is compared with cash inflows during the life of the project.
PERIOD END ADJUSTMENTS
Financial accounting adjustments which are designed to more accurately measure accounting profit. These adjustments typically comprise: Depreciation, Accruals, Prepayments, Closing Stock and Debtors adjustments.
PREFERENCE SHARES
Shares which have limited voting and dividend rights, but which will be repaid before ordinary shares if the issuing company goes into liquidation.
PREPAYMENTS
A prepayment is an item of expenditure, which has been paid during an accounting period, which must be included in the expenditure of a subsequent accounting period. Prepayments are often unsupported by specific invoices and must, therefore, be estimated.

PRICE/EARNINGS (P/E) RATIO

A measure of the amount of time an investor will take to recover the current market value of a share from the receipt of dividends. It is calculated by dividing the market price per share by earnings per share.

PROFIT CENTRE

A type of responsibility centre where a named individual is made responsible for designated costs and revenues.

PROFIT AND LOSS ACCOUNT

A primary financial accounting statement that presents the elements of the calculation of accounting profit for the whole accounting period.

PROFIT VOLUME (PV) RATIO

Contribution expressed as a percentage of sales.

RATIO ANALYSIS

A systematic method of examining accounting statements which is based upon the calculation of a number of ratios and statistics.

REDUCING BALANCE METHOD

A method of calculating depreciation which charges proportionately more depreciation to the Profit and Loss Account early in the asset's useful life and lower amounts of depreciation later in the asset's useful life.

RESPONSIBILITY ACCOUNTING

A control technique whereby named individuals are made responsible for Responsibility Centres.

RESPONSIBILITY CENTRE

An organizational sub-unit for which a named individual is made accountable. Responsibility Centres may give an individual responsibility for costs (Cost Centre), costs and revenues (Profit Centre) or costs, revenues and capital expenditures (Investment Centre).

RETURN ON CAPITAL EMPLOYED (ROCE)

A method of assessing the profitability of a business by comparing profit with capital employed.

STANDARD COSTING

The use of detailed predetermined estimates of costs and revenues for control purposes.

STRAIGHT LINE DEPRECIATION

A method of depreciation that charges equal amounts of depreciation to the Profit and Loss Account during the useful life of an asset.

'T' ACCOUNT

A text book representation of a nominal ledger account.

TREND ANALYSIS

A method of interpreting financial statements whereby revenues, expenditures, assets and liabilities are expressed in terms of index numbers corresponding to a base period. Thus changes over several accounting periods may be assessed.

TRIAL BALANCE

A list of nominal ledger account balances which forms the basis for the preparation of financial accounting statements.

VARIANCE

The difference between a budgetary target and the corresponding actual value. Variances which exceed the target are said to be favourable. Variances which do not meet the target are said to be adverse.

VARIANCE ANALYSIS
The calculation and investigation of variances for monitoring and control purposes.
VARIABLE COSTS
Costs which vary with output or sales.
VERTICAL ANALYSIS
A method of interpreting financial statements whereby Profit and Loss Account values are expressed as a percentage of sales and Balance Sheet values are expressed as a percentage of net assets.
WORKING CAPITAL
Net Current Assets
ZERO BASED BUDGETING (ZBB)
A method of producing a budget which ignores historical precedents.

INDEX

Accounting
  equation 1
  for credit transactions 26–32
  historical review of 12
  systems 5–10
  ratios (see Ratio Analysis)
  rate of return 249–253
  profit 1–2, 42–44, 46–48
Accounts
  annual accounts 42
  balancing 32–35
  consolidated/group 94–95
  interpretation 129–130, 132–149
  ledger 14–15
  published 80, 93–101
  'T' accounts 14
Accruals 63
Acid Test Ratio 142
Annual Report
  narrative reports 95–98
  numerical reports 95, 98–101
Audit
  report 95, 97
ARR 249–253
Assets 1–2, 44–45
  fixed 45
  current 45
  turnover 143–144
Average Cost 167–168

Bad Debts 59, 63–64
Balance Sheet 44
  example 46, 49, 52, 67
  partnership 77
  company 81

Balancing Accounts 32–35
Book-keeping 7–9
Books
  cash book 7
  day book 8
  nominal ledger 8
Break Even Analysis 185–198
  break even point 185
Budget
  reasons for 203–204
  budgetary control 217–218
  cash budget 210–212
  definition 203
  fixed 218
  flexible 218–219
  example 205–215
  master 211–215
  production 206–207
  sales 206
  traditional method 205–215
  ZBB (Zero Based Budgeting) 215–217

Capital
  account 15
  expenditure 43
  working 144
  share 78
Capital Investment Appraisal
  NPV 243–244
  IRR 244–246
  Payback 247–248
  ARR 249–253
Cash
  budget 210–212
  liquidity 140–141

versus profit 43–44
Cash Flow Statement
    layout 103–104
    direct/indirect method 104–110
    notes 118–121
    net debt 119–120
Chairman's/Chief Executive's Report 95–96
Closing Stock 64
Company
    private 77
    public 77–78
    accounting statements 78–85
    shareholders 78
    directors 80
    dividends 79
    Profit & Loss Account and Balance Sheet
        80–85
Consolidated Accounts 94–95
Contribution
    method of calculating 183
    use for decision making 184–198
Control
    budgetary 217–219
    accounting systems 9–10
Corporate Report 93
Cost Centre 164
Cost of Sales 47–48
Cost Unit 164
Costs
    direct and indirect 164–165 ✓
    fixed 182
    labour 168–169
    materials 165–168
    variable 182
Creative Accounting 103
Credit 13
Creditors 27
Credit Sales/Purchases 26–32
Current Assets 45
Current Ratio 141–142
Current Liability 45

Debit 13
Debtors 27
    bad 63
    doubtful 63, 65–66
Depreciation 59–62
Direct Cost 164
Direct Labour 165
Direct Materials 164
Direct Expenses 165
Direct Method for Cashflow Statements 104–105

Directors 80
Discount Factors 242
Discounted Cash Flow 243–244
Discounting 243
Dividends
    ordinary shares 79, 85
    preference shares 79, 85
    method of calculating 79
Double Entry System 12–20, 26–38
    history 12
    debit 13
    credit 13
    trial balance 35–38
    period end adjustments 59–67
    credit transactions 26–32

Earnings per Share 147
Efficiency Ratios 143–145
Entities
    limited companies 77–78
    sole traders 73
    partnerships 74

FIFO (first-in-first-out) 166–167
Financial Accounting ✓
    users of information 93–94
    and management accounting 158–159
First-in-first-out (FIFO) 166–167
Fixed Budget 218
Fixed Assets 45
    depreciation 59–62
Fixed Costs 182
Flexible Budget 218–219
Format
    of Balance Sheet 49. 81
    of Cash Flow Statement 103–104, 118–121
    of Profit & Loss Account 47, 80

Gearing Ratio 146
Gross Profit
    calculation of 46–47
Group Accounts 94–95

Holding Company 94
Horizontal Analysis 133–134

Indirect Costs (see also Overheads) 165
Indirect Method, Cash Flow Statements
    105–110
Internal Rate of Return (IRR) 244–246
Interpretation
    methods 132–135

ratio analysis 135–149
Investment Ratios
  capital gearing 146
  dividend cover 148
  dividend yield 148–149
  earnings per share (EPS) 147
  price/earnings ratio (P/E ratio) 148
Inventories (see Stock)

Last-in-first-out (LIFO) 167
Liabilities 45
LIFO (Last-in-first-out) 167
Limiting Factor 193
Liquidity Ratios 140–142
Luca Pacioli 12

Management Accounting
  and financial accounting 158–159
Marginal Costing (see Variable Costing)
Master Budget 211–215
Multiple Ownership Entities 73

Net Assets 49
Net Current Assets 49
Net Present Value (NPV) 243–244
Net Profit 46–47
NPV (Net Present Value) 243–244

Operating Activities, Cash Flow 105–110
Operating Profit 105
Ordinary Shares 78
Overheads
  in unit cost calculation 170–172
  in financial accounting 46

P/V (Profit/Volume) Ratio 185
Pacioli, Luca 12
Partnership
  accounts 74–77
  profit sharing 75–76
  capital account 74–75
  current account 74–75
Payback 247–248
Period End Adjustments 59
PLC (Public Limited Company) 77–78
Prepayments 59
Price/Earnings Ratio (P/E Ratio) 148
Private Company 77
Profit
  gross 46

net 46–47
Profit & Loss Account
  format 47, 80
Project Appraisal 240–254

Ratio Analysis 135–149
Reducing Balance Method 60–61
Responsibility Accounting 217
Return on Capital Employed (ROCE) 136–139
Revenue Expenditure 43
ROCE (Return on Capital Employed) 136–139

Share Capital 78
Sole Traders 73
Standard Costing 222–237
Stock 59, 160–161, 144
Straight-line Depreciation 60

Taxation (of Companies)
  accounting treatment of 79–80
Trading Account 46
Trend Analysis 134–135
Trial Balance 35–38

Unit Cost 164
Users of Accounts 93–94

Variance Analysis 236–237
Variances
  Production Cost Variances 226
  Variable Overhead Variances 228, 230, 232
  Fixed Overhead Variances 228
  Formulae 229–232
  Materials Variances 226–227, 230–231
  Labour Variances 227–228, 230–231
  Sales Variances 232–233
  and absorption costing 234
Variable Costing Statements 183
Variable Costs 182
Vertical Analysis 132–133
Vertical Format 45

Wage Rate Variance 227, 230
Wage Efficiency Variance 228, 231
Working Capital 144

Year End Adjustments (see period end
  adjustments)

Zero Based Budgeting (ZBB) 215–217